YOUR PERSONAL
LEGAL GUIDE

MICHAEL LYNN GABRIEL

Copyright © 1993 Michael Lynn Gabriel

All rights reserved.
No part of this book may be reproduced or transmitted in any form or by any means, electronic or mechanical, including photocopying, recording, or by any information storage and retrieval system, without permission in writing from the Publisher.

Produced by Wieser & Wieser
118 East 25th Street
New York, NY 10010

Designed by Tony Meisel

Printed in the United States of America

ISBN 0-944297-06-4

CONTENTS

1. INCOME TAXES

2. DRUNK DRIVING

3. SMALL CLAIMS COURT

4. IMMIGRATION

5. CHILD CUSTODY AND SUPPORT

6. UNWED PARENTING AND ADOPTIONS

7. LANDLORD-TENANT

8. REAL PROPERTY

9. ESCROW

10. TORTS

11. PROBATE

12. ESTATE PLANNING

INDEX

SAMPLE FORMS FOR REFERENCE THROUGHOUT

INTRODUCTION

This book was written to help the reader better understand certain areas of law covered in this book. It was designed with the intent to serve as a guide and tool with which to help the reader cut through legal jargon and understand and appreciate the reader's rights under the law.

This book is different from nearly all of the legal self-help books on the market. It does not dwell upon the legal procedures needed to be followed in order to achieve a desired result. This is not a "HOW TO" book in any sense of the word. Instead, it is intended to aid the reader in discovering his or her legal rights so that the proper decision on a course of action can be made.

As a practicing attorney, I receive many telephone calls each month from people with general legal questions. Most of their question are answered for free on the phone.

For several years, I have hosted a radio legal talk show on KXBX radio station in Lake County, California. Listeners with legal questions call the show and I attempt to answer their questions as best I can with the facts given me.

From this experience, I have come to realize that a void exists in the general public's mind regarding their basic understanding of the law. Many people have simple questions regarding the law that they would like answered. Yet for various reasons, cost being one, they are reluctant to pay for an attorney consultation to have them answered.

I have attempted through this book to answer the basic questions that the general public has on many areas of law.

In my practice, I have handled cases in all the areas of the law discussed in this book. I have relied upon my education and experience to draft the most informative questions and answers that I could .

There are many "How To" books on the market. This book is not intended to be one. It does have the effect, however, of rendering some such books unnecessary. For example, the small claims chapter addresses most of the questions a person would have in a small claims action. As such, the average reader would not have to purchase one of the many "How To" books on small claims. In addition, the chapters on Landlord Tenant or Real Property may make respective "How To" books redundant.

This book serves as a mini-encyclopedia of the areas covered herein. It was written to be the most useful and interactive book of its type available. REMEMBER, THIS BOOK IS NOT INTENDED TO REPLACE AN ATTORNEY. It is written to give the most current general legal information available. Some answers may seem to be short and others unnecessarily long, but that was intentional. The answers are designed to be explicit enough to explain the law with examples given, if necessary.

Generally, the average person will have no difficulty in understanding the questions or answers. For a more specific and detailed understanding of the law in a particular state, the reader must still, in certain instances, cross check the information in this book with the law of that state. This book helps guide the reader to the legal principles needed to begin such a legal research. THIS BOOK IS A STARTING POINT FOR THE READER. IT IS INTENDED AS AN AID TO THE UNDERSTANDING OF THE READER'S LEGAL RIGHTS AND, WHERE APPROPRIATE, TO HELP DIRECT THE LEGAL RESEARCH ON PARTICULAR QUESTIONS.

1
INCOME TAXES

1. INCOME TAXES

In this chapter will be addressed those basic federal income tax questions that most frequently arise. This chapter can not possibly answer all of the tax questions raised by the over 8,000 code sections in the Internal Revenue Code. Therefore, this chapter has been devoted to the questions of the greatest interest to the greatest number of readers.

To accomplish this avowed goal, the fundamental tax questions have been answered in such a way so as to create a basic understanding of the tax law. This basic understanding is then utilized to answer more involved, informative and personal tax questions.

Income Tax is an important consideration in many people's lives. It is effect of income taxes on a person's paycheck that determines the take home pay and the amount of disposable income the person has to spend. As such, income taxes directly affect the quality of life of every taxpayer. Businesses live or die by their ability to master the tax code. Thus, the welfare of all employees are affected by the obscure rule and regulations implemented to enforce the Internal Revenue Code.

The purpose of this chapter is to help the reader understand and truly appreciate the Internal Revenue Code's complexity.

1. WHAT SERVICES DOES THE IRS PROVIDE FREE?

The IRS provides free tax information and services. The IRS publication 910, Guide to Free Tax Services, describes the publications and services available to taxpayers. There are over 100 publications by the IRS containing tax information.

Videotaped instructions for completing tax returns have been prepared by the IRS in both Spanish and English. They are available in some public libraries.

Braille materials are also available at regional libraries in conjunction with the Library of Congress. The IRS offers the TELE-TAX service. It is a telephone service that provides recorded tax information on over 140 subjects.

It call also tell a taxpayer the status of his or her refund.

There is telephone service for hearing impaired persons who have access to TDD equipment. Call 1-800-829-4059. The IRS provides toll-free numbers for every state for taxpayers to call regarding tax questions not covered in the IRS publications.

2. WHAT CAN BE DONE WITH UNRESOLVED TAX PROBLEMS?
Congress mandated that the IRS create a Problem Resolution Program for taxpayers that are unable to resolve their problems with the IRS. A taxpayer may write to the local IRS District Director or call the local IRS office and ask for Problem Resolution Assistance. This problems resolution officer will advise the taxpayer of the Taxpayer's Bill of Rights and help clear up problems. It can not change tax law or technical decisions but can assist in other ways.

3. WHAT IS MEANT BY FILING STATUS?
A taxpayer's tax rate, filing requirements and standard deduction is determined by his or her filing status. The five filing statuses are:

    1. Single—Unmarried or legally separated on the last day of the tax year. State law determines if a person if married or legally separated.
    2. Married filing jointly
    3. Married filing separately
    4. Household - A qualifying widow or widower with a dependent child
    5. Qualifying widow or widower

4. WHAT IS A TAX EXEMPTION?
Tax exemptions reduce a taxpayers income before tax is computed. In 1990, each exemption was worth $2,050. There are two types of tax exemptions, personal exemptions and dependency exemptions.

A taxpayer is entitled to one exemption for himself and if married for his spouse. These are the personal exemptions. An exemption for a spouse with gross income can only be taken if a joint return is filed.

5. WHAT ARE DEPENDENTS?
The dependency exemption of $2,050 is permitted for each dependent of a taxpayer. As with a personal exemption, each dependency exemption reduces the taxpayers' gross income before tax calculation. There are five tests for dependency that must be met before an exemption is

allowed.

Member of Household or Relationship Test - the dependent lives with the taxpayer or is a relative.

2. Citizenship Test - the dependent is U.S. citizen, resident or national or a resident of Canada or Mexico.

3. Joint Return Test - the dependent has not filed a joint return with his or her spouse.

4. Gross Income Test - Generally, a dependency exemption is unavailable if the person sought to be claimed has earned more than $2,050 for the year. This does not apply to the earnings of a child or a student under 24 years of age.

5. Support Test - More than half of the support of the person must be provided by the taxpayer during the year.

6. WHAT IS A MULTIPLE SUPPORT AGREEMENT?

A situation may exist where several persons contribute to the support of a person, such as an elderly parent by the children . In such a case, no one individual may meet the support test. When this happens, the persons providing over ten percent (10%) of the support may agree among themselves to let one of them claim the exemption. Each person agreeing not to claim the exemption must sign a written statement to that effect. Form 2120 is used for that purpose. It must be filed with the tax return of the person claiming the exemption.

7. IS EVERYONE ALLOWED EXEMPTIONS?

Not everyone is allowed an exemption. The amount that a taxpayer may claim as a deduction is gradually phased out once the taxable income exceeds a certain level for that taxpayer's filing status.

Filing Status	*Taxable Income Subject to Exemption Phaseout*
Single	$97,620
Married filing jointly	$162.770
Married filing separately	$123,570
Head of Household	$134,930
Qualifying Widow(er)	$162,770

If the taxable amount is more than the amount shown in the above table, the taxpayer continues to deduct the exemptions on the Form 1040 as usual. The amount of the exemption phaseout is computed using the tax rates schedules.

8. MUST AN INCOME TAX RETURN BE FILED FOR A DECEDENT?

The personal representative or surviving spouse must file the final income tax return and any other return still due for the decedent. The person acting as the fiduciary, such as executor or administrator, must file Form 56, Notice Concerning Fiduciary Relationship with the IRS.

The personal representative and the surviving spouse may file a joint return for the decedent and the surviving spouse. The surviving spouse may file the joint return alone if no personal representative has been appointed before the filing date. A joint return may not be file if the surviving spouse remarries before the end of the tax year in which the decedent died.

The final tax return is due when the the decedent's tax return would have been due had the person not died.

9. WHAT IS A REQUEST FOR PROMPT ASSESSMENT?

The IRS usually has three (3) years in which to assess (charge the taxpayer) for any additional tax that may be due. This may cause uncertainty among the heirs of the decedent. A request for prompt assessment can shorten that time. It reduces the time for assessing (charging) additional tax for an estate to eighteen (18) months from the date the request is received. This permits quicker settlement of the tax responsibility of the estate and earlier distribution of the decedent's assets.

10. WHAT DEDUCTIONS, CREDITS AND EXEMPTIONS ARE ALLOWED ON A DECEDENT'S FINAL RETURN?

The standard deduction is available to calculate the taxable income on the decedent's final return. An exception exists when the surviving spouse files a separate return and itemized deductions are elected by one spouse. If either spouse elects to itemize deductions, then both spouses must itemize their deductions.

If the decedent used the cash method of accounting, only those expenses actually paid before death are deductible. If the decedent used the accrual method of accounting, only those expenses accrued before death are deductible.

Normally, the decedent's standard deduction is the same as it would have been had the decedent not died. However, a higher standard deduction is allowed to a decedent that was blind or over 65 at the time of death. If the decedent was a dependent of another, the standard deduction may be reduced.

The personal exemption is allowed in full on a decedent's final tax return unless the decedent is claimed as a dependent by another taxpayer.

Income tax withheld from a decedent's pay, pensions or annuities before death along with any estimated tax payments must be claimed on the final return.

11. WHAT IS INCOME IN RESPECT OF THE DECEDENT?

Income in respect of the decedent is income that the decedent had a right to receive and that is not includible in the final return of the decedent. This income is included, for the tax year received as follows:

1. The decedent's estate, if the estate acquired the right to receive the amount from the decedent, or

2. The person to whom the right to the income passed directly if the estate did not receive that right from the decedent, or

3. Any person to whom the estate properly distributes the right to receive that amount. The character of the income received in respect of the decedent is the same as it would have been had the decedent continued to live. For example, capital gain income to the decedent will remain capital gain income to the person receiving it as income in respect of the decedent.

12. WHAT IS THE CASH METHOD OF ACCOUNTING?

Under this method of accounting, the taxpayer reports all items of income in the year that they are actually or constructively received. The taxpayer will only deduct, under the cash method of accounting, those expenses actually paid. This is the tax method that most individuals utilize.

Income is considered constructively received by a taxpayer when

when it is credited to a taxpayer's account or is set apart in any way that makes it available to the taxpayer. Actual possession of the income is not necessary.

If person cancels a debt that is owed to a taxpayer, the amount of the canceled debt is income to the taxpayer and must be reported.

Income received by an agent of a taxpayer is constructively received by the taxpayer and must be reported.

13. WHAT IS THE ACCRUAL METHOD OF ACCOUNTING?

Under the accrual method of reporting, a taxpayer reports income when earned not when received. Likewise, expenses are deducted when incurred not when paid.

Prepaid income is generally reported when received regardless of the method used if the funds are available to the taxpayer.

Advance payments for services to be performed by the end of the tax year can be deferred from income until the taxpayer actually earns them by performing the services. The taxpayer must be on the accrual method of reporting to defer the payments. Publication 538 Accounting Periods and Methods covers in detail the advantages and detriments of both methods.

Once an accounting method is chosen it can not be changed without IRS approval. However, a taxpayer can use a different method for each business the taxpayer may have. If the taxpayer wishes to change his accounting method, Form 3115 Application For Change of Accounting Method is used.

14. WHAT ARE EXPIRED TAX ITEMS?

In 1991, there were important tax changes. Some expired tax items, items that can no longer be claimed are:

1. Personal interest- beginning in 1991 personal interest, such as for car loans or credit cards is no longer deductible.

2. The exclusion for employer-provided educational assistance no longer exists.

3. The exclusion for employer-provided group legal assistance no longer exists.

4. The 25% deduction of health insurance cost for self employed individuals is eliminated

5. Targeted job credits were eliminated.
6. Business energy credit was eliminated
7. Low-income housing credit was eliminated
8. Research and experimentation credit was eliminated.

15. WHAT IS THE CEILING FOR SELF-EMPLOYMENT TAX?

The combined tax rate on self-employment tax is 15.3%. The rate consists of a 12.4% component for old-age, survivors and disability insurance and a 2.9% component for hospital insurance (Medicare).

In 1991, the maximum amount of net earnings from self-employment subject to the 12.4% tax was increased to $53,400. The maximum amount of income subject to the 2.9% medicare component is $125,000.

16. ARE FRINGE BENEFITS TAXABLE?

Fringe benefits received by an employee from the employer are considered compensation and is fully taxable unless specifically excluded by law or the employee pays fair market value for them.

There are some fringe benefits that have been specifically excluded by law for taxation. They are as follows:

1. Those fringe benefits that incur no additional service cost. These are benefits or services that do not cost the employer little or nothing to furnish the employee. An example is free telephone service to phone company employees or free stand-by flights to airline personnel.

2. Qualified Employee Discounts are not taxable if
   (i) the discount is not greater than the gross profit percentage on the price the property is sold to customers, or
   (ii) the discount is not greater than 20% of the price at which the goods or services are offered to the public.

3. A Working Condition Fringe Benefit is not taxable. That is a fringe benefit that the taxpayer would be allowed as a business deduction if the taxpayer had to pay for them. Examples of such are parking lots provided by an employer.

4. De Minimis Fringe Benefits are not taxable. These are fringe benefits that are so small in value that it would be unreasonable or impractical for an employer to account for them.

17. HOW ARE TIPS TAXED?

All tips are taxable income and are subject to federal income tax. An employee must give the employer a written report of the tips received for each month by the 10th day of the next month. This report is required for each month that the employee receives tips in excess of $20.00.

The employer must withhold social security or railroad retirement tax and income tax on any tips reported by a taxpayer. The employer usually deducts the withholding due for the tips from the employee's wages.

If the tips exceed $20.00 but were not reported, the employee must figure the social security tax on the unreported tips. This is done using Form 4137 Social Security Tax on Unreported Tax Income. The employee must also include this unreported tips on line 7 of Form 1040. When there is unreported tip income, the employee may not use Form 1040EZ or Form 1040A.

18. WHAT IS THE W-4?

Income tax is withheld from every employee's paycheck. The amount that is withheld depends on the the following:
1. The amount that the taxpayer earned, and
2. The information given the employed in the Form W-4, Employee's Withholding Allowance Certificate. The W-4 tells the employer the following:

   1. Whether the taxpayer wants the withholding to be based on the single person rate or that of the lower married rate.

   2. How many withholding allowances, dependents, are claimed. Each allowance reduces the amount withheld.

   3. Whether the taxpayer wants additional amount withheld.

If not enough taxes are withheld, that taxpayer must pay the balance along with any penalties when the tax return is filed. A taxpayer can claim an exemption from withholding only if the taxpayer had no tax liability for the previous year and expects none for the current tax year. An exemption is good only for one year. It must be filed for each year in which it is claimed.

19. IS THERE WITHHOLDING ON TIPS?

The tips received while working on a job are considered part of a taxpayer's job. As such they must be reported on the taxpayer's return the same as regular pay. Because of its nature, tax is not withheld directly from tip income. Regardless of that, the tips reported to the employer are taken into account when the employer calculates how much to withhold from the taxpayer's wages. Publication 531, Reporting Income From Tips covers tip reporting requirements.

The employer can figure the withholding in one of two ways:

1. By withholding at the regular rate on the sum of you pay plus your reported tips, or

2. By withholding at the regular rate on your pay plus an amount equal to 20% of your reported tips.

The employer should not withhold income tax, social security tax or railroad retirement tax on any allocated tips. Withholding is based only on the taxpayer's pay plus reported tips. Any incorrectly withheld tax should be refunded.

20. IS THERE WITHHOLDING ON FRINGE BENEFITS?

The value of noncash fringe benefits that an employee receives from his or her employer is considered part of the taxpayer's pay. The employer is then required to withhold income tax on those fringe benefits from the taxpayers regular pay for the period the benefits are paid or treated as paid.

The employer may either add the value of the fringe benefit to the employee's regular pay and figure income tax withholding on the total or withhold 20% of the fringe benefit's value.

If the benefit's actual value cannot be determined when it is paid or treated as paid, the employer may use a reasonable estimate. The employer must report on the W-2, Wage and Tax Statement, the total of taxable fringe benefits paid or treated to be paid during the taxable year.

21. IS THERE WITHHOLDING ON PENSIONS AND ANNUITIES?

Normally income tax will be withheld from a taxpayer's pension and annuity distributions, unless the taxpayer chooses not to have it withheld. This withholding applies to distributions from:

1. An individual retirement account (IRA),
2. A life insurance company under an endowment or life insurance contract,
3. A pension, annuity or profit-sharing plan,
4. A stock bonus plan, and
5. Any other plan that defers the time the taxpayer receives compensation. The amount withheld depends on whether the taxpayer receives the payments spread out over more than one year (this is called periodic payments) or whether the taxpayer receives all of the payments in one tax year (this is called nonperiodic payments). A part of the annuity and pension may not be taxable. Generally, if the taxpayer did not pay any part of the cost of the pension plan or annuity, the amount received under the pension or annuity will be fully taxable. If the taxpayer pays part of the cost for the pension or annuity, the taxpayer will not be taxed on the part of the annuity or pension that represents a return of the taxpayer's cost. The rest of the amount will be taxable.

22. WHAT IS THE ESTIMATED TAX?

The estimated tax is the method used to pay tax on income that is not subject to withholding. Such income includes income from self-employment, unemployment compensation, interest, dividends, alimony, rent, gains from sale of assets, prizes and awards. Estimated tax must also be paid if the amount withheld from a taxpayers' salary, pension or other income is not enough. To determine the amount of estimated tax a person should pay use Form 1040 ES, Estimated Tax For Individuals.

Estimated tax is used to pay both income and self-employment tax as well as the other taxes reported on a Form 1040. A taxpayer should expect to pay estimated tax if, after subtracting withholding and credits, the taxpayer is expected to owe at least $500.00 and the withholding and credits are expected to be less than:
1. 90% of the present year's taxes or
2. 100% of the previous year's tax.

23. WHEN ARE THE ESTIMATED TAX PAYMENTS DUE?

The Internal Revenue Code divides the taxable year into four quarters for estimated tax purposes. Each quarter has a specific date for the payment of estimated taxes. If the taxpayer fails to make the required payment by that date or underpays the estimated tax, the taxpayer may be charged a penalty even if the taxpayer is due a refund when the tax return is filed. The payment periods and due dates are as follows:

For the Period Due Date Jan 1 through March 31, April 15
April 1 through May 31, June 15
June 1 through August 31, Sept. 15
September 1 through Dec. 31, Jan 15 of the next year

The last payment does not have to be made if the taxpayer's income tax return is filed by the last day of the first month after the end of the tax year and all taxes are are paid with the return.

24. WHAT IS THE PENALTY FOR UNDERPAYMENT OF THE ESTIMATED TAX?

A penalty for underpayment will generally not be assessed if any of the following applies to the taxpayer:

    1. The total of the taxpayer's withholding and estimated tax payments were at least as much as the previous year's taxes and the estimated taxes were paid on time,

    2. The tax balance is no more than 10% of your total tax for the year and all required estimated tax payments were made on time.

    3. Your total tax for the year minus the withholding is less than $500.00

    4. You did not owe tax for the previous year. The penalty is figured separately for each payment period. It is therefore possible for a taxpayer to owe a penalty for a period even if later the taxpayer makes it up in a later period. Furthermore, a taxpayer may be assessed a penalty for failure to file or pay even though the taxpayer in the end be owed a refund when the tax return is filed. The underpayment penalty is figured on Form 210: Underpayment of Estimated Tax by Individuals and Fiduciaries.

25. WHAT IS GROSS INCOME?

The general rule is that everything received in payment for personal services is gross income. this includes wages, salaries, commissions, fees and tips. Also included in gross income is other forms of compensation such as fringe benefits.

In addition, gross income includes interest, dividends, rental income, pensions and annuities, part of social security benefits, part of railroad retirement benefits, alimony, bartering income, canceled debt income, gain on the sale of personal assets, gambling winning, activities not for profit, royalties, recoveries of amounts previously deducted, estate and trust income, partnership income and S corporation income.

Gross income generally does not include life insurance proceeds, part of scholarships and fellowship grants, welfare and public assistance benefits, military allowances, interest on state and local obligations, accident and health insurance proceeds, gifts and inheritances and housing allowances for clergy.

26. WHAT ARE TAX-EXEMPT STATE OBLIGATIONS?

The interest on state and local government obligations is generally tax exempt. This includes obligations of a state or one of its political subdivisions, the District of Columbia, a possession of the United States, or one of its political subdivisions used to finance governmental operations. This includes interest on certain obligations issued after 1982 by Indian tribal governments recognized by the secretary of the Treasury as having the right to exercise one or more sovereign powers.

Interest on arbitrage bonds issued by state and local governments after October 9, 1969 and interest on private activity bonds are generally taxable. For more information on whether interest on governmental obligations is taxable or exempt see Publication 550, State or Local Government Obligations. Even if the income is tax-free, it still must be reported on the taxpayers return. This is just an information reporting requirement.

27. WHAT IS A RETURN OF CAPITAL?

A return of capital is a corporate distribution that is not paid out of the earnings and profits of a corporation. It is a return of the taxpayer's investment in the stock of the corporation. The taxpayer receives a Form 1099-DIV or similar statement stating the what part of the distribution is a return of cap ital.

A return of capital reduced the basis in the taxpayer's stock and is not taxed until the taxpayer has fully recovered his basis in the stock. Once the basis has been reduced to zero, the taxpayer reports further returns on capital as capital gains.

Liquidating distributions, sometimes called liquidating dividends, are distributions received during a partial or complete liquidation of the corporation. These distributions are, at least in part, return of capital. Any liquidating distributing is not tax able until the basis has been recovered in the stock. Afterward, it is reported as capital gain.

28. WHAT IS RENTAL INCOME?

Rental income is any payment received for the use or occupation of property. Generally, a taxpayer must include in gross income all amounts received as rent.

Advance rent is any amount received before the period that it covers. Advance rent is included in the rental income for the year the taxpayer receives it. It is included in gross income of the year received regardless of the period it covers or the accounting method the taxpayer uses.

Security deposits are not include into the rental income of the landlord if the taxpayer plans to return it to the tenant a t the end of the lease. However if during the year, the landlord keeps all or any part of the security deposit, then that amount is treated is rental income and must be reported.

If the landlord receives property or services in lieu of rent, the fair market value of said property or services is rental income and must be reported.

29. WHAT IS THE RENTAL INCOME OF A HOME?

If a taxpayer rents his or her home, the rental deductions and income depends on how may days it was rented. A taxpayer that rents a dwelling unit, used as a home, for less than 15 days during a tax year, the rental income is not reported nor can the rental expenses be deducted. The taxpayer can still deduct allowable interest, taxes, and casualty or theft losses on Schedule A of Form 1040 if the taxpayer itemizes.

If the taxpayer uses the dwelling unit as a home and rents it for more than 15 days per tax year, all of the rental income is taxable and reportable. The taxpayer must divide the expenses between personal and rental use based on the number of days used for each purpose. If the taxpayer has a net profit from the rental, then the taxpayer may deduct all of the rental expenses. If there is not a net profit, the taxpayer can only deduct the rental expenses up to the amount of rental income.

If the total of rental expenses exceeds rental income, the unused rental expenses may be carried over to the next year.

30. WHAT IS DEPRECIATION?

Depreciation is the annual deduction a taxpayer takes to recover the cost of property that is used in business for more than one year.

The main factors used to determine the amount of depreciation that may be deducted are:

1. The basis of the property, and

2. the recovery period of the property. There are three systems of depreciation involved in computing depreciation. These systems depend on when the property was placed into service. These systems are:

1. MACRS for property placed in service after 1986,

2. ACRS for property placed in service after 1980 but before 1987, and

3. Straight line depreciation or accelerated depreciation, if placed in service before 1981. The most utilized system is MACRS, Modified Accelerated Cost Recovery System. In that system, all property is characterized by its recovery life. That is it is placed in one of the following classes:

1. 3 year property,
2. 5 year property
3. 7 year property
4. 10 year property
5. 15 year property
6. 20 year property
7. Nonresidential real property and
8. Residential rental property.

For each class, the IRS has published tables that gives the percentage of depreciation for each year of the property contained in the class. The taxpayer multiplies that percentage by the cost of the item and gets the deduction for the year.

31. IS THERE A LIMIT ON RENTAL LOSSES?
A taxpayer may not generally deduct losses from rental real estate activities unless the taxpayer has income from other passive activities.

At risk rules limit the amount of deductible losses from holding real property placed in service after 1986. A taxpayer is allowed to deduct up to $25,000 ($12,500 if married filing separately and living apart from your spouse the entire year) of the losses from rental real estate in which the taxpayer participated during the tax year. The taxpayer is allowed this offset for otherwise unallowable losses from real estate activities from other income (nonpassive income). The $25,000 ($12,500) figure is reduced if the taxpayer's adjusted gross income is more than $100,000.00.

The active participation is met if the taxpayer or the taxpayer's spouse owns more than 10% of the rental real property.

32. WHAT ARE PASSIVE ACTIVITY LOSSES?
Passive activity losses may not generally be deducted from nonpassive income (wages, interest, dividends). Similarly tax credits for passive activities are limited to the tax allocable to such activities only. Passive activity rules apply to individuals, estates, trusts and personal service corporations.

A passive activity is one that involves the conduct of a trade and business in which the taxpayer does not materially participate. Any rental activity is a passive activity regardless of whether the taxpayer materially participates.

Generally, an individual will be considered as materially participating in an activity if one of the following tests are met :
1. the taxpayer participates more than 500 hours,
2. the taxpayer's participation constitutes substantially all of the activity,
3. the taxpayer participates more than 100 hours and no one else participates more,

4. a fact and circumstances test shows that the taxpayer participated on a regular, continuous and substantial basis. Portfolio income such as from interest, dividends, annuities and royalties is not passive income and the activities generating the income are not passive activities.

33. ARE PENSIONS AND ANNUITIES TAXABLE?

If an employee did not pay any part of the cost of his pension or annuity, and the employer did not withhold part of the cost of the contract from the employee's pay, the amounts that the employee receives is fully taxable.

If the employee pays part of the cost of the annuity, the taxpayer is not taxed on the part of the annuity received that represents the return of the cost. The rest is taxable. The taxpayer will use either the General Rule or the Simplified Rule to determine the taxable and nontaxable parts of the payments.

Under the General Rule, apart of each payment is is non taxable because it is considered a return of your cost. The remainder is fully taxable. The calculation is complex involving actuarial tables. Publication 539 Pension General Rule covers the procedure for the determination of nontaxable amounts.

The Simplified General Rule is available for annuities starting after July 1, 1986 and the recipient was under 75 years of age when the payments started or the payments were to last less than 5 years. Generally the simplified general rule is more advantageous and easier to use than the general rule.

34. IS A DEATH BENEFIT TAXABLE?

The pension or annuity received by beneficiary of a deceased employee or former employee because of that persons' death may qualify for a death exclusion benefit.

There is a death benefit exclusion of $5,000.00. It applies to the amount by which the survivor annuity, figured as of the date of the employee's death, exceeds the larger of: (1) the employee's total regular contributions to the plan, or (2) the amount the employee had a nonforfeitable right (a right that can not be taken away) to receive just before death.

If the beneficiary is eligible for the exclusion, it is added to the cost or unrecovered cost of the annuity when the beneficiary figures the cost at the annuity start date.

An exception exists if the beneficiary is the survivor under a joint or survivor annuity. The exclusion applies in that case only if:

1. the decedent died before receiving or being entitled to receive the retirement or annuity payments, or

2. the decedent received disability payments that were not treated as pension or annuity income. Publication 575 Pension and Annuity Income covers death benefit exclusion.

35. WHAT IS A LUMP SUM DISTRIBUTION?

A lump sum distribution is a distribution from a qualified retirement plan within a single year of the employee's entire balance. Excluded from the distribution are any amounts forfeited or subject to forfeiture, from all of the employer's qualified pension plans, all of the employer's qualified stock bonus plans, or all of the employer's qualified profit-sharing plans.

The distribution must be paid: 1. Because of the employee's death, 2. After the employee reached 59 years of age, 3. Because the employee separates from service, or 4. After a self-employed individual becomes totally and permanently disabled. That portion of the distribution that is a return of the employee's nondeductible contributions is tax free to the employee.

The remaining balance is taxable. The employee may elect long term capital gain treatment if the employee was born before 1936. If so, the distribution is taxed at a 20% rate for the portion earned for participation prior to 1974.

A special averaging method is available to employees born before 1936. The lumps sum distribution may be rolled over without taxation to a eligible retirement plan, such as an IRA.

36. ARE SOCIAL SECURITY BENEFITS TAXABLE?

A portion of a taxpayer's social security benefits may be taxable. The amount of benefits that must be included in income is the lesser of one-half of the benefits received for the year or one-half of the excess of the taxpayer's combined income over a specified base amount. The combined income is the taxpayer's modified adjusted gross income plus one-half of the social security benefits. Modified adjusted gross income is the taxpayer's adjusted gross income plus (a) any tax-exempt interest, and (b) amounts earned in a foreign country or U.S. possession, or Puerto Rico that are excluded from gross income.

The taxpayer's base amount is (a) $32,000 if his filing status is married filing jointly, (b) zero if married filing separately and the taxpayer lived with his or her spouse during the year, and (c) $25,000 for any other filing status.

37. HOW IS DISABILITY INCOME TREATED?
Whether a recipient must report disability pension or annuity payments as income depends on how the pension plan was financed.

The general rule is that any amount received for a disability through an accident or health insurance plan paid for by the employer is taxable.

If the plan requires the employee to pay part of the cost of the disability pension, any amounts that the employee receives that are due to the employees' payments are not taxed. Said payments are treated as benefits received under an accident or health insurance policy bought by the employee. The employee must include the rest of the payments that are due to the employer's payments.

If part of the disability pension is worker's compensation, that part is not taxable. A credit may be claimed if the recipient is over 65 or totally disabled.

38. ARE RAILROAD RETIREMENT BENEFITS TAXABLE?
A portion of a taxpayer's tier 1 railroad retirement benefits may be taxable. The amount of benefits that must be included in income is the lesser of one-half of the benefits received for the year or one-half of the excess of the taxpayer's combined income over a specified base amount. The combined income is the taxpayer's modified adjusted gross income plus one-half of the tier 1 rail road retirement benefits. Modified adjusted gross income is the taxpayer's adjusted gross income plus (a) any tax-exempt interest, and (b) amounts earned in a foreign country or U.S. possession, or Puerto Rico that are excluded from gross income.

The taxpayer's base amount is (a) $32,000 if his filing status is married filing jointly, (b) zero if married filing separately and the taxpayer lived with his or her spouse during the year, and (c) $25,000 for any other filing status.

Tier 2 railroad retirement benefits will be taxed in the same manner as private employer retirement plans.

39. IS A COURT AWARD TAXABLE?
A court award for the following must be included as income and thus is taxable:

1. Interest on any court ordered award.

2. Compensation for lost wages or lost profits.

3. Punitive damages awarded in cases not involving physical injury or sickness.

4. Amount received in settlement of pension rights (if there was not employee contribution)

5. Damages for: a. Patent or copyright infringement, b. Breach of contract, c. Interference with business operations.

Not included in income is an award for the following:

1. Personal injury or sickness.

2. Damage to a person's reputation.

3. Alienation of affection.

40. IS A CANCELED STUDENT LOAN TAXABLE?
There is no tax on a canceled student loan if it was cancelled because the taxpayer performed required services under the contract. Under the terms of the contract, the borrower must be required to work for a specified period of time in certain professions. To qualify the loan must have been made by:

1. The government-federal state or local.

2. A tax exempt public benefit corporation running a government hospital.

3. An educational organization that was provided funds from an entity in (1) or (2) to make the loan.

41. IS AN ACTIVITY NOT FOR PROFIT TAXABLE?
Even though an activity was not intended to make make a profit, if it

does so then that income must be reported. Deductions for activities not intended for profit are severely restricted. Such deductions can not exceed the income derived from the activity and can only be taken if the taxpayer itemizes his deductions.

The activity will be presumed to be for profit if it produces a profit three out of five consecutive years. However when the activity in question involves the breeding of horses, the period for profitability is two years out of seven.

If the activity has been carried on for less than three years, the taxpayer may postpone the determination that the activity is not for profit by filing Form 5213 Election to Postpone Determination.

42. IS A CANCELED DEBT TAXABLE?

A canceled debt or a debt paid for by another person is generally reportable income to the debtor. It should be reported on line 22 of Form 1040. This is a discharge of indebtedness and usually results in taxable income to the debtor. A discount offered by a financial institution for the prepayment of a mortgage loan is income from the cancellation of the debt. However there is no income on the cancellation of a debt, if the cancellation was intended as a gift.

If the debt is canceled in a bankruptcy (title 11) or when the debtor is insolvent, the discharge of the debt is not income.

43. CAN THE TAX ON THE GAIN FROM A SALE OF A HOUSE BE POSTPONED?

A taxpayer must postpone the tax on the gain of the sale of the taxpayer's primary home if the taxpayer buys a new home with in the replacement period and it costs as much or more as the adjusted sales price of the old home.

The tax on the gain of the old home is not forgiven but merely postponed. Any gain that is not taxed in the year of the sale of the old house is subtracted from the basis of the new house. This gives the new house a lower basis. If the new house is sold later, the gain can be postponed again if a new house is purchased.

The taxpayer must buy or build the replacement home within 2 years after the date of the sale of the old home to postpone the gain on the sale of the old home.

44. CAN THE GAIN FOR THE SALE OF A HOUSE BE EXCLUDED?

A taxpayer may choose to exclude from income $125,000 of gain on the sale of the taxpayer's main home ($62,500 if the taxpayer is married filing a separate return) if the following requirements are met:

    1. The taxpayer is over 55 years of age on the date of the sale.

    2. The taxpayer lived in and owned the home for three of the five years prior to the sale.

    3. Neither the taxpayer or the taxpayer's spouse has excluded gain on the sale of a home since July 26, 1978. This is a one-time exclusion and can not be used more than once following July 1978.

45. WHAT IS AN INDIVIDUAL RETIREMENT ACCOUNT?

An individual retirement account is a personal savings plan that offers the taxpayer advantages to set aside money tax-free for retirement. If the taxpayer is self-employed, the taxpayer may be able to deduct contributions to Simplified Employee Pension plans (SEP) that involves the use of IRSs (SEP-IRAs).

To be eligible to open a IRA, the taxpayer must have taxable compensation and not have reached the age of 70 If the neither the taxpayer or spouse is an active participant in a retirement plan, then the IRA contribution is fully deductible (up to $2,000 for worker, $2,250 with nonworking spouse. If either the taxpayer or spouse participates in a retirement plan, then the amount of the deductible IRA contributions depends on the taxpayers' adjusted gross income. The $2,000 maximum ($2,250 spousal IRA) deduction is reduced as the earnings of an employee in a qualified retirement plan increases.

A qualified retirement plan is any pension or profit-sharing plan described in the Internal Revenue Code and generally includes any properly adopted 401 (a) plan, 401(k) plan, defined benefit plan, defined contribution plan or simplified employee plan. Anyone making an IRA contribution must first determine the amount that can be deducted in accordance with the IRA rules.

46. WHAT ARE CAPITAL ASSETS?

A capital asset is generally any property not used in a trade or business. It is primarily property held by a taxpayer for personal purposes, pleasure or investment. A capital asset is not, for tax purposes, one of

the following:
1. Property or inventory held mainly for sale to customers.
2. Depreciable property used in the taxpayer's trade or business.
3. Real property used in the taxpayer's trade or business.
4. A copyright, a literary, musical or artistic composition, a letter or memorandum or similar property that was created by the personal efforts of the taxpayer.
5. Accounts or notes receivable acquired in the normal course of a trade or business.
6. U.S. Government publications that the taxpayer received from the government.

47. WHAT IS CAPITAL GAIN OR LOSS?
The gain or loss from the sale or exchange of a capital asset is characterized as long term or short term capital gain or lo ss. An asset held more than one year is a longer term capital asset. An asset held less than one year is a short term capital asset. he net long term capital gain or loss is added to the net short term gain or loss to arrive at the net overall capital gain or loss. If capital gains exceed capital losses, the overall gain is included on the taxpayer's return and taxed at regular tax rates.

If capital losses exceed capital gains, the overall losses are subject to deduction limitations.

48. WHAT IS A CAPITAL LOSS CARRYOVER?
If a taxpayer's capital losses exceed capital gains, the taxpayer may deduct up to $3,000.00 ($1,500 if married and filing a single return) of the excess for the tax year.

The unused capital loss may be carried over to succeeding years until it is used up. When carried over the capital loss retains its initial character as long term or short term loss.

A decedent's capital losses are not carried over. The excess of the decedent's capital losses are deductible only on the final return of the decedent. The loss may not be carried over to the decedent's estate.

49. WHAT IS COST BASIS?
Basis is a way of measuring the taxpayer's investment in property for

tax purposes. Cost basis is the amount of cash or its equivalent that the taxpayer pays for the property. It includes the fair market value of services and other property that is provided for the purchase. Cost basis also includes:
1. the sales tax charged for the purchase,
2. freight charges for the property
3. installation and testing charges.

50. WHAT IS ADJUSTED BASIS?
The cost basis, investment in the property, is adjusted for changes in the property. As the basis increases, gain (profit) decreases and thus taxes due as a result of the sale of the property are reduced. As the basis decreases, gain (profit) increases and taxes due on the sale of the property likewise increases.

Improvements are adjustments to the basis of property wherein additional investments are made in the property. The value of the improvements are added to the cost basis.

Just as a cost basis may be increased it may be decreased. Items that represent a return of capital operate to reduce the cost basis. Some such items are depreciation, casualty losses and thefts which when deducted operate to reduce the property's basis.

51. WHAT IS THE BASIS OF PROPERTY ACQUIRED BY GIFT?
To determine the donee's basis in property received as a gift it is necessary to know the donor's adjusted basis in the property and the property's fair market value.

If the fair market value of the property is less than than the donor's adjusted basis, then the donee will use the donor's adjusted basis as the basis for the property for calculating depreciation, depletion, amortization and gain on the sale of the property. The basis for any loss on the sale of the property will be its fair market value.

If the fair market value of the property is equal or greater that the adjusted basis, the the donee will use the donor's adjusted basis for all purposes.

The adjusted basis for the gift will be increased by the amount of any gift tax actually paid.

52. WHAT IS THE BASIS OF PROPERTY ACQUIRED FROM A SPOUSE?

The basis of property transferred from one spouse to another or in trust by one spouse for another or by a former spouse if the transfer is incident to a divorce is the same as the transferor's adjusted basis in the property. However, the basis for the spouse receiving the property is adjusted for any gain recognized by the transferor on a transfer of property in trust in which the sum of the liabilities assumed, plus the sum of the liabilities to which the property is subject, is more than the adjusted basis of the property.

The transferor must provide the transferee with records necessary to determine the adjusted basis and holding period of the property as of the date of transfer.

53. WHAT IS THE BASIS OF INHERITED PROPERTY?

The basis of inherited property is usually its fair market value as of the date of the death of the decedent from whom it is inherited. If a federal estate tax return was filed, the basis in the inherited property can be its fair market value at the alternative valuation date if the estate elects to use alternative valuation. If a federal estate tax return was not filed, the basis of t he property is its appraised value set at the date of death.

Special valuation alternatives exists for special farm or closely held business real property. Publication 448, Federal and Estate Gift Taxes covers the various alternative methods of valuation.

54. WHAT IS A LIKE-KIND EXCHANGE?

Certain trades and exchanges of property are nontaxable. As such, gain from the exchange of the property is not taxed nor can loss form the exchange be deducted.

To be nontaxable, a like kind exchange must meet the following six requirements:

    1. The property must be business or investment property

    2. The property must not be property held for sale. It must be property held for investment or productive use in the the taxpayer's trade or business.

    3. There must be an exchange for like kind property. The exchanged property must be similar in nature and function.

    4. The property exchanged must be tangible property. A like kind

exchange is not permitted for stocks, bonds, notes and other intangible interests.

5. The exchanged property must be identified within 45 days of the exchange.

6. The exchange must be completed by the earlier of 180 days or the end of the tax year when the exchange occurred.

55. WHEN SHOULD DEDUCTIONS BE ITEMIZED?
A taxpayer should itemize if the taxpayer can not take the standard deduction. Some reasons for not being able to take the standard deduction are:
   1. the taxpayer is married filing separately
   2. the taxpayer is filing s return for a short tax year.
   3. the taxpayer is a nonresident or dual status alien. A dual status alien is one who was both a resident and nonresident alien during the tax year. A taxpayer should take the standard deduction if itemized deductions are less than the standard deduction.

Significant deductions that may be lost if not itemized are:
   1. large uninsured medical and dental expenses;
   2. taxes and interest paid on a home,
   3. large charitable contributions,
   4. large casualty and theft losses,
   5. moving expenses,
   6. employee business expenses
   7. miscellaneous expenses.

If these deductions plus others exceed the standard deduction, then the taxpayer should itemize.

56. WHAT IS A CASUALTY LOSS?
A casualty loss is the loss suffered as a result of damage, destruction to property resulting from an identifiable event that is sudden, unexpected, or unusual. A sudden event is defined as one that is swift, not gradual or progressive. An unexpected event is one that is ordinarily unanticipated and not intended. An unusual event is one that is not a day to day occurrence and that is not typical in the activity the taxpayer was engaged.

A casualty loss may also include a government ordered demolition or relocation of a structure declared unsafe because of some disaster. Casualty losses may result from the following causes but are not limited to them: earthquakes, hurricanes, floods, volcanoes, shipwrecks, cave-ins, vandalism. There is no casualty loss permitted for termite damage, disease to trees or shrubs, drought, or progressive deterioration due to age.

57. WHAT IS A THEFT LOSS?
Theft is the unlawful taking and removing of the property of another with the intent to permanently deprive the owner of it. Theft includes but it not limited to larceny, robbery and embezzlement. Money taken by way of threats, extortion and blackmail are also theft losses. The taxpayer need only show that the property was taken illegally under the state law where it occurred and that it was done with criminal intent.

The lost of property through normal negligence is not theft. However, the accidental disappearance may qualify as a casualty if the loss occurs from an identifiable event that is sudden, unusual and unexpected. An example would be a person accidentally tripping another person causing the victim to break a string of pearls. The loss of the pearls would be a casualty loss.

58. WHAT IS A LOSS OF DEPOSITS?
A loss of deposits occurs when a bank, credit union or other financial institution becomes insolvent and can not pay depositors. Such a loss can be deducted as a nonbusiness bad debt, a casualty loss or as an ordinary loss.

A nonbusiness bad debt loss is treated as a capital loss and is subject to the yearly deduction limit of capital gain plus $ 3,000 ($1,500 for married individuals filing separately).

A casualty loss is an itemized deduction and as such is balanced against the standard deduction. An ordinary loss deduction is limited to $20,000 per year ($10,000 if married filing separately). It is taken as an itemized deduction. An ordinary loss deduction is not permitted if any part of the loss is federally insured.

59. WHAT ARE MOVING EXPENSES?
If a taxpayer has moved to take take a new job or change job location, the taxpayer may deduct the expenses incurred in moving, if the taxpayer itemizes the deductions.

To be deductible, the move must be more than 35 miles from the taxpayer's old residence and the taxpayer must be fully employed for at least 39 weeks on the next year. If the taxpayer is self-employed he must be fully employed for 78 weeks in the next two years.

If the requirements are met, the taxpayer may deduct the reasonable expenses of: 1. moving household goods 2. traveling to the new home 3. househunting before actually moving 4. living temporarily in the new area 5. settling an old lease and signing a new one.

60. ARE EMPLOYEE BUSINESS EXPENSES DEDUCTIBLE?
An employee can deduct expenses for business related travel, transportation, meals, entertainment and gifts if the expenses were incurred as both necessary and ordinary expenses.

An ordinary expense is one that is common and accepted in the taxpayer's trade, business or profession. A necessary expense is one that is helpful and appropriate for the taxpayer's business. An expense is not required to be indispensable in order to be considered necessary for a taxpayer's business.

If an employee is not reimbursed for his business expenses by his employer, the employee must complete Form 2106 Employee Business Expenses and itemize the deduction.

61. ARE COMMUTING EXPENSES DEDUCTIBLE?
Transportation expenses incurred by an employee to and from work are personal expenses and are not deductible regardless of how far the employee has to travel to get to work. Such travel expenses are not deductible even if the taxpayer works during the trip.

Transportation expenses incurred in traveling from one work place to another in the course of a taxpayer's trade, business or profession are ordinary and necessary expenses.

The use of a personal car to advertise the taxpayer's trade, business or profession does change the personal use of the vehicle to business use. If the car is used to commuting back and forth to work, the expenses are still not deductible.

Trips to a union hall to get work assignments are not deductible. They are treated as commuting expenses to work.

62. WHAT IS CREDIT FOR THE ELDERLY AND DISABLED?

A 15% tax credit for the elderly and totally disabled applies to citizens and residents who are either: 1. 65 years of age before the end of the tax year, or 2. under 65 years of age and retired on a disability and were permanently and totally disabled when they retired. Married taxpayers must file a joint return to claim the credit unless they lived separate and apart for the entire tax year. Permanent and total disability exists when the taxpayer cannot engage in any gainful activity because of the physical or mental condition. A physician must certify that the condition has lasted or can be expected to last continuously for 12 or more months or that the condition can be expected to result in death.

63. HOW ARE AUDITS SELECTED?

An audit begins when the IRS notifies the taxpayer that the taxpayer's return has been selected for review. The IRS informs the taxpayer as to what information, documentation and records the taxpayer must produce.

Returns are chosen for examination using several methods. Some returns are selected randomly. Most returns are selected by a computer program called a Discriminant Function System (DIF). Other returns are selected because they had claims for refunds or credits. In short, the returns raised attention to themselves by their claims.

64. CAN AN AUDIT BE RECORDED?

An audit can be recorded by either the IRS or the taxpayer. If the taxpayer wishes to record the audit, the taxpayer is required to give 10 days written notice of the intent to record the audit. The taxpayer is to bring his or her own recording equipment.

If the IRS records the audit, it will notify the taxpayer 10 days before the audit. The taxpayer can get a copy of the audit tape at the taxpayer's own expense.

65. HOW IS AN APPEAL HANDLED?

The taxpayer can appeal the findings of the examination within the IRS through its Appeals Office. The Appeals Office a separate branch of the IRS and is independent of the Service Center Director and the District Director.

If the matter can not be settled administratively, the taxpayer may take the dispute to court.

66. WHAT IS THE TAX COURT?

The U.S. Tax Court is a special court system set up only to hear tax cases. It is usually the best forum in which a taxpayer can litigate disputed tax issues.

To be able to go to Tax Court, the taxpayer must file a Tax Court Petition within ninety (90) days of receipt of the formal Notice of Deficiency telling the taxpayer that the IRS claims additional tax is due. If the taxpayer fails to file the Tax Court Petition within the 90 day period, the taxpayer loses all right to go to Tax Court and the IRS can immediately start collection procedures.

The biggest mistake that taxpayers routinely make is to ignore the chance to go to Tax Court. Once that option is lost, all power shifts to IRS and they begin collection virtually unhindered.

67. CAN THE TAXPAYER GO TO FEDERAL COURT?

A taxpayer can file a complaint in Federal Court of the U.S. Claims Court over a disputed debt but first the taxpayer must pay the disputed tax. This is the real difference between these courts and the Tax Court. The taxpayer does not have to pay the disputed tax prior to commencing the suit in Tax Court.

It poses a real burden on a taxpayer to have the pay the tax in full before commencing a suit for a refund. It often takes years to fully pay off the disputed amount before the taxpayer then has the right to file a suit. It is for this reason that a taxpayer should never lightly give up his right to go to Tax Court.

The IRS only follows Supreme Court decisions. The IRS has repeatedly stated that if it feels it is right, it will continue to follow its own interpretation of the law regardless of how many times it loses in the lower courts.

2
DRUNK DRIVING

2. DRUNK DRIVING

This chapter deals with the law surrounding drunk driving also called driving while intoxicated (DWI) or driving under the influence (DUI). As everyone is aware, drunk driving is a crime. Every year tens of thousands of persons are killed or horribly maimed in accidents involving drunk drivers.

To stem the seemingly endless onslaught of drunk drivers against the world at large, all of the states have passed increasingly onerous drunk driving laws. These laws have not been as effective as originally thought in curbing drunk drivers.

The prime weapon against drunk driving was to make it a crime to drive with a certain blood alcohol level which has constantly been lowered. This lowering of the blood alcohol level needed for a conviction has turned otherwise sober and safe drivers into criminals merely because they have failed a blood, breath or urine test.

If convictions for drunk driving are to be based, as they are in many case, solely upon the results of blood, breath or urine tests, then every driver should be aware of what those tests actually entail and their reliability.

This chapter addresses those questions most often posed by the general public regarding drunk driving laws, their enforcement and the possible defenses to the alleged charges.

1. WHAT IS DRUNK DRIVING?
All states makes it a crime to drive while under the influence of alcohol (DUI) to such an extent that the vehicle can not be operated in a safe manner.

It is legal in every state to drink alcohol and then drive provided the alcohol imbibed does not impair the driver's ability to safely operate the vehicle.

Because it is possible to safely operate a vehicle with alcohol in the driver's system, it has proven difficult to determine the point when alcoholic impairment of the ability to operate a vehicle occurs. To accomplish this, law enforcement officers have had to rely on field sobriety tests and their own observations to determine whether the vehicle can be operated safely. Interpretation of the results of the field sobriety tests are subjective and therefore open to considerable dispute.

2. WHAT IS DRIVING WITH AN ILLEGAL BLOOD ALCOHOL LEVEL?

To address the problem of the subjective nature of the field sobriety test, nearly all states have passed special drunk driving laws making it illegal to operate a vehicle on public roads when the driver has an alcoholic blood level over a fixed percentage. Over the years, California has reduced the level of blood alcohol permitted by a driver from .15% to .08%.

A person driving a vehicle with a blood alcohol content over the state limit is guilty of drunk driving regardless of the fact that he or she may be able to handle the vehicle in a perfectly safe manner.

A person with a blood alcohol level less than the state limit may still be charged with drunk driving under the general drunk if the driver appears not to be able to safely operate the vehicle because of the alcohol in his or her system.

3. MAY A DRIVER REFUSE A FIELD SOBRIETY TEST?

Most states now require that driver of a vehicle perform the field sobriety test when requested by a police officer or have the driver's license automatically suspended. Surprisingly, not all states have that requirement. Not until 1991 did California make the refusal to take a field sobriety test grounds for automatic suspension of the driver's license.

There is no standard field sobriety test used throughout the United States. The most common tests are the walking the straight line, standing still, leaning backwards, touching the nose with eyes closed, the touching the fingers of a hand, counting backwards and the Nystagmus test. It is one of the strange effects of alcohol that a person under its influence may pass several field sobriety tests and totally fail others. Because of the possibility of conflicting results, usually more than one test is used to cross check eachother. That is one of the reasons that the field sobriety test results are not always viewed as conclusive in determining whether the driver was under the influence of alcohol.

4. CAN A DRIVER REFUSE TO TAKE A CHEMICAL TEST?

Every state has adopted an implied consent law. Under this law, the state holds that any person driving on its highways or roads and implicitly consented to give undergo a chemical test when stopped by a police officer for suspicion for driving under the influence of alcohol.

Under the implied consent laws, a refusal to take a chemical test results in a suspension of the right to drive a vehicle in the state usually for six (6) months. If the driver is charged and convicted for driving, this suspension is in addition to any punishment meted out for the conviction.

It is the threat of the license revocation that forces nearly all drivers to consent to take a chemical test. Usually state law gives the driver the option to take a blood, breath or urine test provided the driver can complete the chosen test. Failure to complete the test means the driver complete one of the other tests or have it deemed a refusal.

5. CAN BLOOD TESTS BE FORCED?

Even though a driver may refuse to take a chemical test and elect to have his or her license suspended, the United States Supreme Court has held that police officers may nevertheless force a person to take blood test. The only proviso is that they must not use excessive force. Schmerber vs. California 384 U.S. 757 . There is no constitutional violation or argument against self-incrimination if the police force a blood test as long as they do not use excessive force. As a rule, except when there is felony drunk driving involving serious bodily injury, the police will not bother to force a blood test. They would be more than satisfied with the license suspension even if they can't get the conviction.

6. WHAT IS A CHEMICAL TEST?

There are three general types of chemical test available These tests are the:

    1. A blood test,

    2. An urine test, and

    3. A breath test.

Many states, including California, can require a blood test in addition to a breath test. The reason for this is that a person may be on a drug other that alcohol and the blood test will detect it.

7. MUST THE VEHICLE ACTUALLY BE MOVING FOR A DRUNK DRIVING CONVICTION?

The majority of states have held that drunk driving does not require the actual movement of the vehicle. The majority instead asserts that a driver under the influence has control over the vehicle and can be charged with drunk driving. There are many cases in California where a person was sitting in a parked car with the engine running and was convicted of drunk driving. This trend may be changing in California. In 1991, the Supreme Court held that in a license revocation case, actual movement of some type was necessary. The test in the majority of states is the person excercising all of the control over the vehicle that a driver would exercise. If so, the driver could be charged with drunk driving even if the car was not moving.

A minority of states do not take the expanded view. These states require actual movement of the vehicle, even if only a few inches, to demonstrate the operation of the vehicle.

8. MUST AN OFFICER HAVE PROBABLE CAUSE FOR THE STOP BEFORE THERE CAN BE A DRUNK DRIVING ARREST?

No police officer may wantonly and indiscriminately require the driver to undergo chemical or field sobriety tests. The officer musts have "probable cause", a reasonable belief that the driver might be violating some law prior to the stop.

A drunken driver stopped without probable cause can not be convicted. A pretext stop is the term of art given for stopping people for non-existent or minor violations in order to observe and test them for intoxication. Pretext stops are improper but as a practical matter they are hard to prove.

At night, police routinely look for anything suspicious so as to be able to pull drivers over. The most common stop is for "weaving in the lanes". Another common stop is for having the license plate light out. These reasons have been upheld in court as valid reasons for stopping a car and speaking with a driver. If the officer smells alcohol, the officer can then validly order a field or chemical test.

9. DOES THE SMELL OF ALCOHOL MEAN A PERSON HAS BEEN DRINKING?

This was a trick question. Pure alcohol has no smell. It is only the additives placed in the alcohol that gives the combined drink its taste, color and smell. The general public has long mistakenly assumed alcohol to have a smell. Thus the general public believes, sometimes wrongly, when an officer testifies that a person smelled of alcohol that the driver had been drinking alcohol.

There are non-alcoholic beer and wine products on the market. A person may drink a entirely non-alcoholic beverages or a mixture of both alcoholic and non-alcoholic beverages and thus have a strong smell and yet still not be legally drunk. A police officer in a blind smelling test would be unable to identify the non-alcoholic from the alcoholic beverage.

10. IS AN ARREST AT A DRUNK DRIVING ROADBLOCK VALID?

For years sobriety roadblocks were challenged as unconstitutional pretext searches. Several states held that the roadblocks violated the U.S. Constitution as unreasonable searches. Finally, after several years of argument, the U.S. Supreme Court held that sobriety roadblocks are valid.

Basically all that can be done at such roadblocks is to stop the car and speak with the drivers. Unless the officers observe something giving rise to probable cause to order the field sobriety or chemical test, the officer must let the driver alone. If the officer smells what he believes to be alcohol (see question 9) then the officer can order the tests be done.

11. WHAT IS THE MOST ACCURATE TEST?

Each of the three chemical tests blood, breath and urine, have their own characteristics. The one most problematical and therefore most popular with drivers is the breath machine.

The breath machine can be the most unreliable because it measures alcohol in the breath and converts, it through a mathematical formula, into the amount of alcoholic content in the blood. Common sense points out that someone being tested immediately after drinking an alcoholic beverage will have a highly inaccurate reading because the alcohol will not have had time to enter the bloodstream.

The urine test utilizes concerts, through a mathematical formula, the alcoholic content in the urine into the alcoholic content in the blood. Urine tests have been repeatedly attacked as unreliable because they measure alcohol that has already passed through the person to determine what is presently in the person. The inability to completely empty the bladder prior to the test can lead to false readings.

The most accurate test is the blood test provided it is done within a timely manner. A blood test, however, does require taking a blood sample and given today's fear of AIDS most people shy away from that test.

Generally, if a person has been drinking, the easiest one to attack is the breath test followed by the urine test. If a person hasn't been drinking for several hours, the blood test is definitely the most reliable to prove innocence.

12. WHAT IS THE STANDARD FOR THE USE OF SCIENTIFIC EVIDENCE IN COURT?

The standard by which the court must judge the admissibility of scientific evidence is set forth in the Frye Rule (Frye vs. United States (1923) 293 F. 1013. All states follow the Frye Rule and as did California in People vs. Kelly 17 C3d 24). The rule has been recently restated in People vs. Brown (1985) 40 C3d. 512 when the California Supreme Court held: "In Kelly, supra, this court affirmed California adherence to the rule first announced in Frye, supra, for the admissibility of a new scientific technique: the technique must be "sufficiency established to gained general acceptance in the particular field to which it belongs." Under the Kelly/Frye rule, the proponent of the scientific evidence must establish 1. the (generally accepted) reliability of the method ... usually by expert testimony, and 2. (that) the witness furnishing such testimony (is) properly qualified as an expert to give an opinion on the subject.

Additionally, the proponent must "demonstrate that the correct scientific procedures were used in the instant case."

In People vs. Adams (1976) 59 Cal.App.3d 559, the court ruled that

results of breath analysis machines were governed by the Kelly/Frye Rule. The court held that before the results could be introduced into court, the district attorney had to show:
1. The apparatus was in proper working order
2. The test was properly administered, and
3. The operator was competent and qualified.

These requirements must be met every time the prosecution seeks to have a person convicted because of a failure of a chemical test. If it can be shown that one of those requirements were not met, then the court should not admit the results into evidence.

13. BREATH ANALYSIS MACHINES CERTIFIED FOR ACCURACY?
The United States Department of Transportation (DOT) tests breath analyzing machines for reliability. The Department of Transportation places the breath machines that it finds accurate to its standards on a "Conforming Products List" in the Federal Register Vol. 49, 242.

Over 40 states simply take the machines off the list and use them. Those states do not perform independent certification. The DOT by its regulations require all modifications to a machine on the list to be retested for accuracy. This is a point that could be important in a case where the machine was modified by the agency using it but never retested for reliability afterward.

14. DO THE POLICE HAVE A DUTY TO PRESERVE BREATH SAMPLES?
The United States Supreme Court in California vs. Trombetta (1984) 467 U.S. 479 held that the defendant's breath sample, although collected by the police, had not been destroyed in bad faith. Furthermore the Court held that the defendant failed to meet the new materiality standard. This standard requires the defendant to that the exculpatory evidence was apparent before it was destroyed, that the evidence might be expected to play a significant role in the defendant's defense and the defense is unable to get the evidence by other reasonable available means.

State law may be more liberal than the federal standard. California use to to require keeping of the breath sample, if possible prior to the

Trombetta decision. It no longer does. However other states may require it. It certainly is relevant because the sample can be retested to prove guilt or innocence.

15. MAY A JURY DISREGARD THE RESULTS OF A BREATH MACHINE?

The obvious answer is yes. However, in the real world it is difficult to get a jury to see anything other than the reading on the machine.

The jury is ultimate trier of fact. As such they decide what to believe or not to believe. Unfortunately many jurors believe despite all the instructions to the contrary that they must find a person guilty if the breath machine says so. Many jurors fail to realize that the breath machine is just a machine and capable of error even more readily than a person if improperly maintained or operated.

A properly instructed jury will understand its duty to consider whether the machine was an accurate machine, properly maintained and properly operated before accepting the results.

16. WHAT IS THE NYSTAGMUS TEST?

Nystagmus means jerking of the eyes. Many police check as part of their field sobriety test the "Horizontal Gaze Nystagmus." This is the nystagmus that occurs when the eyes gaze to the side. Many people will show some jerking if the eyes move far enough to the sides. When a person is intoxicated, however, three signs will be observed:

1. The jerking of the eyes will occur much sooner. The more intoxicated the person, the sooner his eyes will jerk when moved to the side

2. The greater the intoxication, the greater will be the jerking at the extreme gaze to the side.

3. If the subject is intoxicated, then the suspect can not smoothly follow a slowly moving object with his eyes. The testing officer uses a point system to determine the degree of impairment on the above observations, when a certain an arrest occurs.

17. IS THE NYSTAGMUS TEST ACCURATE?

The Nystagmus test is not a valid scientific test. At most, it gives an possibility of being under the influence. The U.S. Department of

Transportation, National Highway Traffic Safety Association (NHTSA) published a manual for Improved Sobriety Testing.

The NHTSA discussed in its training manual the Nystagmus test. The manual states the problems with the nystagmus test. It states: "Nystagmus may be due to causes other than alcohol in three or four percent of the population. These other causes include medications, barbituates and other depressants. A large disparity between the right and left eye may indicate brain damage."

When everything is considered, no one should ever be convicted on the Nystagmus test alone. The test does not meet the standards for a scientific test. For that reason, some courts do not even admit its results.

18. CAN A BLOOD ALCOHOL LEVEL BE ZERO AND STILL HAVE A POSITIVE URINE RESULT?

A urine test measures the alcohol content in the urine after it passed through a body. Therefore alcohol in the urine is obviously is not in the blood. Some alcohol in the urine is burnt up by the body and the rest has to be expelled.

The Journal of the American Medical Association had an article where a person drinking alcohol the previous night had a zero blood alcohol level but still had a measurable amount of alcohol in his urine.

A urine test conducted properly is designed to prevent a false positive. The suspect voids his or her bladder and then waits 20 minutes before giving the sample to be tested. This sample contains most, if not all of the alcohol that that body processed during that time period.

A common complaint heard by defense attorneys is that the police did not have the suspect void his bladder and use the second sample. Many defendants have claimed that only one sample was given without prior voiding. If this can be proven, a difficult matter because the suspect's word against the police, the results would be thrown out.

19. DOES RADIO FREQUENCY INTERFERENCE EFFECT A BREATH MACHINE?

There are significant radio frequency interference (RFI) problems breath machines. A federal study entitled "Limited Electromagnetic

Interference Testing of Evidential Breath Testers" by the National Highway Safety Administration (NHTSA) DOT-HS806 concluded that there is a problem with RFI, and that it cannot be proven that any approved breath test machine is free of RFI.

As such, the defense should include testimony from persons in and near the sight of the test regarding what radios were present, what radios and transmitting antennas were near and whether or not any transmitting may have been been going on during the test.

20. IS THERE A RIGHT TO JURY TRIAL?

The Sixth Amendment of the United States Constitution does not require a defendant be given the right to have a jury trial for petty crimes. Petty crimes are defines as those crimes which carry a maximum jail term of six months or less or with additional penalties so severe that the total punishment shows an intent to treat the crime as a "serious" offense.

Generally, drunk driving cases carry a maximum jail time of six months. Therefore in most states a jury trial is not mandate d by Federal Law. Some states, like California, give the defendant the right to a jury trial even in "petty" misdemeanor cases.

21. CAN A VEHICLE BE SEARCHED AFTER AN ARREST HAS BEEN MADE?

It has long been settled that after an arrest of an individual for drunk driving, the police can search the vehicle without a warrant. Several theories support the search, looking for weapons, inventorying the contents so they won't be lost, looking for evidence, etc.

Any search of the vehicle must conform to the individual state law where the arrest occurred but the general view that normal searches following an arrest are valid.

22. WHAT IS RECKLESS DRIVING?

Reckless driving is the crime of intentionally driving a vehicle with knowledge that injury to another was probable or with wanton disregard of the safety of others and in reckless disregard for the consequences of the actions.

Reckless driving is not a lesser included offense of drunk driving.

A person can be driving a vehicle in a perfectly safe and sane manner and simply have a higher than a .08 blood alcohol level.

Reckless driving usually carries the same criminal penalty as drunk driving. The difference between the two crimes is that a reckless driving conviction does not carry with it the automatic license restrictions or the requirement to attend drunk schools that a criminal conviction for drunk driving carries.

On weak case or case with low blood alcohol, the prosecution often offers to reduce the drunk driving charge to reckless driving. The advantage for the defendant is that this is not a drunk driving charge and therefore there is requirement to attend drunk school in order to keep the driver's license.

23. WHAT IS A PRIOR ENHANCEMENT?
A prior enhancement is an allegation in the complaint or indictment that the defendant has committed the crime before. Many states will punish a repeat offender for the same crime harder than it did on the first offense.

All states punish repeat drunk drivers harder as the number of times they are caught increases. This increased punishment is not considered a violation of double jeopardy guarantee of the Fifth Amendment or equal protection clause.

To validly have a enhanced punishment, the prosecution merely has to show after the conviction for the current drunk driving offense that there was a prior conviction for drunk driving. The prosecution must also show that, if the defendant pled guilty to the prior offense, he did so with full knowledge and understanding of his rights.

24. WHAT IS A WET RECKLESS?
Some states have passed laws, like California, whereby the district attorney can reduce a drunk driving offense to reckless driving but if the defendant is convicted of another drunk driving offense within a fixed period, usually seven years, the reduced reckless driving charge will be treated as a regular drunk driving conviction for enhancement purposes.

A regular reckless driving conviction can not be used to enhance a drunk driving conviction but a wet reckless conviction can be used to so enhance a drunk driving conviction.

25. HOW ARE JUVENILE DRUNK DRIVERS TREATED?

Most states treat juvenile drunk driver differently from adults. Some states try the juvenile in juvenile court system rather than in the regular court system.

Nearly all state have laws declaring a juvenile driving with a blood alcohol level of .05% guilty of drunk driving as opposed to .08 or higher for adults in most states.

A juvenile drunk driver upon conviction usually has his or her license revoked until reaching the age of 18 years. In some states, it is restricted until 21 years of age.

At trial the juvenile has the same rights as an adult. The right to an attorney and to call witnesses. The right to a jury trial is not available in a juvenile court even though imprisonment may exceed six months. The reason for this is that juvenile court is not for punishment but rather rehabilitation of the juvenile. For that reason, different treatment is permitted for the juvenile offender that is not meted out to the adult.

26. WHAT IS ADMINISTRATIVE REVOCATION?

Many states, including California, have adopted a administrative procedure whereby a person accused of drunk driving may have his or her license revoked prior to actual criminal trial or conviction for drunk driving.

Basically, the states having this program will have an administrative hearing before their Department of Motor Vehicles with in 45 to 60 days of the drunk driving arrest. At the hearing, if it can be shown that the person was driving a vehicle while having a blood alcohol level over the legal limit, the person's driver's license is suspended.

This suspension is in addition to whatever happens in the criminal case. Constitutional arguments have been raised this procedure. It is possible for the driver to be found not guilty at the criminal trial and still have his license revoked administratively. In other words, 12 people on the jury could find the chemical inaccurate for the criminal case and yet one administrative judge might find the same test valid for revocation of the license.

Some states have addressed the effect of revocation after being found not guilty at the criminal case but allowing the defendant to administratively appeal the revocation after the acquittal.

3
SMALL CLAIMS COURTS

3. SMALL CLAIMS COURTS

Small claims court is truly the People's Court. For most people, it will be their only contact with the judicial system except for the occasional traffic ticket.

Small claims court exist as an alternative to the highly structured, complex and expensive traditional court system. Small claims courts exist to provide a cheap, fast and efficient means to settle disputes concerning small amounts of money not worth hiring an attorney to bring a lawsuit in the traditional sense.

There are many "how to" books on the market that instruct in great detail what a person must do to file a small claims action. Generally, such books are unnecessary. This chapter answers most of the important and fundamental questions most people have concerning small claims court The expensive "how to" books merely expand the information contained herein.

After reading these questions, most people should be able to understand the small claims court procedure. Afterward, they should be able to go to the clerk of the small claims court, pick up the forms along with the local rules of court and intelligently start the action. In the same vein, most defendants, after reading this chapter, should be able to understand how to competently present their case

1. WHAT IS SMALL CLAIMS COURT?
The small claims court is a specially created court in which most disputes can be tried inexpensively and quickly. The rules of the court are simple and court procedure is relatively informal. Lawyers are not permitted to present or try the case. Claims in small claims cases vary from state to state. In California for instance, disputes up to $5,000 can be heard in a small claims court. The regular filing fee for most small claims court is between $6.00 and $15.00.

The trial of a small claims case is usually heard within 40 to 70 days from the filing of the claim. While most small claim cases involve money damages, most small claims court have the power to grant other remedies such as ordering a person to so or not do something if the value of the act ordered or restrained is within the monetary limits of the court.

2. WHO CAN SUE IN SMALL CLAIMS COURT?

Nearly anyone can sue in small claims court. The person bringing the suit is called the plaintiff and the person being sued is the defendant. An individual can sue other individuals or businesses and vice versa.

Most states deny collection agencies the right to sue in small claims court. Nor can someone file a small claims action for another. Most states deny assignees, persons who buy a debt of another, to sue in small claims for collection of that debt.

To file in small claims court, a person must be an adult, over 18 years of age, and mentally competent. The plaintiff need not be a U.S. citizen to file a small claims complaint. The plaintiff does not have to speak English to file the the complaint. Interpreters are permitted in court if a witness does not speak competent English.

3. CAN AN ATTORNEY APPEAR IN SMALL CLAIMS COURT?

An attorney is not permitted in small claim court as an advocate of a party. The attorney can give legal advice in court to either the plaintiff or defendant. Nor can an attorney comment in court as to the presentation of evidence.

The parties are permitted to speak with attorneys out of court and ask for advise in preparing their cases. An attorney is permitted to testify as a witness in a small claims action. There is no prohibition to calling an attorney or other profession to present facts and testimony germane to the case. The attorney is simply prohibited from assisting a party while in the courtroom.

4. WHERE IS A SMALL CLAIMS ACTION FILED?

It is imperative that a plaintiff file a small claims action in the proper court. Failure to file in the proper court may result in the action be transferred to proper court or dismissed altogether.

Generally, a small claims action is filed in the court whose judicial district or area covers where the defendant lives, or if a business, where the business is located.

Sometimes the small claims court rules for a state permits the plaintiff to sue in the court district where an accident or tort, a civil wrong, occurred even if it isn't where the defendant lives. Also most states permit a small claims suit involving a breach of contract to be

filed:
1. where the defendant lives
2. where the defendant signed the contract
3. where the defendant lived when the contract was signed
4. where the contract was to be performed.

If it is possible to file in more than one judicial district, the plaintiff may choose the one most convenient for the plaintiff and witnesses. However if a judicial district is chosen that is not the where the defendant lives, then a longer notice requirement may apply which would make it longer for the case to be heard.

5. WHEN CAN A SMALL CLAIMS ACTION BE FILED?
Every claim had a statute of limitations which is a period of time in which a lawsuit must be filed or the right to bring the lawsuit will be lost. Statute of limitations vary from state to state.

In California, claims for personal injury have a one year statute of limitation. In California breaches of a written contract have a four year statute of limitation while oral contracts have a two year statute of limitation. Checking the Civil Code for the state where the small claims court is located will give the appropriate statute of limitations.

Suits against most governmental agencies require special handling. First the plaintiff must file a claim with the agency within a certain period of time following the injury or breach, normally around 100 days but this varies. Then after the agency rejects the claim, the plaintiff must file his or her action within a very narrow time period, usually six months but this varies, or lose the right to sue altogether. Claims against government agencies should be pursued with all dispatch.

6. HOW IS A DEFENDANT IDENTIFIED?
On most small claims forms the plaintiff must state the names and addresses of the defendants, those people or business being sued.

If the defendant is a business or corporation, the business' legal name and address can be found by checking with the city's licensing agency, the tax assessor's office, the fictitious business names files in the County Clerk's Office, or the Office of the Secretary of State's corporate division. All corporations incorporated in a state and foreign corporations doing business in a state are usually required to designate a person to receive process (service of complaints) for the corporation.

The correct names and addresses of the defendants are needed so that they can be properly served with the complaint.

7. WHERE ARE THE FORMS FOR SMALL CLAIMS COURT OBTAINED?

All of the forms for small claims court are obtainable from the clerk of the small claims court. In addition, many stationary stores sell the small claim forms and do-it-yourself small claims manuals often include them.

8. WHAT DECIDES THE AMOUNT OF THE CLAIM?

The most important consideration in a small claims case is the amount of the claim sought. A plaintiff can not go over the jurisdictional limit of the court. If a plaintiff asks for more than the court is allowed to award, the entire case may be dismissed.

If the plaintiff sues for less than is owed, the plaintiff forever waives the balance. For instance, if the plaintiff is owed $20,000 and sues for $5,000, the plaintiff forever loses the right to sue for the remaining $15,000. In such an example, the plaintiff could have sued in a regular court for the full $20,000. However in such an event, the Plaintiff might have had to wait years to have the case heard and incurred large fees and cost in the meantime preparing for the trial.

9. IS THERE A FILING FEE?

There is always a filing fee. In California the basis fee was $6.00 per case. Multiple filers, those with over 13 cases per year, pay, in California, $12.00 per case.

A person unable to pay the filing fee can, in most states, file for a waiver of fees. This waiver is called a Forma Pauperis, Latin for Form of a Pauper. If the plaintiff qualifies the fee is waived and subsequently recovered if the plaintiff wins the case. In such an event, the defendant pays the filing fee as a cost to the plaintiff.

10. WHAT COSTS ARE RECOVERABLE?

Most of the costs related to pursuing a small claims actions are recoverable from the defendant if the plaintiff wins. Court costs that are recoverable are filing fees, service of process fees, witness fees and mileage. There is usually no recovery for expert witness fees in small claims cases. Also recoverable are fees for subpoena of individuals and for subpoena duces tecum for documents. Interest on the judgment is always awarded and sometimes it is awarded before judgment. Prejudgment interest, interest running from a date prior to the date of judgment, is governed by the laws of each state. A plaintiff should always investigate to determine if it is awardable in his case.

After the trial, the plaintiff presents a summary of his or her costs to the court for approval.

11. CAN WITNESSES BE SUBPOENAED?

Some states permit statements by witnesses in small claim actions to be used instead of the witness actually appearing. In such states, the statements must be in writing and signed under penalty of perjury. The statement should state, "Signed under penalty of perjury that the foregoing is true and correct." It is always best to have your witnesses available at trial. Since the other party can not question a witness, Judge's do no have to accept the statement or it it much effect.

A plaintiff can subpoena a witness. A subpoena is a court order that the person appear at the court to testify or face charges of contempt of court. Likewise, a subpoena duces tecum can be issued for documents. A subpoena duces tecum requires the person served with it to bring specified documents to court on a day of trial. A subpoena can only be served in person. It can not be mailed.

The person serving the subpoena must be over 18 years of age. In some states the plaintiff can serve the subpoena in other states the plaintiff can not serve it.

Whoever serves the subpoena must fill out a Proof of Service stating the date and location where the person was served. The Proof of Service is filed with the court. If it becomes necessary to compel attendance, the court will rely on the Proof of Service for jurisdiction over the witness.

Most states require the party issuing the subpoena to pay the witness a daily fee and mileage round trip. In California for example this is presently $35.00 per day and $.20 per mile.

Always bear in mind that a subpoenaed witness may be hostile to a case and it might be better not to subpoena a witness who might "forget" or "misremember" key items.

12. HOW IS A DEFENDANT SERVED?
A defendant must be served and given the small claims complaint in such a manner that the court will know for sure that it was done. The procedural requirement as to how service is performed must be correctly followed or the action may not proceed and may be dismissed altogether.

A plaintiff can not serve the small claims action on the defendant. In some states such as California, the court clerk will mail the complaint to the defendant's address by Certified Mail. If the defendant signs for it, then service is made. The fee for this is $3.00 in California. If the defendant does not accept delivery of the Certified Mail, the plaintiff must serve the defendant another way.

The defendant can be served by personal service. Personal service requires a person over 18 years of age to personally deliver the complaint to the defendant. A sheriff will do it for about $25.00 or a commercial process server will do it for about $50.00.

Once the complaint is filed a Proof of Service is filed with the court stating the date and location when filed. The case will not be calendared for trial until the Proof of Service is filed with the court.

In most states, the defendant may be served by substituted service. Substituted service requires the process server to leave a copy of the complaint with a identified person at the business or residence of the defendant and to mail a copy of the complaint to the defendant at that address within 10 days. A proof of service must be filed by the process server stating the name of the person that the complaint was given.

13. CAN THE SMALL CLAIMS ACTION BE SETTLED BEFORE TRIAL?
A small claims action can always be settled by the parties. The Plaintiff merely files a Dismissal with the Court. The plaintiff should hold off filing the dismissal until the check, if any, clears the bank. If the check does not clear, then the plaintiff would not have to refile the small claims action.

If periodic payments are to be made, the parties should write a settlement agreement describing the rights and duties of the parties. Then instead of dismissing, they should have the court adopt it as its judgment in the case. Once done, the settlement agreement becomes enforceable by the court if either party defaults in the performance under the settlement agreement. Another alternative if payments are made is to dismiss without prejudice which allows the plaintiff to refile if the payments are not made.

14. WHAT HAPPENS IF THE DEFENDANT DOES NOT APPEAR?

If the defendant does not appear at the trial what happens next depends on whether the defendant was properly served. The court will determine if the Proof of Service is valid. If the proof of service is procedurally invalid, the court will dismiss the case for want of jurisdiction over the defendant. If the proof of service was valid, meaning the complaint was properly served on the defendant, then the case will continue.

Judgment is not automatic for the plaintiff just because the defendant fails to appear. The Plaintiff must still put on evidence proving the plaintiff's entitlement to damages. This is called a "Prove up" hearing. The Judge will hear only the plaintiff's case and decide if under state law damages should be awarded. Just because a defendant does not show up does not mean that a judge can award damages when no liability can be shown or in violation of state or federal law.

If the judge can issue a valid judgment, he will do so. The judgment will include the award for the proper damages suffered by the plaintiff, the court costs in bringing the suit and the amount of interest permitted under state law.

15. CAN A DEFENDANT FILE A CLAIM AGAINST THE PLAINTIFF?

The defendant may file a claim against the plaintiff in small claims court. The claim does not have to be over the same fact pattern as the plaintiff's claim. For example, the plaintiff may be suing over a car accident and the defendant may be suing over a broken refrigerator totally unrelated to the car accident.

The defendant's claim is subject to the same restrictions as the plaintiff's claim. The defendant may not sue for damages over the court's jurisdictional limit and must comply with the statute of limitations. The amount over the defendant's claim is forever waived as with the plaintiff's claim.

The defendant may file his complaint in the regular court, Municipal Court, Superior Court, District Court or whatever that state calls its courts or even in Federal Court if appropriate. The plaintiff's small claim action will be transferred to the regular court if it arises from the same fact pattern as the defendant's action. In such an event, the plaintiff may increase his or her claim for damages and them hire an attorney and handle the action as a regular lawsuit.

16. IS A SMALL CLAIMS JUDGMENT APPEALABLE?
In most states, including California, a plaintiff may not appeal the judgment in a small claims action. If the plaintiff loses the case is over and can not be relitigated.

The defendant, however, can appeal the judgment of a small claims court. Usually in an appeal, the case is retried again in a regular court and before a real Judge. The new trial is called a "Trial De Novo" which means a completely new trial. In California , small claims appeals are heard in the Superior Court, except for that the trial is conducted as before without attorneys.

A plaintiff is entitled to appeal a judgment awarded against the plaintiff on the defendant's claim. Whereas, a defendant is not entitled to appeal a judgment on his or her claim against the plaintiff.

17. HOW IS THE JUDGMENT COLLECTED?
Once the court issue a money judgment, the prevailing party becomes a Judgment Creditor of the losing party who is now the Judgment Debtor.

The judgment may specify that the amount of money is to be paid in full to the Judgment Creditor or allow the Judgment Debtor to make periodic payments. Periodic payments are usually ordered in the judgment only if the parties had entered into a settlement agreement ordering them. Interest is usually awarded on a judgment from that date of its award. The legal rate of interest varies from state to state but is around ten percent (10%) per year.

Once the judgment is issued it is up to the judgment creditor to collect. Collecting a judgment is the most frustrating part of the small claims process. A judgment does not guarantee payment. A judgment creditor may be without assets, "judgment proof", or be uncooperative causing extra effort or costs.

The court is not a collection agency. As such, it will not collect the award for the Judgment Creditor. It will supply orders and documents to help collect the judgment. To collect the judgment, often an attorney or collection agency is hired.

18. CAN WAGES BE ATTACHED TO PAY A SMALL CLAIMS JUDGMENT?

The court issues its judgment in favor of the prevailing party. The prevailing party is the winner and can be the plaintiff winning on his complaint or the defendant winning a judgment against the plaintiff on the defendant's claim. The judgment is taken by the winner to the clerk of the court. The clerk of the court issues a Writ of Execution containing the information in the judgment. A Writ of Execution is a court order directing the Sheriff or Marshal to take control or "levy upon" the assets of the losing party to satisfy the judgment. It is the responsibility of the Judgment Creditor to tell the marshal or sheriff where the property is located so it can be seized.

Wages can be attached, "garnished" to pay the judgment. Most states have laws to prevent employees from being fired just because their wages have been attached.

All states provide debtors statutory exemptions from collections. A debtor is allowed to earn a certain amount of money in wages and have a certain amount of property that can not be attached or seized to satisfy the judgment. Only property over these statutory amounts can be taken to satisfy a judgment.

19. CAN REAL PROPERTY BE SEIZED TO PAY A SMALL CLAIMS JUDGMENT?

Real property can be seized and sold by a marshal or sheriff executing on a small claims judgment. Every state has its own procedure for execution on real property. In essence, the sheriff or marshal advertises in a newspaper of general circulation that on a certain date usually after 30 to 60 days notice to the debtor, that the real property will be sold to the highest bidder at a public auction at the Sheriff or Marshal's Office.

At the sale, highest bidder purchases whatever interest the debtor had in the property. If the debtor owes $100,000 on the real property, the purchaser will take the real property subject to that $100,000. In other words the $100,000 debt still remains on the property.

In all states, a person can file a homestead on the real property the debtor owes and resides. The statutory amount varies from $20,000 to $40,000. This means that if the real property is seized and sold, the debtor is first given the homestead amount before any proceeds are applied to the judgment. As such, a court will not permit execution on real property unless the debtor has equity in the property over the homestead amount because the creditor won't receive anything anyway.

20. CAN A LIEN BE PLACED ON THE DEBTOR'S PROPERTY?

A judgment creditor can request that the clerk of the court issue a Abstract of Judgment. An Abstract of Judgment is an official recordable court document. When recorded in the County Recorder's Office, the Abstract of Judgment places a lien on all of the real property of the debtor in the County where the Abstract is recorded.

As a lien is placed on the real property, anyone purchasing the property in the future also purchases the lien. As such, no one will ever purchase the property without having the lien taken off. This is the cheapest way of getting paid. Often when an abstract is filed it stays on the real property for 10 years. It can then be renewed along with the judgment for another 10 years. When the property is ultimately sold, the lien must be paid along with all interest before clear title can be passed.

21. HOW DOES THE DEBTOR'S BANKRUPTCY AFFECT A SMALL CLAIMS ACTION?

When a debtor files bankruptcy, there is an "Automatic Stay" on any collection lawsuit against the debtor. In other words, a person in bankruptcy can not be sued in small claims court.

If a person intentionally tries to sue a person in bankruptcy, any judgment received would be void. Furthermore, any person who knowingly filed such a suit might face fines or penalties for deliberately violating the law and wasting the court's time.

Furthermore, under the bankruptcy law all judgments obtained within three months of a debtor's bankruptcy are set aside and must be relitigated again in the bankruptcy court. Older judgments are treated as unsecured claims in the bankruptcy proceeding. That means they are paid in percentage to the amount that remains in the estate after all allowable expenses and secured claims have been paid.

22. WHAT HAPPENS AFTER THE JUDGMENT IS PAID OFF?

When everything works right, the party with the judgment, the Judgment Creditor, is paid in full or whatever lesser amount that might be agreed among the parties.

After the judgment has been paid, the Judgment Creditor is required to immediately file a Satisfaction of Judgment with the Court. The recordation of Satisfaction of Judgment removes the liens placed on the debtor's property by virtue of the recording of an Abstract of Judgment.

Failure to file an Abstract of Judgment could expose the Judgment Creditor for a lawsuit on Slander of Title. Failure to file the satisfaction could keep a lien on the debtor's property and thus prevent the obtaining of loans or sale of the property. Such would make the creditor liable for extensive damages. So to avoid that the creditor must open the law and when paid off file the satisfaction of judgment.

23. CAN A DEBTOR BE EXAMINED TO DISCOVER PROPERTY?

It is the judgment creditor's responsibility to collect the award. Toward that end, the creditor is given certain rights in order to assist him.

Many courts require the debtor to file out a Statement of Assets once the the judgment in entered. From this Statement of Assets the creditor is able to obtain the Writ of Execution from the Court Clerk.

All states permit the creditor to apply for an Order to Appear for A Judgment Debtor's Examination. This is order from the court that the debtor appear on a certain date and time to be questioned, under oath, about the debtor's money, property and locations of the same.

A judgment debtor's exam is usually limited to just one every six months until the judgment is satisfied. Following this chapter is the Judgment Debtor's Statement of Assets form used in California. A debtor is required to fill it out as a tool for the creditor in discovering property that can be seized and sold to pay the judgment.

24. WHO HAS THE BURDEN OF PROOF IN THE SMALL CLAIMS ACTION?

The burden of proof is borne by the party seeking some form of relief from the other. The Plaintiff has the burden of proof on his or her claim against the defendant. If the defendant files a claim against the plaintiff, then the defendant has the burden of proof of his or her claim against the plaintiff.

The burden of proof is the standard of evidence needed to prevail in a case. In a small claims action, the party having the burden of proof must convince the Judge that it is more likely than not that the proponent should win. In a fifty-fifty case, one person's word against the other person, judgment should go to the defendant. Without this standard, anyone could sue and collect judgment without ever being damaged. The result would be unfair.

Before anyone files in small claims, he or she should consider whether there is enough evidence to convince a total stranger to render judgment in their behalf.

25. HOW LONG SHOULD IT TAKE TO PRESENT A CASE?

Experience as shown that the average small claims case takes both sides between 10 minutes to 15 minutes to present their case. To speed the case along, most courts require the parties to stand unless they are disabled. Standing causes the parties to quickly present their case in a short and concise manner. It has been shown that where the parties in the small claims case are seated, the presentation usually takes over a half an hour to present.

The use of witnesses will obviously extend the case. However, most small claim cases do not involve more than one witness.

26. WHO CAN TRY A SMALL CLAIMS CASE?

Most small claim court judges are full judges of the local court. However many states permit private attorneys to sit as temporary small claim court judges called Judges Pro Tem.

In order to hear a small claims case as a Judge Pro Tem, the attorney can only do so with the written consent of both parties. If both parties agree to have a private attorney serve as the Judge, the attorney will try the case and render the decision in the same manner as a regular Judge.

The Judgment of an attorney serving as a Judge Pro Tem is treated for all purposes as a valid court judgment.

If the parties do not stipulate to the use of a private attorney, the case will be continued to a time in the future where a regular judge is available. Usually, the first time become aware that a regular judge is not available is the date of trial when the clerk asks the parties to stipulate to a private attorney.

27. WHO CAN REPRESENT A PARTY?

With only a few exceptions a party in a small claims action must represent himself or herself. A lawyer is not permitted to represent a party in a small claims action.

A corporation may appear in a small claims court only through an employee or an officer or director of the corporation. A corporation may not be represented in small claims court by someone whose job is to represent the corporation in small claims court.

Certain businesses and entities other than corporations, such as partnerships or joint ventures, may appear in small claims court only through a regular employee of the entity. The representative may not be someone whose sole job is to represent the business entity in small claim court.

A trust may be represented in small claims court by the Trustee of the trust.

28. CAN GOVERNMENTAL AGENCIES BE SUED IN SMALL CLAIMS COURT?

The general rule is that a governmental agency can be sued in small claims court if the amount of the claim is within the jurisdictional limit of the court.

However individual state law must be complied with when suing a governmental agency. All states have some type of claims statute which requires that a claim be presented to the agency and rejected before a lawsuit may be filed.

Because of the special claim requirement, suits against most governmental agencies require special handling. The claim must be filed with the agency within a certain period of time following the injury or breach, normally around 100 days but this varies. The agency usually given 60 days to accept the claim or it is automatically rejected. After the agency rejects the claim, the plaintiff must file his or her action within a very narrow time period, usually six months but this varies, or lose the right to sue altogether. Claims against governmental entities must be made promptly and with attention to all time limitations.

29. CAN AN UNLAWFUL DETAINER ACTION BE BROUGHT IN SMALL CLAIMS COURT?

An unlawful detainer action is a legal action to oust a person from real property usually for nonpayment of rent. A small claims court has the power to try the case and order the eviction along with payment of back rent and damages. The landlord filing the suit is still limited by the jurisdictional amount of the court. In California, for example, the landlord may not sue in small claims court for more than $5,000. Any damages or lost rent over $5,000 are waived if suit is filed in small claims court.

All states have special statutes governing unlawful detainer. These statutes permit a landlord to quickly file a lawsuit and get preference on the the trial calendar for the trial to evict a tenant. Usually an unlawful detainer case takes about a month to get to trial. Suing in small claim court takes a lot longer to get to trial, usually two months. This is an extra month without being paid rent.

Another big liability in filing an unlawful detainer action in small claims court is that if the the tenant appeals, the judgment is stayed until the appeal is heard. In California, on a small claims appeal there is a complete new trial, the Trial De Novo. The appeal takes, at least, another 20 days during which the tenant still stays in the premises without paying rent.

As a rule, it is not a good idea to file an unlawful detainer action in small claims court. Following this chapter is California's Small Claims form for unlawful detainer, most states use similar forms.

30. CAN A SUIT FOR BAD CHECKS BE FILED IN SMALL CLAIMS COURT?

Every state has some type of bad check law that permits a business, and in some instances individuals, to sue for several times the amount of the bad check. In California, Civil Code Section 1719 permits a suit to be filed for value of the check plus three times the amount of the check. The additional amount will be at least $100 with a maximum of $500.

Some states, like California require that the debtor be given notice by certified mail of the bad check before the court will award the additional amount.

Regardless of whether the additional sum is sought as penalty under a bad check law, anyone given a bad check can always sue in small claims court.

31. WHEN WOULD THE SMALL CLAIMS JUDGMENT BE ISSUED?

After both sides have presented their case, the judge will make a decision. Often the decision is announced in open court before the parties. Occasionally, the judge will take the case under submission and decide the case later.

A case is taken under submission for several reasons. The Judge may want to conduct research, conduct an investigation or simply not want to upset the parties while in court.

When the case is taken under submission, the Judge's decision will usually be mailed to the parties within a month. The Judgment will contain any monetary award along with any court costs that the Judge finds should be recovered.

32. IS A SMALL CLAIMS JUDGMENT VALID ELSEWHERE?

A small claims judgment is a valid judgment by a state court. As such, a small claims judgment is fully enforceable throughout the state in which it was issued.

Under the United States Constitution all judgments of a state must be given Full Faith and Credit by other states. As such, a small claims judgment is fully enforceable in another state. The normal procedure of which would be to have it adopted by the court of another state as a Sister State Judgment. Doing so, makes the creditor's small claims judgment fully enforceable under the other state's law and gives the debtor full access to that state's collections procedures.

An out of state small claims judgment can serve as lien on the real property of the out-of-state debtor if the proper steps have been done to have it adopted as a Sister State Judgment. Once adopted as a Sister State Judgment, an abstract of judgment can be recorded to place the lien on the real property.

33. CAN A DEFENDANT BE PUNISHED FOR FILING A FRIVOLOUS APPEAL?

Some states, such as California, permit a judge to fine a defendant for filing a frivolous appeal. This is an appeal that was intended for harassment without a good faith belief in its merit.

In California, if the court finds that the appeal was frivolous, it can award the plaintiff up to $250 as attorney fees. Generally, it is rare that the court will find that the appeal was frivolous. By frivolous, it is meant the appeal was without merit and intended solely to harass, delay or encourage the other party to abandon the claim. However if the state law does permit sanctions for filing a frivolous small claims appeal, there is no harm in asking for them.

4
IMMIGRATION

4. IMMIGRATION

Immigration Law is one of the most difficult areas of law in which to practice. No one should ever ever attempt to tackle an immigration question without qualified legal assistance. Immigration Law is a branch of law generally called Administrative Law. What is meant by this is that judicial functions in this area that would normally be handled by a real court and judge are instead handled by an Administrative Law Judge who is employed by and works for the Immigration and Naturalization Service (INS).

When a visa is denied by the INS, the initial review is not by a Federal Judge but instead by the Administrative Law Judge. If the denial is upheld by the Administrative Law Judge, then any appeal to the Federal Court is usually limited to whether the Administrative Judge abused his discretion rather than have an entirely new trial. There are only a few situations when a Federal Court will hold a completely new trial on whether a visa should be issued to the applicant.

This chapter was written to help the reader understand the various types of visas which are available and the working of the INS so as not to be intimidated when consulting an immigration advisor. This chapter can in no way replace a qualified advisor but it can help ease the fears and concerns attendant in applying for immigrant status.

1. HOW IS IMMIGRATION REGULATED?
The Immigration Act of 1990 (IA90) amended the Immigration and Nationality Act (INA). Specifically, the 1990 Act revised the numerical and preference system used to regulate legal immigration.

Section 201 of the INA pertaining to Worldwide Levels of Immigration was drastically revised. The 1990 Act created three types of legal immigration: Family Sponsored, Employment-based and Diversity-based. Special provisions were also enacted which broadened the scope of eligibility and thus increased the number of persons applying to immigrate.

Section 202 of the INA pertaining to the Per Country Levels of Immigration was also drastically revised. The per county limits on preference immigrants was changed and the specific provisions for

Hong Kong visa applicants were adopted.

2. WHAT ARE THE WORLDWIDE NUMERICAL LIMITS OF IMMIGRATION?

Under the 1990 Act, the total annual number of immigrant visas is capped at 700,000 for fiscal years 1992-1994. These 700,000 visas per year are divided as follows:
1. 465,000 visas go to Family Sponsored Immigrants
2. 140,000 visas go to Employment Based Immigrants
3. 55,000 visas for Spouse and Children of Newly Legalized Aliens
4. 40,000 visas for Special Transition Programs

In 1995, the worldwide cap decreases to 675,000 persons per year. The visa will be allocated as follows:
1. 480,000 visas for Family Sponsored Immigrants
2. 140,000 visas for Employment Based Immigrants
3. 55,000 visas for Diversity Immigrants

3. WHAT ALIENS ARE NOT SUBJECT TO THE NUMERICAL LIMITATIONS?

The following immigrants that are covered included in the numerical limitations of the Immigration Act:
1. Former citizens who wish to reapply for citizenship.
2. Refugees and asylumees
3. Aliens granted amnesty
4. Aliens granted a suspension from deportation
5. Aliens granted registry
6. "Immediate Relatives"
7. Aliens born to an alien admitted for permanent residence during a temporary visit abroad.

Certain transition visas are also exempt from the numerical limitations. These are:
1. 12,000 annual visas for 1991 to 1993 for certain employees of U.S. companies working in Hong Kong.
2. 1,000 visa in the three years period from 1991 to 1994 for displaced Tibetans.

4. WHAT IS FAMILY SPONSORED IMMIGRATION?

Of the 700,000 visas allocated per year, 465,000 will be allocated to family-sponsored immigration. The 465,000 annual visas include both immediate relatives and family preference immigrants.

"Immediate relatives" are defined as children and spouse of U.S. citizens and parents of U.S. citizens over 21 years of age, and widows and widowers of U.S. citizens where the marriage occurred at least two years before the death of the citizen spouse. No restrictions exist on the number of immediate relatives of a U.S. citizen who can immigrant to the U.S. each year.

A minimum of 226,000 visas are set aside for other family based immigration. This minimum protects the family preference category from being consumed by the immediate relative category.

5. WHAT ARE THE FAMILY PREFERENCE CATEGORIES?

The 226,000 visas are distributed as follows:

1. FIRST PREFERENCE: UNMARRIED SONS AND DAUGHTERS OF U.S. CITIZENS. The visas available to adult unmarried children of U.S. citizens were reduced from 54,000 to 23,000. In 1989 only 13,259 such applicants applied for immigration.

2. SECOND PREFERENCE: SPOUSES, SONS AND DAUGHTERS OF LAWFUL PERMANENT RESIDENTS. There are 114,000 visas allocated to this category. In addition, all of the unused visas in the first category are added to this category.

3. THIRD PREFERENCE: MARRIED SONS AND DAUGHTERS OF U.S. CITIZENS. The number of approved visas in this category was reduced from 27,000 to 24,000 plus any unused visas from the first two categories.

4. FOURTH PREFERENCE: BROTHERS AND SISTERS OF U.S. CITIZENS. There are 65,000 visa allocated to this category.

6. WHAT IS EMPLOYMENT BASED IMMIGRATION?

Congress feels that the nation would be benefited by the increased immigration of skilled workers. The 1990 Act eased restrictions that limited the number of highly skilled or needed foreign-born workers.

The law created five categories of employment-based visas: CATEGORY ONE: Priority Workers, CATEGORY TWO: members of the professions holding advanced degrees or persons of exceptional ability, CATEGORY THREE: skilled workers, professionals and other workers, CATEGORY FOUR: special immigrants as defined in INA section 101(a)(27), CATEGORY FIVE: investors who hire U.S. Citizens or lawful permanent residents as workers.

7. WHO ARE PRIORITY WORKERS?
The priority workers category is composed of three subgroups:
1. aliens with extraordinary ability;
2. outstanding professors and researchers; and
3. certain multi-national executives and managers.

This category is allotted a total of 40,000 visas along with any unused visas from the special immigrant and employment creation categories.

8. WHO IS AN ALIEN WITH EXTRAORDINARY ABILITY?
An alien with extraordinary ability is one that:
1. must have extraordinary ability in sciences, arts, education, business or athletics which has been demonstrated by sustained national or international acclaim and whose achievements have been recognized in the field;
2. must seek to enter the U.S. to continue to work in the area of extraordinary ability; and
3. the alien's entry must substantially benefit prospectively the U.S. Applicants in this category are not required to provide employer sponsorship. Such an alien can be self-employed in his or her own field. This is beneficial to artists and entertainers.

9. WHAT ARE DIVERSITY PROVISIONS?
Congress has been concerned that previous immigration systems did not provide for enough diversity of immigrants to the U.S.

Section 131 of the 1990 Act creates another means of immigration to the U.S. For aliens not qualifying for family sponsored or employment based visas, the diversity provisions provide an opportunity to immigrate.

The diversity provisions of the 1990 Act are intended to implement the Congressional intent to "further enhance and promote diversity of immigrants." There have been allocated 55,000 visas for diversity immigrants.

10. WHO IS A DIVERSITY IMMIGRANT?
A diversity immigrant is defined in section 131 of the 1990 Act. The requirements for qualification are:
1. The alien must be a native of a "low" admission country as defined by the Act.
2. The alien must at least possess a high school education or its equivalent, or in the alternative have within the five (5) years previous to the date of the application for immigration worked two (2) or more years in an occupation requiring at least two (2) years of training or experience.

11. WHAT ARE HIGH ADMISSION STATES?
High admission states are countries in which no diversity visas are to be allocated to their nationals. The thirteen countries classified as "high admission states" are Canada, Colombia, Dominican Republic, China, El Salvador, Haiti, India, Jamaica, Korea, Mexico, Philippines, Taiwan and the United Kingdom.

12. HOW ARE IMMIGRANTS FROM HONG KONG TREATED?
Hong Kong is recognized for immigration purposes as a separate foreign state and not as a colony or other component or dependent area of another country. The total number of immigrant visas available to Hong Kong under the family sponsored and employment based categories is limited to 10,000 per year for fiscal years 1991 through 1993.

In October 1993, Hong Kong will be treated in equal terms as other countries with respect to the per country numerical limitations. Starting in fiscal 1994, seven percent (7%) of the combined family-sponsored and employment based visas will be available for Hong Kong immigrants.

Section 124 of the 1990 Act allocates 12,000 visas for three years to Hong Kong residents employed in qualifying U.S. companies. The 12,000 visas are in addition to the per country limitation available to Hong Kong.

13. WHAT IS THE SPECIAL IMMIGRANT CATEGORY?

Special immigrants are defined as those immigrants that fall into one of the following categories:

1. Persons seeking reacquisition of U.S. citizenship
2. Returning residents
3. Religious workers, spouses and children
4. Certain overseas employers of the U.S. government, their spouses and children.
5. Panama Canal treaty employees, their spouses and children
6. Foreign medical school graduates who entered on an H or J visa prior to 1978, their spouses or children.
7. Retired officer's spouse, unmarried sons and daughters or widow or retired employees of international organization.
8. Aliens declared dependent on a juvenile court who have been deemed eligible for long term foster care.

14. WHAT ARE THE ELIGIBILITY REQUIREMENTS FOR RELIGIOUS WORKERS?

To qualify for special immigrant status, a religious worker must:
1. have for at least two (2) years immediately proceeding the time of application, been a member of a religious denomination having a bona-fide, nonprofit, religious organization in the U.S., and 2. seek to enter the U.S.: (a) solely to carry on his or her vocation as a minister or (b) before October 1, 1994, to work for the organization at the request of the organization in a professional capacity or to work for an organization or Section 501 (c)(3) affiliate in a religious vocation or occupation; and 3. have been carrying on such vocation, professional work or other work continuously for the same two (2) year period in which they were a member of the denomination.

15. WHAT IS THE B VISA WAIVER PILOT PROGRAM?

Under this program, the visa requirement is waived for business visitors and tourists from designated countries. Citizens from France, Italy, Japan, the Netherlands, Switzerland, Germany, Sweden, the United Kingdom and Germany can visit the U.S. for up to ninety (90) days without having to obtain a B-2 visa from a U.S. consular post overseas.

The foreign visitor from a pilot program country must present a passport. The applicant must also have a round trip ticket although that requirement may be waived. The alien must have transportation from the U.S. in the event that the alien is inadmissible or deportable.

16. WHAT IS A D VISA?

A D visa is the non immigrant visa required to be held by a crewman of a vessel to land temporarily in the U.S. Crewman is defined in the INA as "a person serving in any capacity on board a vessel or aircraft."

In order to qualify for the temporary D visa, a crewmember must intend to land "temporarily and solely in pursuit of his calling as a crewman and to depart from the U.S. with the vessel or aircraft on which he arrived or some other vessel or aircraft."

A crewman is not entitled to nonimmigrant status if he or she intends to perform work during a labor dispute. Nor may a crewman perform longshore work in U.S. ports or coastal waters.

17. WHAT IS AN E VISA?

The INA permits an alien and certain employees of qualifying entities to enter the U.S. on special E series visas. Under the E-1 visa, such individuals are permitted to travel in the U.S. to carry on "substantial trade" between the U.S. The E-2 visa permits investors or certain employees of qualifying entities to enter the U.S. to develop and direct the operations of an enterprise in which the qualifying investor or entity has invested or is investing "a substantial amount of capital." Both E-1 and E-2 visas normally require the existence of treaties between the U.S. and the alien's country.

For the purposes of the E visa, the term "substantial" is determine to be "such amount of trade or capital as is established by the Secretary of State." In practice an investment has been held to be substantial when it was an "amount considered necessary to establish a viable enterprise of the nature contemplated."

18. WHAT IS THE STUDENT F-1 VISA?

To obtain a F-1 visa, an alien student must:
1. have a residence in a foreign country,
2. have no intention of abandoning the home in the foreign country,

3. be a bona fide student pursuing a full course of study at an established college, university, seminary, conservatory, academic high school, elementary school or other academic institution or in a language program in the U.S.

19. CAN A STUDENT WORK ON A F-1 VISA?
The attorney General can grant a F-1 students permission to work off-campus in a field unrelated to their course of study under certain circumstances:
1. the student must have completed one full calendar year in F-1 status. Students attending school in another status will not qualify.
2. the student must be maintaining good academic standing the academic institution. The employer of a F-1 student must provide the secretary of Labor and the student's academic institution an attestation of the following:
1. that the employer has recruited for the position for at least sixty (60) days,
2. that the employer will pay the F-1 student the actual wage level for the place of employment or, if greater, the prevailing wage level for the occupation in the area of employment, and
3. will not employ the F-1 student more than twenty (20) hours per week during the academic term.

20. WHAT IS THE H-1 VISA?
Under the Immigration Nursing Relief Act of 1989 (INRA) an exclusive classification for registered nurses was created designated as H-1A.

In order to obtain the services of a foreign registered nurse, the employer must file with the Department of Labor (DOL) a complex attestation. The attestation must:
1. demonstrate that there would be a "substantial disruption" of the employer's of health services without the employment of foreign nurses.
2. demonstrate that the employment of a foreign nurse will not affect wages or working conditions for U.S. nurses.
3. demonstrate that it will pay the foreign nurse equally to U.S. nurses.
4. demonstrate that it taking significant steps to recruit U.S. nurses.
5. demonstrate that there is no strike or lockout at the facility.

6. demonstrate that the employer notified the U.S. nurses bargaining unit of the H-1 petition.

21. WHAT ARE H-1B VISAS?
Aliens employed in "Specialty Occupations" are required to have the H-1B visa. Specialty occupations are defined as those that require highly specialized knowledge and a bachelor's degree or its equivalent.
   The specialty occupation requirement can be met by:
1. attainment of full licensure, if license is required to practice in the state of intended employment.
2. completion of the required bachelor's or higher degree;
3. equivalent experience in the specialty, together with recognition of related expertise through progressively responsible experience.

22. WHO IS ELIGIBLE FOR THE H-2B VISA?
A temporary nonagricultural worker is eligible for a H-2B visa if:
1. the alien has residence in a foreign country,
2. the alien does not intend to abandon his or her foreign country,
3. unemployed persons can not be found in the U.S, capable of performing the service or labor cannot be found; and
4. the alien is coming to the U.S. only temporarily to perform temporary nonagricultural service or labor.

23. WHO ARE H-3 TRAINEES?
An alien is eligible for a H-3 visa if:
1. the alien has residence in a foreign country,
2. the alien does not intend to abandon his or her foreign country.
3. the alien is coming to the U.S. only temporarily to complete a training program.
4. the training program is not designed primarily to provide productive employment.

24. WHAT IS THE L-1 INTRACOMPANY TRANSFEREE VISA?
The intracompany transferee visa (L-1) allows organizations with

multi-national operations to transfer certain designated personnel to the United States temporarily. The personnel can be transferred to temporarily to fill permanent positions with the company. This category permits nonimmigrants to enter the U.S. and be employed if:
1. they had previously been employed abroad as managers, executives or in a capacity involving specialized knowledge,
2. they will continue to work in those capacities for the same employer or its U.S. subsidiary or affiliate.

Nonimmigrants with L-1 visas can remain in the U.S. for up to six years. Between 60,000 and 65,000 aliens are admitted in the U.S. each year.

25. WHO QUALIFIES FOR THE O VISA?

The O category visa was created in the 1990 Act. It is set aside for aliens with "Exceptional" ability in the sciences, arts, education, business, or athletics. Family members of such aliens also qualify for the O visa. There is a general test to determine extraordinary ability and a special test for aliens in the motion picture industry.

26. WHAT IS THE GENERAL TEST FOR EXTRAORDINARY ABILITY?

The general test for extraordinary ability requires demonstrating "sustained national or international acclaim". The aliens must be entering the U.S. to work in their field and the Immigration and Naturalization Service (INS) must determine that their entry will substantially benefit the United States.

Under this test, businessmen will not normally apply. Consultations with labor unions are mandatory under the 1990 Act in determining if the alien meets the extraordinary ability test.

27. WHAT IS THE SPECIAL TEST FOR EXTRAORDINARY ABILITY IN THE MOTION PICTURE INDUSTRY

The special test for aliens working in the motion picture industry requires proof of the alien's extraordinary ability through "a demonstrated record of extraordinary achievement."

28. WHO IS COVERED UNDER THE O-2 VISA?

The O-2 visa is for aliens who seek to enter temporarily and solely for the purpose of assisting in the artistic performance by an alien admitted under an O-1 visa. The immigrant must be an integral part of the actual performance for which the principal alien was admitted or have critical skills and experience with the principal alien that are not of a general nature and that can not be performed by other individuals.

The O-2 applicant must demonstrate that he or she has a foreign residence and has no intention of abandoning it. The 0-3 visa is for the family members of those persons holding a O-1 or O-2 visa.

29. HOW LONG ARE PERSONS ADMITTED UNDER AN O VISA?

There is no fixed period of time for which a persons holding an O visa can remain in the U.S. Instead, the law grants the INS the discretion to admit O aliens for the period of time needed to "provide for the event for which the nonimmigrant is admitted." This definition does not assist those persons offered temporary jobs not related to a certain specific event.

30. WHO ARE P VISA ALIENS?

A class of new temporary nonimmigrants was created under the 1990 ACT with relation to certain performing artists and athletes. The category consists of four subcategories:
1. (P-1) internationally recognized athletes and entertainers,
2. (P-2) reciprocal exchange artists and entertainers
3. (P-3) culturally unique artists and entertainers, and 4. (P-4) family members of those P-1, P-2 or P-3 aliens. All P immigrants must demonstrate their intention not to abandon their foreign country.

31. WHO IS ELIGIBLE FOR THE Q VISA?

The Q visa is a newly created category for certain participants in cultural exchange programs designated by the INS. The program must provide practical training, employment, and the "sharing of history, culture, and traditions" of the alien's homeland.

The holder of a Q visa must demonstrate foreign residency with the intention of returning after the program is completed.

32. WHO ARE COVERED BY THE R VISA?

The 1990 Act created a new nonimmigrant category for religious workers. Under this new category the following persons can enter the country:

1. ministers of a religion
2. professional workers in religious vocations or occupations,
3. other religious personnel who work for a religious nonprofit organization or related tax-exempt entity,
4. family members of the above. To be eligible for R classification, an alien must have been a member of the religious organization for at least two years immediately preceding admission to the U.S.

Holders of R visas may be admitted for up to five years. An application for an R visa can be made directly to a consular officer. The INS does not have to pre-approve the petition for R classification.

33. WHAT ARE THE GROUNDS FOR EXCLUSION OF AN ALIEN APPLYING TO ENTER THE UNITED STATES?

There are nine (9) major grounds for excluding an alien from entry into the United States. These grounds are:

1. Health Related Grounds
2. Criminal and Related Grounds
3. Security and Related Grounds
4. Public Charge
5. Labor Certification
6. Illegal Entrants and Immigration Visitors
7. Documentation Requirements
8. Ineligible for citizenship
9. Miscellaneous: (a) Practicing polygamists, (b) Guardians required to accompany excluded alien, (c) International child abduction.

34. WHAT ARE CRIMINAL GROUNDS FOR EXCLUSION?

The 1990 Act lists six (6) subcategories for criminal ground for exclusion. These are:

1. conviction or commission of crimes involving moral turpitude
2. violation of laws relating to controlled substances
3. conviction of two or more offenses
4. engaging in illicit drug trafficking

5. engaging in prostitution; and
6. commission of a serious crime for which diplomatic immunity has been asserted.

35. WHAT IS MEANT BY PUBLIC CHARGE?
The exclusion for public charges is new to the 1990 Act. It means that an alien can be excluded if at the time of application, it appears that the person will be unable to care for himself and thus seek welfare or other relief from the government.

36. WHAT IS THE LABOR EXCLUSION FOR AN ALIEN?
Aliens seeking to enter the United States for the purpose of performing skilled and unskilled labor are excludable unless they can first prove:
1. there are no U.S. workers willing, able or qualified to do the same job; and
2. their employment will not adversely affect thee wages and working conditions of similarly employed U.S. workers.

37. WHAT ARE THE ILLEGAL ENTRANTS AND IMMIGRATION VISITORS EXCLUSIONS?
The grounds for exclusion for illegal entrants and immigration visitors are as follows:
1. aliens previously excluded;
2. aliens previously deported;
3. aliens who have committed fraud or material misrepresentation;
4. stowaways;
5. smugglers; and
6. aliens who have committed document fraud.

38. CAN THE INS WAIVE ILLEGAL ENTRANTS EXCLUSION?
A waiver for an illegal entrant or immigration visitor may be granted for "Humanitarian purposes, to assure family unity or when it is otherwise in the public interest." The waiver is limited. To be eligible, the applicant for the waiver
1. must be a lawful permanent resident who temporarily proceeded abroad not in response to an order of deportation,
2. must be admissible as a returning resident, and

3. must have aided the aliens' spouse, parent, son or daughter (but no other individual) to enter the United States in violation of the law.

39. WHAT IS THE RE-ENTRY DOCTRINE?
Under U.S. immigration law, an alien who intentionally departs from the U.S. for however a brief a period of time is subject to exclusion upon his or her return. This is the RE-ENTRY DOCTRINE of immigration law. Under this doctrine, an alien who commits an act in the U.S. or changes his or her status into one that is excludable but not a deportable, upon leaving the country will be subject to exclusion upon his or her return. The standards are different for exclusion and deportation. An act that may support excluding an alien from entering the country might not be sufficient for deporting an alien who is already in the country legally.

40. WHAT IS THE FLEUTI DOCTRINE AND HOW DOES IT RELATE TO THE RE-ENTRY DOCTRINE?
The United States Supreme Court held in Rosenberg vs. Fleuti 374 U.S. 449 that a lawful permanent resident who visited Mexico for a few hours did not leave the country for purposes of the immigration law and thus was not subject to exclusion.

The Supreme Court stated that in such cases the INS must look to the following factors to determine if the alien intended an innocent and brief departure. These factors are:
1. length of absence,
2. purpose of the visit, and
3. procurement of travel documents.

41. WHAT ARE THE GROUNDS OF DEPORTATION?
There are five (5) separate topics with sub-topics that cover the grounds for deportation. These are:
1. Classes of deportable aliens (A) Excludable at the time of entry (B) Entered without inspection (C) Violated nonimmigrant status or condition of entry (D) Termination of conditional permanent residence (E) Smuggling (F) Failure to maintain Replacement Agricultural Workers status (G) Marriage Fraud
2. Criminal Offenses (A) General crimes (B) Controlled substances (C)

Firearm offenses (D) Miscellaneous crimes
3. Failure to register and falsification of documents (A) Change of Address (B) Failure to register and falsification of documents
4. Security related grounds: (A) Activity in violation of the law relating to espionage, other criminal activity that endangers public safety (B) Terrorist activities (C) Foreign policy
5. Public charge.

42. WHAT IS MARRIAGE FRAUD?
An alien is deportable, under immigration law, when 1. the alien obtains an immigrant visa on the basis of a marriage entered into within two years prior to the alien's entry and that marriage is terminated within two years after any entry of the alien unless the alien establishes to the satisfaction of the Attorney General that such marriage was not contracted for the purpose of evading immigration laws, or 2. it appears to the satisfaction of the Attorney General that the alien has failed or refused to fulfill the alien's marital agreement. This generally means supporting the alien's spouse or family.

43. WHAT IS A DEPORTABLE FIREARM OFFENSE?
Any alien convicted of violating any law regarding the purchasing, selling, using, or carrying a firearm or destructive device is deportable.

Relief from deportation based upon a firearm offense is very restricted. Some federal courts and the U.S. Attorney General have adopted the view that relief for deportation is unavailable where firearm violations are involved.

44. WHAT IS AN ORDER TO SHOW CAUSE IN A DEPORTATION ACTION?
An order to show cause is a legal document served upon an alien that requires the alien to come, on a certain date and time, before an Immigration Judge for a hearing. At the hearing, it is to be determined whether the alien should be allowed to remain in the United States or be excluded or deported.

The order to show cause must be served in person on the alien unless for some reason it is found to be impracticable. If the personal service is impracticable, then the order to show cause may be served by certified mail.

An alien that fails to appear when properly served will have judgment rendered against him or her by default, that is without the presentation of any evidence at the hearing on the alien's behalf.

45. WHAT IS CONTAINED IN AN ORDER TO SHOW CAUSE?
An order to show cause is required to specify with particularity:
1. The nature of the proceedings against the aliens,
2. The legal authority under which the proceedings are conducted,
3. The acts or conduct alleged to be in violation of the law,
4. The charges against the alien and the statutory provisions alleged to have been violated,
5. That the alien may be represented by counsel and, upon request, the alien will be provided with a list of counsel,
6. That the alien must provide the INS with the alien's address and phone number at which the alien can be contacted.

46. WHAT IS AN ABSENTIA ORDER OF DEPORTATION?
If the alien fails to appear at the hearing after being served with an order to show cause, the alien will be order deported in absentia once the INS establishes that the alien was served with the order to show cause and the offense committed by the alien was a deportable one.

47. CAN ABSENTIA ORDER BE RESCINDED?
An absentia order may be rescinded for one of three situations:
1. Exceptional circumstances such as serious illness of the alien or death of an immediate relative of the alien, not including less compelling circumstances beyond the control the control of the alien. The motion to reopen the hearing must be filed within 180 days after the date of the order of the deportation.
2. Failure of the alien to receive notice of the hearing through certified mail or personal service will result in the deportation order to be rescinded. There is no time limit to challenge the validity of the order based upon failure to give notice of the hearing to the alien.
3. An alien ordered deported in absentia may have the order rescinded if the failure to appear was due to the fact that the alien was in federal or state custody and failed to appear through no fault of the alien's.

There is no time limit for filing a motion to reopen based on this situation.

48. CAN A COURT REVIEW AN ABSENTIA DEPORTATION ORDER?

A petition for judicial review of an absentia deportation order must be filed in Federal Court within sixty (60) days of the date of the order of deportation.

The appeal of the deportation order is limited to the following issues:
1. the validity of the notice contained in the order to show cause;
2. the reasons that the alien failed to attend the hearing; and
3. whether unequivocal evidence of deportability was established.

49. HOW IS AN ALIEN WHO COMMITS AN AGGRAVATED FELONY TREATED?

Congress is very concerned with the treated of aliens by the INS who commit aggravated felonies. For that reason, the 1990 Act states that an alien convicted of an aggravated felony:
1. is no longer entitled to asylum;
2. is not entitled to an automatic stay of deportation upon filing a petition of review;
3. may not establish good moral character;
4. may not re-enter the U.S. for twenty years unless the alien has received permission from the Attorney General.
5. is subject to mandatory detention upon completion of a sentence;
6. is considered to have committed a "particularly serious crime for purposes of withholding deportation".

50. WHAT IS AN AGGRAVATED FELONY?

Under the 1990 Act, the commission of aggravated felonies may constitute separate bases for deportation. Under the 1990 Act aggravated felonies are defined as: Murder, any illicit trafficking in any controlled substance, including any drug trafficking crime as defined in Section 924(c)(2) of Title 18, U.S.C, or any illicit trafficking in firearms or destructive devices as defined in Section 921 of such title, any offense described in Section 1956 of Title 18, U.S.C. (relating money laundering) or any crime of violence (as defined in Section 16 o f the title 18 USC, not including a purely political offense) for which a term of five years of imprisonment was imposed (regardless of any suspension of imprisonment) or any attempt or conspiracy to commit such an act."

51. DOES AN EMPLOYER FACE RESTRICTIONS IN HIRING AN ALIEN?

The immigration law requires employment verification be conducted by all employers, recruiters and referrers for a fee. An employer is prohibited from knowingly hiring, recruiting or referring for a fee an unauthorized alien.

Aliens hired prior to November 6, 1986 are exempt from the verification provisions and there is no liability for continuing to employ said alien.

The three ways that an employer may become subject to sanctions are:
1. failure to verify or incompletely verify work authorization on Form 1-9;
2. hiring an unauthorized worker; and/or
3. continuing to hire a person after their work authorization ends.

52. WHAT ARE THE EMPLOYER'S SANCTIONS FOR HIRING AN ILLEGAL ALIEN?

The INS has the authority to seek the following fines against an employer: A. For knowingly hiring or continuing to hire an unauthorized worker:
1. First Offense: $250 to $2,000 per unauthorized worker
2. Second Offense: $2,000 to $5,000 per unauthorized worker
3. Third Offense: $3,000 to $10,000 per unauthorized worker

B. For failing to complete an I-9 form or failure it accurately the fine is between $100 to $1,000 per offense.

C. For overdocumenting or refusing valid documents, an employer may be fined $100 to $1,000 per person discriminated against.

D. For unfair immigration related employment practices:
1. First Offense: $250 to $2,000 per individual
2. Second Offense: $2,000 to $5,000 per individual
3. Third Offense: $3,000 to $10,000 per individual

53. WHAT AUTHORITY DOES THE INS HAVE TO REMEDY DISCRIMINATION?

In addition to ordering back pay, reinstatement and attorney fees for employer discrimination, the INS can order the employer:
1. to post notices to all employees about their rights;
2. to educate all personnel involved in hiring with compliance with employment verifications;
3. to order the removal of false performance reviews or false warnings from an employee's personnel file; and/or
4. to order the lifting of any restrictions on the employee's assignment, shift or movements.

54. WHAT ARE DEFENSES CAN AN EMPLOYER RAISE IN DEFENSE TO A CLAIM OF DISCRIMINATION?

An employer may raise the following defenses to a claim of discrimination under immigration law:
1. The INS has no jurisdiction over the employer because the employer has three or fewer employees,
2. No jurisdiction because the claim is covered by Title VII,
3. The discriminatory acts are required by law, regulation, or executive order because it is essential to do business with an agency or department of the government.
4. The right to prefer an equally qualified citizen over an alien.
5. The individual is not a citizen, national or "protected individual".
6. The discrimination complaint for filed late. The time limit for filing such a complaint is 180 days.

55. WHAT IS TEMPORARY PROTECTED STATUS?

The 1990 Act created a new immigration class known as Temporary Protected Status. This status is for individuals from countries which the Attorney General designates to be in a state of armed conflict, natural or environmental disaster, or subject to extra ordinary and temporary conditions which prevent the safe return of its citizens.

Aliens receiving temporary protected status are permitted to remain in the U.S. and are authorized to work for as long as the extraordinary conditions exist in their homeland.

56. WHO ARE ELIGIBLE FOR TEMPORARY PROTECTED STATUS?

To be eligible for temporary protected status, an alien must:

1. have been continuously physically present in the U.S. since the most recent designation of Attorney designating the citizens for the alien's country eligible for temporary protected status;
2. have resided in the U.S. since the date established by the Attorney General;
3. be admissible as an immigrant, not have been convicted of a felony or two or more misdemeanors, and
4. apply for temporary protected status in the manner approved by the Attorney General.

57. WHAT IS THE PROCEDURE FOR NATURALIZATION?

Naturalization starts with the applicant filing a sworn application with the INS in duplicate. The INS then conducts an investigation of the person. The investigation may be waived by the INS. The examiner makes a determination if the application is to be granted or denied.

If the application is granted, the applicant has the option to have the Attorney General or a court to give the oath of allegiance.

If the application is denied, the applicant is entitled to a hearing before an immigration officer. If the immigration upholds the denial, the applicant can seek review in federal court.

In federal court, the court will conduct a trial de novo, a complete new hearing on the issue. The federal court has the authority to overrule the INS and grant citizenship.

58. MUST AN APPLICANT FOR NATURALIZATION SPEAK ENGLISH?

An applicant for naturalization is required only to be able to speak "simple words and phrases". A person over fifty five years of age who has been a lawful permanent resident for fifteen years or longer is excused from the English language requirement.

59. ARE FILIPINO VETERANS ELIGIBLE FOR NATURALIZATION?

Filipinos veterans are eligible for naturalization if:
1. they were born in the Philippines;

2. they resided in the Philippines before joining the U.S. Armed Forces;
3. they served honorably in the U.S. Armed Forces, Philippine Army or Philippine Scouts any time between September 1, 1939 and December 31, 1946;
4. they applied for naturalization by November 29, 1992.

5
CHILD CUSTODY AND SUPPORT

5. CHILD CUSTODY AND SUPPORT

Family law is the generic term for the body of law dealing with the personal relationships of families and the rights of all members therein. Family Law is is the most litigated field of all civil (non-criminal) law. As much as sixty percent (60%) of all civil filings (requests for relief from a court) involve some area of Family Law. The most commonly contested area of Family Law is, not unexpectedly, child custody and support.

In the last few years, many states have eliminated the requirement of fault as a necessity for granting a divorce. As such, the only areas of contention left in a divorce are property divisions, spousal support, child custody and child support.

With the recent influx of women into the non-traditional work force, the traditional nuclear family has greatly disappeared. As there are more working mothers, courts have begun to rethink their traditional notions of always awarding custody of the children to the mother. Many states have enacted laws that requiring joint child custody and even mandate that judges consider fathers to be equal with mothers in ability to rear their children.

All of these actions have served to increase litigation in the area and fill the already crowded court dockets. This chapter is intended to help answer and resolve common questions hopefully without having to go to court.

1. WHO MAKES THE DECISION ON CHILD CUSTODY AND SUPPORT?

In every state, the judge of the court having jurisdiction over the child and one of the parents is the person who makes the decision regarding child custody and support.

In making its decision, the court determines what is in the best interests of the child. While the parents may agree among themselves how the child custody should be handled and what the amount of the child support should be, the the court is not bound by their agreement. The court will not award child custody to a parent, it deems is unfit.

2. WHAT FACTORS DOES THE COURT RELY ON IT MAKING ITS DECISION?

The court looks at many factors when it makes its decision as to what is in the best interests of the child. Some of the factors that it looks at are:

1. the age, health and sex of the child,
2. the age, sex and health of each parent,
3. the home environment of each parent,
4. the character of each parent,
5. any criminal record of any parent,
6. the financial ability of each parent to provide for the child.

To aid in its determination, the court may appoint a social worker to investigate the parents and make a recommendation. The traditional view, still held by many judges, is that the mother should always have custody. In many states, it is now recognized that since many mothers work the traditional reason for awarding custody to the mother, that she was always at home to care for them, no longer exists. in such states, fathers are to be given equal preference in custody petitions.

3. CAN CHILDREN SELECT THE PARENT WITH WHOM THEY WILL LIVE?

Children can not select the parent in whom their custody will be given. However most courts will, at least, listen to their preference and try to understand the reason for it.

The children's preference may be a factor to be considered by the court but it is not the only one. The court still must do what it considers to be in the best interests of the child.

When everything is taken into consideration, the preference of the child may be an important factor. The court however will consider the weight to be given the request. A younger child's desire will naturally be of less weight than that of a teenager.

4. IF A PARENT MOVES IN WITH A PERSON OF THE OPPOSITE SEX WILL THE COURT DENY THAT PARENT CUSTODY?

It was not so long ago that that a parent living with another person of the opposite sex was automatically denied custody. Such conduct was immediately perceived as immoral and created a harmful environment in which to raise children.

As a result of the sexual revolution, today's view of such conduct is not so well defined. The court is required to do what is in the best interest's of the child. Toward that end the court must determine, on somewhat subjective bases, whether such a relationship will harm the moral or psychological character of the children.

Many court, particularly in California will not consider such a relationship in itself destructive to the normal development of children. Other courts have gone so far as to order the unmarried visitor out of the home whenever the children visit. It is all dependent on the development of the child and effect of such a relationship will have on the child.

5. CAN A CUSTODIAL PARENT TAKE THE CHILDREN OUT OF THE STATE?

The custodial parent can take children out of the state. However if the move will adversely affect the visitation rights of the noncustodial parent then the court may order restrictions placed on the move. The factors that the court looks at in making its decision are:

1. the length of time the children will be out of the state,
2. whether the move is permanent,
3. the effect of the move on the visitation rights of the noncustodial parent,
4. the closeness of the relationship with the noncustodial parent
5. whether the move is just to deny visitation to the noncustodial parent.

6. CAN THE COURT TAKE THE CHILDREN AWAY FROM BOTH PARENTS?

Courts are guided solely by what is in the best interests of the child. Towards that end if the court finds that neither parent is capable of providing for the needs of the child, then the court may, if it feels the child's welfare is in jeopardy, order the child put into a foster home. In an extreme case, the child may even be placed up for adoption.

Such interference in the parental rights of both parents is extreme.

It is justified only where the court feels that the absolute safety of the child is in jeopardy if the child were to left in the environment.

7. WHAT IS JOINT CUSTODY?

Joint custody exists in two parts: 1. Physical custody which determines the amount of time the child spends with each parent, and 2. Legal custody which requires the parents to jointly make the decisions about the child's education, health and overall welfare. Joint custody is used by divorcing couples who feel that it affords the best means to provide the most stable environment in which raise their children.

The concept of joint custody has been gaining ground in the last few years. Some states, such as California require preference to be given to joint custody petitions unless it is in the best interests if the child not to do so.

The traditional form of custody was sole legal and physical to the custodial parent. The noncustodial parent, usually the father, had no say in the raising of the child. This was recognized as weakening the parental bond with the child and fostering juvenile delinquency. Joint custody was thought to be a way of instilling more stability into the child's life.

8. DOES JOINT CUSTODY ALWAYS WORK?

Joint custody works best when the parents work together and agree on the goals that they wish to obtain. In a situation where one parent or both parents hate each other and can not work together, joint custody is a failure waiting to happen.

Where the parents can not or will not agree on how to raise their child, the court will terminate joint custody and award one parent sole legal and physical custody.

9. WHO DETERMINES IN WHAT RELIGION A CHILD WILL BE RAISED?

In general the parent having physical custody of the child is responsible for the child's discipline, education, health, and care. However, it is the religion upbringing that often poses the hardest dilemmas on a court.

In the case where the parents are of different religions, there can be a dispute as to what religion the child may be raised. The court hesitates to get involved in such disputes. Both parents are two obviously moral persons wishing their child to be raised with the same moral values. A court that decrees in which religion that child will be raised may be unconstitutionally fostering religion. In more than one case. a parent was ordered to raise a child in a particular religion against the parent's wishes.

Most courts however recognize the value of exposure to different religions and order the child raised in both faiths. Most such courts leave it to the child to ultimately decide what religion the child will finally adopt.

10. IF THE NONCUSTODIAL PARENT REMARRIES, WILL THAT AUTOMATICALLY BE GROUNDS FOR OBTAINING CUSTODY?

Generally most courts feel that it is best for a child to be raised in a two parent home. Thus if the noncustodial parent remarries and seeks custody, the court may consider that an important enough change to change its custody order. The importance of the remarriage in the custody decision increases if the new stepparent is a homemaker and the custodial parent has a full time job. The court may feel that the homemaking stepparent may be able to spend more quality time with the child caring and nurturing it.

If the child is not of school age and the custodial parent must put the child in day care while working, the court could decide that a better environment would be with the other parent who would raise the child at home.

11. CAN THE MOTHER CHANGE THE LAST NAME OF THE CHILD?

The court may permit a woman to change the last name of the child if it is in the best interest of the child. Generally such a request will not be granted if the only purpose is to prevent embarrassment on the part of the mother or to avoid inconvenience of having different last names.

In California a woman who had several children by several different men was permitted to change all of their last names.

12. CAN CUSTODY BE CHANGED IF A STEPPARENT POSES A DANGER TO THE CHILD?

Custody is never final. The court can always change a custody award if it feels that the best interests of the child warrants the name change. If it can be domonstrated that a stepparent poses a danger to a child, the court can and will modify the custody order to protect the child.

The problem with such a scenario is that proof is needed. It has become almost axiomatic in child custody cases for one parent to accuse the other or a stepparent with child molestation, drug dealing or other crimes to get a modification of child custody.

The problem this causes is that it sometimes hides legitimate complaints and concerns. Steps must be taken to protect the child from all dangers that may arise. Toward that end, the parents should amass all the proof that they can muster and pursue relief through the child protective services of their city or county.

13. IF A CHILD IS ADOPTED BY A STEPPARENT DOES THE NONCUSTODIAL PARENT STILL HAVE TO SUPPORT THE CHILD?

Adoption terminates all of the parental rights of a natural parent. If a stepparent adopts the stepchild, the law will treat that child as though it were that person's biological child.

The natural parent will no longer have any rights in the child such as visitation. Nor will the natural parent have any obligation to support the child.

Therefore if a stepmother adopted a stepchild all of the maternal rights that the natural mother had are then transferred to the stepmother. The mother is from then only treated as a legal stranger to the child. The same treatment exists when a stepfat her adopts the stepchild. In such a case, the natural father will then be treated as a legal stranger to the child.

14. CAN A WILL APPOINT THE GUARDIAN OF A CHILD IN THE EVENT OF PARENT'S DEATH?

Many people have a misconception regarding the validity of a clause in a will nominating a guardian of a child. Such a clause only nominates the potential guardian. It is solely within the power of the court to determine who raises a child. The court makes that determination using the best interests of the child test.

A natural parent is presumed to be best the guardian of a child. Priority is given to the natural parent in any custody proceeding. It is up to a person seeking to take custody away from a natural parent to prove that the best interests of the child are served by doing so. financial ability is only one factor the court can look at in determining custodial arrangements. If it were the only factor, nearly every child could be taken away from the parents by persons with more money.

Even if the Will of a parent states that child custody should go to a particular person, the court will not award such custody automatically. The court will never grant child custody to a person who it feels is unfit nor will it deprive a natural parent of custody unless it is in the best interest of the child.

15. MAY A STEPPARENT ADOPT WITHOUT A PARENT'S CONSENT?

A stepparent may not adopt a stepchild without the divorced natural parent's consent unless the parental rights in the child have been terminated. Every state has laws that govern when a parent's rights in a child may be terminated. When those parental rights have been terminated, the child may be placed up for adoption without the knowledge or consent of the parent.

Normally, the grounds for termination of parental rights are:
1. abandonment of the child usually manifested by lack of contact for one or more years with the child,
2. failure to provide support for the child,
3. child molestation, or
4. exposing the child to repeated danger of bodily harm.

16. WHAT RIGHTS DO AN ADOPTING STEPPARENT ACQUIRE IN THE CHILD?

When a stepparent adopts a stepchild, the adopting stepparent acquires all the rights and obligations towards that child as if the stepchild were his or she natural child.

If the natural parent and the adopting stepparent later divorce, the adopting step parent is entitled to visitation and, if appropriate for the best interests of the child, even custody of the stepchild. It is possible that the adopting stepparent may have the custody of the child and the natural parent may only get visitations rights.

The adopting stepparent also acquires the obligations to support and provided for the children. So in the event of a divorce or death of the natural parent, the adopting stepparent will still have the legal responsibility to raise the child.

17. WHAT IS CHILD NAPPING?
Child napping is the taking of a child by a parent in order to get custody in violation of a valid custody order. It is a felony in most states punishable by up to five years in prison and the termination of parental rights.

Since most custody awards are to mothers, it is not surprising that most childnappers are the fathers of the child. However, as more courts are rendering joint custody awards the numbers of women engaging in child napping have been steadily increasing.

The reasons for child napping vary but the one most often cited is the feeling that the ex-spouse is raising the child in an immoral atmosphere or exposing the child to danger and that child napping is the only way to protect the child.

18. WHAT SHOULD BE DONE IF A CHILD IS CHILD NAPPED?
The following steps should be taken if a parent commits child napping:
1. The local police should be contacted immediately and a missing persons report filled out.
2. The missing person's report should be entered immediately on the National Crime Information Center's computer of the FBI. If the local authorities refuse to do it, the parent should contact the FBI directly and ask that it be done.
3. Call the National Center for Missing and Exploited Children at 1-800-843-5678 for the local of support groups.
4. Start proceedings to get sole custody of the child if it had not already been awarded.
5. Contact the local prosecutor to determine if criminal prosecution is possible. If there was no custody order entered, then no crime may have been committed until a court issues such an order, after that point then child napping may exist.

19. CAN A SPOUSE DENY CHILD VISITATION DURING A DIVORCE?

Both parents have legal rights and obligations towards their children. Neither parent can unilaterally interfere with those rights and obligations of the other parent.

Even though a divorce is pending, visitation and contact with a child can not be denied without a court order. Usually during a divorce temporary court orders are obtained specifying visitation rights. These court ordered visitation rights are not final and may be modified in the final custody order.

20. CAN CHILD CUSTODY BE MODIFIED IF THE MOTHER MOVES OUT OF STATE?

Child custody is never final. The custody order was made with certain facts in mind. As though facts change, modification of the custody order may be necessary.

The custodial parent can take children out of the state. However if the move will adversely affect the visitation rights of the noncustodial parent then the court may order the custody order modified to maintain contact with the noncustodial parent. The factors that the court looks at in making its decision are:
1. age of the child,
2. the effect on the child in being away from the custodial parent,
3. the effect of the move on the visitation rights of the noncustodial parent,
4. the closeness of the relationship with the noncustodial parent
5. whether the move is just to deny visitation to the noncustodial parent. Moving the child out of state is a common ground for modifying custody orders. In such an event, courts often give the noncustodial parent one or more months of custody during the summer and alternate holidays.

21. CAN GRANDPARENTS VISIT THEIR GRANDCHILDREN?

It has only been within the last twenty years that grandparents have acquired the legal rights to see their grandchildren. In the past, grandparents could and were deprived of all contact with their grandchildren by the custodial parent.

Now all fifty states have enacted laws guaranteeing grandparent visitation rights. The grandparents may petition the court for visitation rights. The court still will use the best interest of the the child as the determining factor in deciding to award visitation rights to the grandparents.

Courts generally agree that it is in the best interest of the child to have loving grandparents around. Therefore unless it can be shown that the contact will be harmful to the child, the courts will grant grandparent visitation.

22. CAN CHILD SUPPORT BE WITHHELD IF VISITATION IS PREVENTED?

In a few states, if the non-custodial parent is denied visitation by the custodial spouse, then the non-custodial parent may be excused from paying child support.

Most states, including California, make the requirement to pay child support totally independent of child visitation. These states feel that the noncustodial parent could always go to court to enforce the visitation and thus there is no reason to resort to self help and withhold child support. In many instances, this has worked an injustice. A father, who has been denied visitation for years, may suddenly be facing criminal prosecution and a huge judgment for back child support.

Recent studies show that when the father is permitted to see the child then support payments are made in over 90% of the cases. When child visitation is prevented by the mother, that figure drops to less than 60%.

23. CAN CHILD SUPPORT BE AWARDED DURING THE DIVORCE?

Both parents have a duty to support their children. The court will not order one parent to bear that burden alone. The custodial parent can petition the court at any time for child support. The court can make temporary child support orders that will remain in effect until the final support order is entered.

A child support order is never final and can be modified at any time when the circumstances of the case have changed so much that a modification is necessary for basic fairness.

24. WHEN DOES CHILD SUPPORT STOP?

A parent's obligation to pay child support stops when the child is adopted, dies or reached maturity. The age of maturity is eighteen years of age in most states and twenty-one years of age in others. The parents may agree in their final court order to pay for support longer than the state's age of maturity. The parents may also agree to support a child through college.

Courts do not have the authority to force a parent to send a child through college or graduate school unless the parent had earlier agreed to do so.

Parents also have the obligation to support their children into adulthood if they are mentally retarded.

25. CAN WAGES BE ATTACHED TO PAY CHILD SUPPORT?

All states permit wages of parents to be attached to pay child support if the parent fails to pay promptly. The court's support order is a judgment that is enforceable like any other judgment.

California is one for the few states that orders attachment of wages automatically without first having to show that the chi ld support payments would be missed.

On a personal level, attachment to secure payment of child support when the parent has never demonstrated a pattern of failing to pay support is a needless indignity.

26. CAN THERE BE INCREASES IN CHILD SUPPORT DUE TO COST OF LIVING?

Child support is never final. It can be modified both up and down depending on the circumstances of the child, the expenses incurred by the custodial parent and the ability to pay of the noncustodial parent.

The most common reasons for increasing child support are clothing, transportation and education. A child with special health or education needs will also have additional expenses.

Many courts approve automatic increases in child support due to cost of living increases. Automatic decreases due to decreases in the cost of living are not approved.

27. HOW CAN CHILD SUPPORT BE COLLECTED?

Failure to pay child support can be criminal contempt of court and expose the parent to jail and a fine. In addition, the custodial parent has the following options available to collect child support:

1. automatic withholding of child support from wages,
2. seizure of income tax refunds,
3. attachment and sale of real and personal property,
4. requiring a bond or other security to be posted with the court to assure future payments.

In every state there is a child support department of the District Attorney's Office to collect court ordered support. This department will seek enforcement of child support orders if the alternative is for the custodial parent to be on welfare.

28. CAN THE PARENTS AGREE AMONG THEMSELVES TO ALTER CHILD SUPPORT?

Only the court has the authority to legally modify child support. Parents can not agree among themselves to change it and have it binding on the parents.

If the custodial parent were to agree to accept less than the court ordered child support without court approval, that parent could years later go to the court and demand the difference. The court would probably order the back payments made because the support was to go to the child not the parent. Child support is not waivable by a parent.

29. HOW SHOULD CHILD SUPPORT PAYMENTS BE MADE?

Child support payments should never be made in cash unless a signed receipt is given for the payments. It is the responsibility of the parent ordered to pay the support to prove that it was actually made. Some parents take the child support in cash and then file for welfare and Aid to Dependent Families (AFDC) claiming that no support is being paid.

Eventually, the public prosecutor sues the parent ordered to pay the support for the alleged non-payment of the support. If the parent can not prove the payments were made, then they must be made again along with interest and possible attorney fees. This is a common scenario with poor parents and should be guarded against.

30. CAN A CHILD FORCE A PARENT TO PAY FOR COLLEGE?

A parent can not be forced to pay for the college of a child unless it was required in the court's divorce order. Many parents put that requirement in the final divorce decree. When that is done it becomes court mandated and enforceable by the court as any other judgment.

31. CAN THE COURT REQUIRE ONE PARENT TO PROVIDE HEATH COVERAGE FOR THE CHILDREN?

A parent has a duty to provide for the welfare of the children. Often a court requires one parent or the other, depending on the circumstances, to carry medical insurance on the children.

Furthermore, it is not uncommon for the court to order the noncustodial parent to also carry medical insurance on the custodial parent. In making such a decision, the court recognizes the value of such insurance on the stability of the child's family and the inability of the custodial parent to pay for it.

32. WHAT IS THE UNIFORM CHILD CUSTODY AND SUPPORT ACT?

The Uniform Child Custody and Support Act is a standard law adopted by nearly every state. The adopting states have agreed that if a parent seeks to modify an out of court child custody or support order, the case will be referred back to the state that entered the original order unless the best interest of the child require the new state to exercise jurisdiction.

The purpose of this law was to prevent forum shopping. It was to keep the parents from looking throughout the country for a court likely to render a more favorable ruling.

Under this Act, which most states have adopted, modification of child custody or support orders must be made before the court the issued them. This prevents both parents from flaunting the court's judgment by simply moving across state lines.

33. WILL CHILD SUPPORT BE REDUCED IF THE CUSTODIAL PARENT REMARRIES?

Remarriage is an important factor for the court to consider in determining whether child support will be modified. However, the child support award may go up as likely as down as a result of the remarriage.

Child support is based upon disposable income, the amount of income a parent had left over after all of the necessities of life have been paid. If a parent remarries, the new stepparent may be contributing to the cost of running the home and thus actually increase the parent's disposable income.

On the other hand, if the stepparent does not work or contribute to the cost of running the home or has new new children, the disposable income may go down. This would be grounds for reducing the child support. Everything depends on the numbers presented to the court.

6
UNWED PARENTING AND ADOPTIONS

6. UNWED PARENTING AND ADOPTIONS

Teenage pregnancy is increasing with alarming rates throughout the United States. The debate regarding abortion rights in America is partially fueled by the seemingly endless rise in teenage pregnancies. While unwed pregnancies are undeniably not confined to just teenagers, it is equally undeniable that statistics show that the majority of unwed pregnancies are by teenagers. It is very real social problem facing this country as to how to adequately deal with the tide of unplanned and, in some cases, unwanted children.

This chapter can not begin to address the social issues that have plagued the social planners of today. Instead, this chapter attempts to deal more pragmatically and practically with the various aspects of the problems.

In particular, this chapter attempts to define and delineate the rights and obligations of both parents to provide for the care and support of their children. In addition, this chapter deals with the practical alternative of placing the children up for adoptions and what that involves in both an emotional and legal sense. It is hoped that this chapter will answer the major questions of the reader and help, in some fashion, to make both the parents' and the childrens' lives a little bit better.

1. WHAT IS AN ILLEGITIMATE CHILD?
A child born out of wedlock is illegitimate. Under the laws of many states an illegitimate child may not inherit from the child's natural father unless the father has acknowledged the child as his.

Acknowledgment can be accomplished by affirming the relationship publicly or taking the child into his home. Many states have abolished the difference between legitimate and illegitimate children. Such is a recognition that in today's society there is no longer the stigma attaching to illegitimacy that it once did. Even so, legitimacy may play a factor in inheriting from grandparents because it is standard clause in wills that distributions can only be made to legitimate heirs.

2. IS A CHILD CONCEIVED DURING A MARRIAGE BUT BORNE AFTER THE DIVORCE LEGITIMATE?

The law tries to make a child legitimate whenever possible. A child conceived in marriage or born in valid marriage is legitimate under the laws of all the states.

3. IF THE MOTHER MARRIES THE FATHER OF AN ILLEGITIMATE CHILD WHAT IS NEEDED TO MAKE THE CHILD LEGITIMATE?

In most states, when a mother marries the father of an illegitimate child, the child will immediately be legitimatized. After the marriage, the mother should apply for a new birth certificate placing the father's name on the new birth certificate if his name is not already on it.

4. WHOSE NAME WILL APPEAR ON A BIRTH CERTIFICATE AS THE FATHER WHEN THE PREGNANT MOTHER MARRIES A MAN NOT THE FATHER?

The husband is always presumed to be the father of all children born of the wife during the marriage. Therefore, a man marrying a pregnant woman is permitted to have his name placed on the birth certificate of the child.

California has statutes permitting the unmarried father to attempt to establish paternity and visitation rights in his child . If the action is started prior to the marriage of the mother to another man, then the court can not use the presumption to cut off the natural father's rights.

5. IF A FATHER ACKNOWLEDGES AN ILLEGITIMATE CHILD, CAN THE BIRTH CERTIFICATE BE CHANGED?

If the father acknowledges the child, then the bureau of vital statistics for the state where the child was born will place the father's name on the certificate.

The procedure for changing the certificate is simple. First write to the bureau of vital statistics and tell it of changes that are to be made. The bureau will send the appropriate forms needed to process the changes.

6. WHAT IS A PATERNITY SUIT?

A paternity suit is a legal complaint filed by a woman against a man.

The lawsuit seeks to have the man declared the father of the child that the mother has borne. The suit also seeks to have the court order child support.

If the court finds that the man is the father of the child, then he will be entitled to all of the rights and obligations of a divorced father. The man would be entitled to child visitation and, in appropriate, custody of the child.

Once paternity has been declared, the court can not put the child up for adoption without terminating parental rights of the man in the child.

7. CAN THE COURT ORDER BLOOD TESTS TO DETERMINE PATERNITY?

All states use blood tests as evidence of paternity. In the beginning, only blood types were used. The blood typing test could prove conclusively that the man was not the father could not prove conclusively if he was the father.

In recent years, the HLA (Human Leukocyte Antigen) test has been developed that is nearly 99% conclusive in determining paternity.

If the court can get jurisdiction over the father, then it can order that he submit to the blood tests. The court's view is that the invasion of privacy to the man is outweighed by the desire of the state to keep children off the welfare rolls.

8. IF THE HUSBAND IS NOT THE FATHER OF THE CHILD WILL HE HAVE TO TO SUPPORT IT?

In most states it will make no difference if the husband is not the father. In those states the husband is required to support all children born by his wife. It is a moralistic view based on the somewhat dated belief that a wife would not commit adultery and therefore the children are the husband's regardless of what he says.

A small minority of states permit a husband to contest paternity for children borne to his wife. In such states, a husband may seek to prove by blood and genetic testing that a child is not his. If the proof is conclusive to the court, then the husband will not have to support the child. The child, in such cases, will then be considered illegitimate.

9. IS A CHILD BORN BY ARTIFICIAL INSEMINATION ILLEGITIMATE?

A small number of states consider a child born of artificial insemination illegitimate unless the woman's husband adopts the child or otherwise acknowledges it.

The majority of states will hold the child legitimate if it was born to a married woman. The courts rely on the general presumption that a child born to a married woman is the child of the husband.

10. MUST A FATHER SUPPORT AN ILLEGITIMATE CHILD?

Every father has a duty to support his children both illegitimate and legitimate. Therefore if a man is declared to be the father of an illegitimate child by a court or otherwise acknowledges the child as his, then he has an absolute duty to support the child.

Failure to support an illegitimate child may expose the father to criminal prosecution.

11. ARE GRANDPARENTS RESPONSIBLE FOR SUPPORTING THEIR GRANDCHILDREN?

Most states do not have laws requiring grandparents to care for their grandchildren. A parent only has to provide support to their children until they reach the age of maturity (18 years of age in most states and 21 years of age in others) or until the child is emancipated by getting married or by moving out and living on the child's own.

A few states, such as Wisconsin, require grandparents to provide support for their grandchildren until their child (the grandchildren's parent) reaches the age of maturity. For example if the grandparents child is 17 and the age of consent is 21, the grandparents must support their child and his or her children until the child reaches 21.

The theory behind the grandparent support laws is that parents should control their minor children and if their minor children act irresponsibly then the parents should bear some of the burden.

12. IS THERE A TIME LIMIT FOR INSTITUTING A PATERNITY ACTION?

Generally, there is no time limit for bringing a paternity action. A parent has a duty to support his or her child throughout the child's minority (until adulthood).

However unless there is a court order or an agreement to provide support, the mother will usually not recover an award for child support spent prior to the paternity action.

In other words, if the mother raises the child for five years before filing the paternity action, the court may, if it fines the man the father order him to pay child support in the future.

However, the court usually will not make an order for back payment of child support.

13. CAN A COURT ORDER TEMPORARY SUPPORT WHILE A PATERNITY ACTION IS PENDING?

The court has the inherent power to order temporary support to be paid by the man against whom a paternity action is filed. The court is willing to err on the side of the child. If the paternity is not established, then the mother will be ordered to reimburse the man. The order will take the form of a judgment. However if the woman is judgment proof (without the means to pay the judgment) then the man will never recover the support payments.

As a practical matter, such is not a real problem because paternity actions usually don't take long. Once the blood tests are taken, the court's decision follows soon thereafter.

14. CAN AN UNMARRIED COUPLE ADOPT A CHILD?

Courts and placement agencies have always given preference to married couples. Adoption agencies tend to be even stricter than the courts because they are aware of the public scrutiny their activities are always under.

Despite the preference for married couples, opportunities do exist for the adoption by unmarried couples. The reasons for this is that society has become more tolerant of an unmarried couple living together and secondly there is a growing need to find good homes for older children that are not as easily placed.

It is not easy for an unmarried couple to adopt but it is at least possible.

15. CAN A SINGLE PERSON ADOPT A CHILD?

Courts and placement agencies tend to give preference to married couples. Adoption agencies tend to be even stricter than the courts because they are aware of the public scrutiny their activities are always under.

Despite the preference for married couples, opportunities do exist for the adoption by single persons. The reasons for this is that that society has become more tolerant and willing to accept a single parent and secondly there is a growing need to find good homes for older children that are not as easily placed.

It is not easy for a single person to adopt but it is at least possible. The person must show that he or she is capable for providing a stable home environment, financial security and a supportive environment.

16. CAN A HOMOSEXUAL ADOPT A CHILD?

Courts and placement agencies tend to give preference to married couples. Adoption agencies tend to be even stricter than the courts because they are aware of the public scrutiny their activities are always under.

Adoption by homosexuals used to be taboo. However California and several other states have laws that prevent discrimination based on sexual preference. These laws have been cited as permitting homosexual adoption. In California, homosexual adoption has occurred many times.

The problems faced by a homosexual seeking to adopt are obvious. There is a concern that such a lifestyle will harm the development of the child and possibly expose the child to danger.

It will never be easy for a homosexual to adopt but it is at least possible. The person must show, as anyone else who seeks to adopt, that he or she is capable for providing a stable home environment, financial security and a supportive environment. When all of that is done, the court must then decide whether the best interests of the child would be served by placement with the person.

If the child sought to be adopted is not easily placeable and the home environment is stable, the court may approve the adoption.

17. WHAT IS A PRIVATE ADOPTION?

A private adoption is an adoption arranged directly between the natural mother and the adoptive parents without going through an adoption agency.

The same formalities have to be followed in a private adoption as when the adoption is done through an adoption agency. All of the state ordered consents must be obtained, changes are made in the birth certificates and there is probationary period before the final court decree in entered.

The only money permitted to be paid in a private adoption is to cover the mother's medical and hospital expenses. Payments involving a bonus or other property to the mother are illegal. The payments may make the adoption invalid and expose the parties to criminal action.

18. SHOULD AN ATTORNEY BE CONSULTED IN AN ADOPTION?

An attorney is definitely an advantage in an adoption proceeding. Regardless of whether the adoption is through an agency or a private adoption, there will be legal forms and procedures with which to comply.

The adoption agency will have an attorney to look out for its interest. Likewise in a private adoption, there is usually an attorney representing the mother. For that reason an attorney should be used by the adoptive parents to protect their interest.

19. WHAT IS THE BABY BLACK MARKET?

The baby black market is a nebulous web of intrigue through out the U.S. whereby children are sold to people wishing to adopt them. The practice is illegal in all states but continues to flourish because of the money involved.

There are women that have children for the express purpose of selling them. Unscrupulous attorneys or other intermediaries make the contact with the prospective adoptive parents and sell the children. The black market continues because for many reasons this may be the only way that the parents can adopt a child. Since the people go into the transactions with their eyes open, they seldom call the police if they are defrauded and receive a less than perfect baby.

20. CAN FOREIGN CHILDREN BE ADOPTED?

Foreign children can be adopted by American citizens but the problems arising from such an adoption are daunting. The paperwork is excessive both in the U.S. and the home country of the child to be adopted.

If the child is not already in the U.S., at least one trip will be necessary to that foreign country in order to obtain permission to adopt the child. Most countries, including the United States, do not make it easy for their children to be taken out of their country. Children fathered in Viet Nam by American servicemen have been waiting years for permission to be adopted by waiting American families.

In order to get the child into the U.S., both exit and entry visas will have to be obtained from the Immigration Service. Once the foreign hurdles are met, the adoption process in the U.S. takes no longer than a normal adoption.

21. ONCE ADOPTED DOES A FOREIGN BORN CHILD AUTOMATICALLY BECOME AN AMERICAN CITIZEN?

Adopting a foreign born child does not automatically confer citizenship on the child. As soon as the adoption becomes final the adoptive parents should file a petition with the U.S. Immigration and Naturalization Service to have the child become a naturalized citizen. There is no waiting period for such a petition.

22. HOW DOES AN ADOPTION AGENCY OPERATE?

Every state has both public and private adoption agencies. Public agencies can be found by contacting the loan department of social services. Private adoption agencies can be found through the telephone book, advertisements, or checking with adoptive parent groups or doctors.

From each agency, the prospective adoptive parents should ask about the availability of children, religious restrictions if any, fees, income requirements, and medical history of the children.

After the agency is selected, it conducts an detailed investigation on the home life of the applicant. After a child is selected for adoption, further investigations will be made on the background of the child. Until the adoption of the child is completed the agency remains the legal guardian of the child.

23. WHAT IS THE LEGAL PROCEDURE FOR AN ADOPTION?
The adoption process begins by filing a petition for adoption with the court. A hearing is then scheduled in court. The hearing will be closed to the public.

If the court feels the adoption is appropriate, then in some states the court will issue a temporary decree of adoption. In some states there is no temporary decree of adoption but the adoptive parents are permitted to care for the child for a probationary period up to 18 months long. After the probationary period, the court holds a hearing to determine if the adoption should be made final. If the court decides to grant the adoption, the final decree of adoption will be executed.

Once the final decree of adoption is issued, an amended birth certificate is prepared listing the adoptive parents as the biological parents.

Adoption records are sealed and not open to the public. Unless the biological parents agreed to have their names released later, the child may never learn the identity of his or her real parents.

24. CAN THE CHILD BE RETURNED IF THE ADOPTION DOES NOT WORK OUT?
Temporary custody is awarded for a probationary period between 6 to 18 months. During this period the adoptive parents are reviewed periodically by caseworkers. The ability of the adoptive parents to care for the child is continuously assessed.

If during this period the caseworker feels that proper care is not being given to the child, then the court can take the child back. In the same vein, the parents can, during the interim period, return the child if they feel that they can not properly care for the child. If the child is returned to the agency, it will then start the adoption process over again for the child.

25. CAN A STEPPARENT ADOPT A STEPCHILD WITHOUT THE NATURAL PARENT'S CONSENT?
A stepparent may not adopt without the consent of both natural parents unless the parental rights in the child have been terminated. Every state

has laws that govern when a parent's rights in a child may be terminated. When those parental rights have been terminated, the child may be placed up for adoption without the knowledge or consent of the parent.

Consent must also be obtained or the parental rights terminated from a natural father who was paying support for the child. Normally, the grounds for termination of parental rights are:
1. abandonment of the child usually manifested by lack of contact for one or more years with the child,
2. failure to provide support for the child,
3. child molestation, or
4. exposing the child to repeated danger of bodily harm.

26. IS PREFERENCE GIVEN TO FAMILY MEMBER SEEKING TO ADOPT RELATIVES?

All states give preference to family members that seek to adopt relatives. This is not the only factor that the court looks at but the court will consider the family relationship in determining whether to permit the adoption.

27. HOW ARE CHILDREN PLACED UP FOR ADOPTION?

There are two main ways of placing a child up for adoption. The first is through a public agency and the second is the private placement.

In the public agency, the mother signs a statement which is a consent form. The consent form states clearly and emphatically that the mother is willingly giving the baby up for adoption and understands that by doing so all of her parental rights in the child are terminated. The agency then takes the baby and arranges placement with a suitable family.

In a private placement, a doctor or attorney acts as an intermediary between the mother and adopting parents. The adopting parents then file the petition for adoption with the court.

There are many states that do not permit private adoptions and require all adoptions to go through agencies licensed by the state.

28. WHAT ARE THE RIGHTS OF THE UNMARRIED FATHER TO GAIN CUSTODY?

The rights of the unmarried father in his child are the last form of legalized discrimination in the United States. Unless the unmarried father has supported the child, most states will treat him as a total stranger and permit adoption of his child without notice. Most states will give no preference in an adoption preceding to an unmarried father.

The discrimination is obvious. A unmarried woman that wishes to raise the child can get a court to order child support over the father's wishes. Likewise a woman that does not want to raise the child can place it up for adoption and terminate both her and the father's rights in the child simply by refusing to let the father support or have contact with the child.

In most states, unless the father has been permitted to care for the child, he will have no rights whatsoever in the child. For this reason, in most states, the unmarried will have complete power over whether the child is placed up for adoption.

The California Supreme Court, in 1992, for the first time held that the parental rights of an unmarried father could not be cut off if the he is a fit parent and wants to raise the child even though the mother wants to place the child up for adoption. This case is the exception to the rule that the unmarried mother can place the child up for adoption without the consent of the father.

29. CAN A MOTHER CHANGE HER MIND ON AN ADOPTION?

During the temporary period of adoption, a mother may change her mind and some states will order the return of the child to the mother.

After the adoption has become permanent, the court will not reverse the adoption and return the baby to the mother except for some for the gravest of reasons.

The court will only set aside a final adoption if the mother's consent was procured by fraud, or a mistake of fact so great that the court feels that due process requires that the adoption be set aside.

30. MUST A STEPPARENT ADOPT A STEPCHILD TO HAVE THE FULL RIGHTS OF A PARENT?

Legally, a stepparent is a stranger to the stepchild. The stepparent has no rights in the stepchild nor does the stepchild have any obligations towards the stepchild.

In order for the stepparent to acquire the full rights and obligations of a parent towards the stepchild, then there must be an adoption.

31. CAN A STEPCHILD INHERIT FROM A STEPPARENT?

A stepchild is considered a stranger to the stepparent. therefore, unless the stepparent adopts the stepchild, the stepchild will not inherit from the stepparent's estate.

This does not mean that the stepparent can not leave property to the stepchild in the stepparent's will. It means that the stepchild will not be treated as a child of the stepparent in the event the stepparent died without a will. In such an event the estate will be distributed by the laws of intestancy and the stepchild will receive nothing from the stepparent's estate.

32. CAN A GRANDPARENT STOP AN ADOPTION?

A grandparent can not stop an adoption of his or her grandchildren. However a grandparent may petition the court to adopt the grandchild. The grandparent's age will be the most important factor against approving the adoption. However if the grandparent has maintained a close relationship with the child and can otherwise care for the child, the adoption will be approved. The grandparent will have a preference over non relatives in the adoption process.

If the grandparent can not adopt, he or she can still seek visitation rights to the grandchild. All states now recognize the benefit of permitting the continuance of such visitation to the well rounded development of the child.

33. IF A SURROGATE MOTHER DECIDED TO KEEP THE BABY, CAN THE COURT FORCE HER TO COMPLETE THE AGREEMENT?

A surrogate mother is a woman who agrees to have a child for a couple. usually the wife is infertile and the husband fathers the child either by artificial insemination or sexual intercourse.

After the child is borne, the surrogate mother required under the contract to allow the father's wife to adopt the child. Case law has not yet developed as to how the courts should treat a surrogate mother that changes her mind about letting the father's wife adopt the child.

The father can sue for custody and may get it given the circumstances of the case. The surrogate mother will undoubtedly be granted visitation.

34. IS A SURROGATE CONTRACT LEGAL?

The law is not fixed on surrogate contracts. Some states make the contracts illegal. These states view surrogate contracts a s similar to adoption for profit. In such a state the contract is void and neither party can be compelled to complete the contract.

Most states permit the father to pay the medical and living expenses of the surrogate mother but do not permit payments to the surrogate for having the child.

Courts in Kentucky and New York have upheld fee payments to surrogate mothers. In these states surrogate contracts may, for the time being, be legal. As the law develops, anyone considering a surrogate contract should check with their current state law.

35. WHAT TYPES OF SURROGACY CONTRACTS ARE THERE?

There are two types of surrogacy contracts. They are as follows:
1. sperm donation contracts. In this type of surrogacy contract, the father contributes the sperm through artificial insemination to the surrogate mother.
2. gestational contracts. In this type of contract, a fertilized egg is contributed by the couple to the surrogate mother. The surrogate mother will not be the biological mother of the child that she carries.

Only eight states, Arizona, Florida, Indiana, Michigan, New Hampshire, New York, Virginia and Washington, have laws that specifically apply to gestational surrogacy. The laws of the remaining seven states which currently have laws dealing with surrogacy apply only to surrogacy involving sperm donation.

36. WHO ARE THE LEGAL PARENTS OF THE CHILD?

Because of the lack on laws on the subject, who the real parent of a child born under a surrogacy contract is very unclear. Under California law, which is being challenged in court, the father of a child born under a surrogacy contract is not the legal father and must adopt his own child. This can be done by taking the child into his home but where the surrogate mother changes her mind, the father will no rights in the child.

Arkansas, however, clearly provides that the intended parents under a surrogacy contract are the legal parents. Several states, Florida, New Hampshire and Virginia presume that the intended parents under a surrogacy contract are the legal parents but give the surrogate mother a fixed length of time to change her mind and keep the child. In Arizona, North Dakota and Utah, the legal parents are the surrogate and the father. The father's wife must adopt the child if she wishes to acquire any parental rights in the child. Such a result might be different if the father's wife contributed the egg to the surrogate mother.

37. MUST COURT APPROVAL BE OBTAINED BEFORE ENTERING A SURROGACY CONTRACT?

Both Virginia and New Hampshire have laws that require before a valid surrogacy contract can be entered, the intended parents must complete a home study program, as well as the surrogate and her husband, if any, to determine all of the parties' suitability for parenthood.

These are the only laws in the country that require court approval in order to father and bear a child. Such laws skirt the edge of constitutionality. The laws are clearly discriminatory but may be constitutional that will be for the courts to decide.

Certainly, husbands and wives are not required for court approval to bear children. Nor is court approval needed by a woman to keep a child, if she is unmarried and the child was fathered in a manner other than a surrogacy contract.

7
LANDLORD–TENANT

7. LANDLORD-TENANT

Unless a person owns the home where he or she is living or is living with a relative, that person is quite probably a tenant. For every tenant, there is landlord with superior ownership rights and control of the property.

At one time, the landlord was supreme and the tenant had virtually no rights in the premises. The property was rented "AS IS" under the doctrine of caveat emptor, buyer beware. The tenant occupancy was solely based upon the payment of rent regardless of the condition of the property.

Over the years, courts and state legislatures have greatly eroded the landlord's omnipotent rights in the property. Tenants, today, have significant rights in their rented properties and the violation of them by the landlord can result is serious fines and penalties.

This chapter was written in the hope of educating both landlords and tenants of their respective rights before any serious disagreements occur. In certain areas, there are splits among the states as to how they are treated. In those instances, the reader must consult the state statutes to determine which view is followed in that state. The purpose of this chapter is to guide the user towards the legal principle of interest that is to be researched.

1. WHAT IS A LEASE?
A lease is a transfer of real property for a period of time called tenancy by a person with a greater interest in the real property to another. The person granting the lease is called a landlord or lessor. The person receiving the lease the leases is called a tenant or lessee. The consideration paid for the lease is called rent. Following this chapter is a general residential lease and a general store lease.

2. WHAT IS A PERIODIC TENANCY?
A periodic tenancy is a lease that runs from period to period such as month to month or year to year. It is automatically re renewed for another period until terminated.

Termination of a periodic tenancy occurs by giving proper notice to the other party of the intent to terminate the lease. In most states, unless

the parties agree otherwise, the notice requirements for the terminations of a periodic tenancy are:
1. For a month to month lease, thirty days.
2. For a quarter to quarter lease, one quarter's notice,
3. For a year to year lease, six months notice.

3. WHAT IS A TENANCY OF WILL?
A tenancy of will is a lease in which either party may terminate at any time. Unless the parties have expressly agreed that they intend the lease to be a tenancy at will, the court will treat it as a periodic tenancy.

A tenancy at will terminates by operation of law when:
1. either party to the lease dies,
2. the tenant commits waste to the property (damages it)
3. the tenant attempts to assign the lease,
4. the landlord sells the property,
5. the landlord executes a lease on the same property with another.

4. WHAT IS AN ESTATE FOR YEARS?
An estate for years is a lease that runs only for a certain period of time and is not automatically renewed. Such a lease expires at the end of the term of the lease and no notice is needed to be given by either party to the other.

5. WHAT IS A TENANCY AT SUFFERANCE?
A tenancy at sufferance arises when the tenant had previously been in lawful possession of the property, such as under a lease or with permission of the owner or landlord, but continued in possession of the property after the tenant's right to possession terminated. Such a tenant is called a holdover tenant and is liable for the payment of rent. No notice is required to end the tenancy.

6. IS A LANDLORD LIABLE TO TENANTS FOR INJURIES CAUSED BY DEFECTS IN THE PROPERTY?
At common law, the general standard used throughout the United States, a landlord was under no obligation to deliver the real property to the tenant in a good or satisfactory state of repair. As such, the lessor was not liable to the tenant or his guests or invitees for injuries suffered

on the real property as the results of the defects on the property.

The lessor's common law immunity for injuries to persons on his property has been greatly reduced. Now liability, in most instances, will be assessed against an owner for injuries caused by the undisclosed defects on the property.

7. WHAT DEFECTS MUST A LANDLORD DISCLOSE TO AVOID LIABILITY?

The landlord is obligated to disclose the existence of latent defects on the property. A latent defect is one that the tenant could not discover after making a reasonable inspection of the property.

The landlord does not warrant that the property is free from latent defects. To avoid liability for injuries, the landlord merely has to disclose the existence of those defects which he actually knows exists or has reason to suspect exists. If the disclosure is made, then the landlord is immune for liability for injuries suffered by the tenant from the disclosed defects.

If the landlord fails to disclose the existence of the latent defects, he is liable to any injuries or damages caused by them.

8. IS THE LANDLORD LIABLE FOR INJURIES SUFFERED IN COMMON AREAS?

The common areas of multi-unit buildings are not part of a tenant's leased property. As such, the responsibility remains with the lessor to maintain the common areas in a safe manner.

Lessors have been found liable for negligence in maintaining the common areas when injuries occurred because of the owner's negligence. The lessor must use ordinary care to make the area safe for tenants and invitees (business guests) to the property.

The latest extension of liability for common areas occurred when courts found lessors liable for crimes committed by third parties. The court have held that the lessors were negligent when they failed to install locks on gates leading to the common areas.

9. DOES A LANDLORD HAVE A DUTY TO MAINTAIN THE PROPERTY?

Under the common law, the lessor had no duty to maintain the rented property unless there was an express covenant in the lease requiring him to do so.

The modern trend in landlord tenant law is for courts to hold that landlords have a general duty to use reasonable care with respect to residential tenants. The landlord will thus be held liable for personal injuries suffered by the tenants and their guests as the result of the landlord's ordinary negligence. Liability will be imposed for such negligence only when the landlord had notice of the problem and failed to repair it after a reasonable opportunity to do so.

The California Supreme Court has gone so far as to hold landlords strictly liable for injuries caused by the defective conditions of their property without proof of negligence (knowledge).

Many courts have held the landlord liable for injuries caused as the result of the landlord's failure to comply with housing codes.

10. WHAT IS THE IMPLIED WARRANTY OF HABITABILITY?

More than half of the states have adopted the implied warranty of habitability. Under this warranty, the courts hold that a landlord is warranting that the residential is reasonably suited for use as a human residence.

The remedies that a tenant has for a breach of the implied warranty of habitability are:
1. The tenant may move out and terminate the lease,
2. The tenant may make the necessary repairs and offset the costs against future rent
3. The tenant may abate the rent, reduce it to the fair market rental value of the property with the defects,
4. The tenant may pay the full rent and sue the landlord for damages caused by the defects.

11. IS THE TENANT LIABLE FOR INJURIES SUFFERED BY THIRD PARTIES ON THE PROPERTY?

The fact that the landlord may have a duty to keep the premises in good repair does not relieve the tenant of his duty to keep the property in reasonably good repair. The tenant will be held liable for injuries suffered by third parties that the tenant could have reasonably prevented.

12. WHAT IS THE EXTENT OF A TENANT'S OBLIGATION TO MAINTAIN THE PROPERTY?

Unless the lease agreement imposes an express duty to do so, a tenant has no duty to make any substantial repairs on the property. The tenant does have the duty to make minor repairs and to take such other steps that are necessary to prevent damage by the elements. If the tenant does not make the minor repairs, the tenant will be liable for the damages caused because the minor repairs were not made but will not be liable for the actual cost of making the repairs.

A small number of states have passed laws specifically requiring tenants to:
1. refrain from violating any housing codes,
2. keep the property free of vermin,
3. use plumbing, utilities and appliances in a reasonable manner.

13. WHAT IS THE EXTENT OF A TENANT'S COVENANT TO REPAIR?

When the tenant covenants to keep the property in good repair, the condition of the property at the beginning of the lease and the end of the lease must be compared to determine if there was a breach.

If the covenant to repair does not contain any exceptions, then the tenant may be liable for normal wear and tear to the property. However if consideration, rent, is given for the use of the property, most courts will exclude normal wear and tear from the duty to repair.

Under the covenant to repair, the tenant is liable to repair the damage to the property regardless of the cause (third persons, act of God) unless expressly excepted.

14. WHAT IS AN ASSIGNMENT?

An assignment is the transfer of all of the leasehold interest by the lessee, hereafter referred to as the assignor, in the real property to another, hereafter referred to as the assignee. In order for the transfer to be an assignment, the following must be met:
1. The transfer must be for the entire remaining term of the lease. A transfer of 6 months on the remaining 9 months of a lease is not an assignment.
2. The assignment must be on the same terms of the original lease. The

original terms of the lease may not be varied.

15. WHAT ARE THE EFFECTS OF AN ASSIGNMENT?
The effects of an assignment are as follows:
1. The assignor stills remains liable to the lessor for performance of the conditions of the lease. If the assignee fails to pay the rent, the assignor can be sued for the unpaid rent.
2. By virtue of the assignment, the assignee has assumed the obligations, along with the assignor, to perform the conditions of the lease such as the obligation to pay the rent.
3. Both the assignee and assignor can be sued together by the lessor of the real property for any breach of the lease.
4. The assignor can sue the assignee for indemnification, repayment, for any damages that the assignor has to pay the lessor due to the assignee's failure to perform the obligations under the lease.

16. WHAT IS A SUBLEASE?
A sublease is a transfer by the lessee of the lease, hereinafter called the Sublessor, to another hereinafter called the Sublessee of less than the Sublessor's entire interest in the lease. As a result, the sublessor still retains the some of the term of the lease for himself.

The sublessor still remains liable for the performance of the lease even though part of it has been subleased.

17. IS THE SUBLESSEE LIABLE FOR THE LEASE?
A sublease does not transfer the tenant's rights or duties thereunder to the sublessee (subtenant). Under this situation the subtenant becomes the tenant of the tenant but not the landlord.

There is no direct legal relationship between the sublessee and the landlord. For that reason, the landlord can not sue the sublessee for any breach of the lease. The sublessee can only be sued for any damages that he or she actually causes to the property under a tort theory.

18. WHAT ARE THE EFFECTS OF CLAUSES AGAINST ASSIGNMENT AND SUBLEASE?
A transfer in violation of a clause in the lease that prohibits assignments or subleasing is either void or voidable depending on the language in

the clause.

A clause that states simply that no assignment or sublease can occur will make the transfer voidable. The landlord must take physical action to prevent the transfer, i.e. go to court or terminate the lease.

A clause in lease may state that any assignment or sublease is void and terminates the lease at the option of the lessor. Such a clause makes the assignment or sublease void ab initio, from the beginning. The lessor need do nothing but tell the parties the transfer is ineffective and may terminate the lease immediately.

19. HOW IS A CLAUSE REQUIRING CONSENT OF THE LESSOR FOR AN ASSIGNMENT OR SUBLEASE BE CONSTRUED?

Most leases contain provisions that assignments or subleases can not be made without the consent of the landlord. If the lease does not contain the provision that such consent shall not be unreasonably withheld then most courts will not add that provision.

However, some courts will require that a denial be based on reasonable grounds. In addition, a landlord that refuses to consent to an assignment or sublease for discriminatory reasons such as race, religion or sexual preference, may be in violation of a state's anti-discrimination laws.

20. WHAT IS SURRENDER?

Surrendering is the yielding or returning of the full possession of the real property back to the landlord. If the landlord accepts the return of the property, then the tenant's liability for future payment of rents ends.

Usually surrender occurs when the landlord and tenant have agreed to terminate a lease. If the unexpired term on the lease is more than a year, the agreement to surrender must be in writing to satisfy the Statute of Frauds.

21. WHAT IS THE COVENANT OF QUIET ENJOYMENT?

Every lease agreement contains an implied covenant of quiet enjoyment. The covenant implies the that landlord will do nothing to interfere with the possessory rights of the tenant.

22. WHAT IS CONSTRUCTIVE EVICTION?

Constructive eviction is some act or failure to act by the lessor when he has a duty to act which makes the property uninhabitable. The following conditions for constructive eviction must be met:

1. The act or failure to act must be by the landlord or his agent, not third parties,
2. The results of the act is to render the property uninhabitable,
3. The tenant must vacate the premises as a direct result of the landlord's act. If the tenant does not move out then there is no constructive eviction. A tenant may declare the lease terminated because of the constructive eviction and sue for damages suffered or sue the landlord for the return of possession and damages suffered.

23. WHAT ARE THE LANDLORD'S REMEDIES WHEN THE TENANT ABANDONS THE LEASE?

When a tenant abandons property with time still remaining on the lease, the landlord has the following options available:

1. The landlord may consider the abandonment as an offer to surrender the property. If the landlord accepts the surrender and resumes possession of the property for himself, the tenant is relived of further liability on the lease. The fact that the landlord enters the property to make repairs or offers to rent the property to other on behalf of the tenant does not constitute acceptance of the surrender.
2. The traditional option, still available in many states, allows the landlord to do nothing and simply sue the tenant each month for the rent as it becomes due or wait for the end of the term and sue for the whole amount.

Many states requires a landlord to attempt to mitigate his damages and try to rent the premises and apply the rent received to the damages owed by the tenant. The tenant is then liable for the difference. If the property can not be rented, the tenant is liable for the full remaining rent owing for the unexpired term of the lease.

24. HOW DOES CONDEMNATION AFFECT A LEASE?

Condemnation which is the taking of real property for public use under the doctrine of eminent domain affects the lease in two ways. If the entire property is taken in the condemnation proceeding, the lease terminates because there is nothing left to rent.

However, if only a portion of the leased property is taken by virtue of the condemnation proceeding, then the lease is not terminated and the duty to pay the full rent continues. However, in such an event the tenant gets his share of the condemnation award which relates to the tenant's damages suffered by virtue of the condemnation.

Many leases have clauses that automatically terminate a lease in the event of any condemnation of the property.

25. WHAT IS HOLDING OVER?

Holding over occurs when a tenant continues to hold possession of the real property after the termination of the tenant's right of possession. The landlord has two remedies against a tenant holding over:

1. Eviction of the tenant under the state's unlawful detainer statutes, or
2. The landlord may, in his sole discretion, bind the tenant to a new lease. The terms of the new lease are generally those of the original lease. If the previous lease was a month to month lease, then the new lease will be a month to month lease. If the old lease was a year to year lease then the new lease will be year to year. The landlord can notify the tenant before the previous lease expires that new terms or changes will be added to the next lease and the tenant will be bound by those new terms if he holds over.
3. In some states, the landlord is entitled to receive double the rent from a tenant that holds over.

26. ARE LEASES REQUIRED TO BE IN WRITING TO BE ENFORCEABLE?

The Statute of Frauds is a law adopted by most states that requires a lease of real property over one year to be in writing in order to be enforceable. There are exceptions to the requirement of a writing. The most important exception is that of a completed contract or lease. In such a situation, the lease or contract will not have to be in writing in order for its terms to be enforced.

27. WHAT IS UNLAWFUL DETAINER?

Unlawful detainer is the legal remedy available to a landlord against a tenant who:

1. holds over after the lease has terminated,
2. continues in possession of the property without payment of rent when due, or
3. continues in possession after failing to perform the duties required under the terms of the lease or after breaching the terms of the lease, or
4. continues in possession after a valid notice to quit has been served. Unlawful detainer is a summary remedy where a notice to quit is served. It calls for the tenant to vacate the premises within a fixed period usually three days. If the tenant does not leave, the landlord files a complaint in court and serves the tenant with it. The tenant will have a short period of time, usually five days, to answer the complaint. If the tenant fails to answer, the court will enter a default judgment against the tenant.

If the tenant does answer, the case is set for preference on the calendar and usually heard within two weeks to a month. The form for the tenant's answer follows this chapter.

Following this chapter is the actual pleadings for an unlawful detainer complaint, including judgment and writ of possession, that was taken in Santa Ana, California. Most states use pre-printed forms for an unlawful detainer action and require the same in formation to be provided. This case is similar in pleading style to those used in most states. Even if pre-printed forms are not used in some states, the information contained in this sample complaint would still have to be provided in the typewritten complaint. Forms for an unlawful detainer can usually be obtained from the Clerk of the Court where the complaint will be filed.

28. WHAT IS RETALIATORY EVICTION?
Retaliatory eviction is the eviction of a tenant for reporting housing codes violations to the proper authorities. Many states, such as California, make it illegal for a landlord to evict a tenant for reporting housing codes violations.

In many states, a landlord may be fined for committing a retaliatory eviction.

29. WHAT DEFENSES MAY A TENANT HAVE TO AN UNLAWFUL DETAINER ACTION?

A tenant may assert as a defense, the following if appropriate:
1. Failure to be properly served with the Notice to Quit,
2. Failure to be properly served with the complaint,
3. compliance with all the terms of the lease,
4. breach of the implied warranty of habitability,
5. retaliatory eviction. If the tenant prevails on the first two defenses, the complaint is dismissed for lack of jurisdiction by the court. If the tenant prevails on any of the other defenses, the court may allow the tenant to stay in the premises and even award damages.

30. MAY A LANDLORD LOCK A TENANT OUT OF THE PREMISES FOR A BREACH OF THE LEASE OR HOLDING OVER?

It used to be permitted for a landlord to lock a tenant out of the premises after the lease expired. This form of self-help was widely used.

However, few if any, states now permit a landlord to unilaterally evict a tenant. All states have unlawful detainer statutes to evict tenants wrongly in possession. The unlawful detainer action is a summary procedure and therefore given preference on the court's calendar.

Most state recognize that self-help can result in breaches of the peace and have abolished it altogether.

31. WHAT IS FORCIBLE ENTRY AND DETAINER?

Forcible entry and detainer is a tort whereby a person, usually the landlord, unlawfully evicts a tenant for the leased premises. States that do not permit self-help remedies to the landlord will find the landlord liable for damages suffered by a tenant who is evicted or whose possession of of the property is interfered.

California makes it a crime for a landlord to shut off utilities to a tenant for any reason and fines a landlord $10,000 per day for any forcible entry or detainer act.

32. WHAT IS A WRIT OF POSSESSION?

If the landlord wins in an unlawful detainer action, the court will enter a judgment in the landlord's favor. The court will also issue an order that the tenant vacate the premises by a certain date. The clerk of the court will issue a certified order called a Writ of Possession.

If the tenant fails to move out by the allotted time, the landlord takes the Writ of Possession to the local Sheriff or Marshall's Office. A police officer will then be dispatched to oversee the removal of the tenant's possessions from the premises.

33. WHAT ARE LIQUIDATED DAMAGES IN A LEASE?

The parties in a lease may agree that in the event of a breach of the lease by either party that the only remedy either party will have is the payment of a fixed amount of money.

Such clauses are enforceable if they represent a true attempt to limit damages before a breach has occurred and are entered into in good faith.

34. WHAT IS A SECURITY DEPOSIT?

A security deposit is a payment in addition to rent that is a guarantee against damages to the premises. From this security deposit, the landlord pays to repair any damages caused by the tenant. A security deposit is not rent. The purpose of the security deposit and its uses are clearly defined by statutes in most states. Many states require a security deposit to be kept segregated in an interest bearing account.

35. CAN A LANDLORD KEEP A SECURITY DEPOSIT?

A security deposit is refundable. The laws of many states, including California, impose penalties on the landlord that wrong wrongly fails to return a security deposit. A security deposit can not be made nonrefundable in most states.

A landlord is required within a matters of days, usually 10, after the termination of the lease to inform the tenant in writing as to how the security deposit was applied to satisfy the damages allegedly caused by the tenant. The landlord then is to return the balance of the deposit.

If the tenant feels that more of the security deposit should have been returned, the tenant should sue the landlord in small claims court for the amount in dispute plus any damages that the state law imposes on a landlord for misusing a security deposit.

36. WHAT IS A LANDLORD'S LIEN?
Under the common law, a landlord was not given a lien in the tenant's property for unpaid rent. The laws of many states now give a landlord a lien for rent upon the property of their tenants and, in the case of agricultural lands, upon the crops grown on the leased land. The legal title to the property still remains with the tenant along with the right to possession but a lien attaches to them.

37. WHAT PROPERTY IS AFFECTED BY THE STATUTORY LIEN?
The property to which a statutory lien of a landlord may attach depends of the statutes of each state. Most states that allow the lien permit it to attach all of the tenant's property on the leased premises. A few states, however, limit the landlord's lien to just certain designated types of property such as growing crops on the leased land, fixtures used in a trade or business, or animals on the leased land.

38. WHAT ARE FIXTURES?
A fixture is personal property that is attached to the real property in such a way as to be considered a permanent part of the real property.

Under the common law, all fixtures became the property of the owner of the property. Thus, any improvements to the real property made by the tenant ended up being owned by the landlord and could not be taken away by the tenant when the lease ended.

Most states have modified the common law on fixture and permit the tenant to remove fixtures provided they can be removed without damaging the real property. To address this problem, many leases contain clauses that state whether fixtures will be considered the property of the landlord or the tenant and if the fixtures can or must be removed upon termination of the lease.

39. IS THERE A STATUTORY LIEN ON FIXTURES?
Some states give a landlord a lien on fixtures placed on the leased property by a tenant. A building placed on the real property is a fixture and a lien could attach to it if permitted by the state law.

In the states allowing a fixture lien, the removal of the fixtures or improvements will not terminate the lien. Therefore in the states that allow the lien, the removal of the fixtures, by the tenant, will still permit the lien to follow the fixtures.

For example, if the landlord has a lien on a building which the tenant later moves off the leased land, the lien still follows the building. If the building is subsequently sold, the lien will still follow the building provided the buyer had actual or constructive notice of the landlord's lien on the building.

40. HOW IS THE STATUTORY LIEN ENFORCED?

The statutory lien must be enforced in accordance to the laws of the state involved which means filing a lawsuit for enforcement. In some states, recording a notice or filing a UCC-1 form with the Secretary of State will serve to give notice to the world of the lien. Such notice will prevent the property from being sold without the landlord being paid.

The lien gives the landlord some preference in bankruptcy as a secured creditor should the tenant file.

41. IS A LANDLORD'S LIEN WAIVABLE?

A landlord may waive his statutory lien both intentionally and unintentionally by his express agreement or conduct.

In most states that permit the lien, if a landlord permits the tenant to remove the property without asserting the right of his lien, then he waives the lien forever on that property.

When the landlord permits the tenant to sell the property on a promise that the proceeds will go to the landlord, the court will find a waiver. If the tenant then decides not to pay the landlord, then the landlord must still sue the tenant.

42. DOES A LANDLORD HAVE THE RIGHT TO ENTER THE PROPERTY?

Generally, a landlord does not have a right to enter into the leased property once it has been leased. If a landlord does enter the property without the consent of the tenant, he has committed a trespass.

Many leasse contain clauses giving the landlord the right to enter the property at reasonable times to make repairs. Likewise, many states give the landlord the right to enter the property under reasonable circumstances to make repairs even if it the lease does not specifically give the landlord that right.

A landlord that enters the property without a proper purpose may violating the tenant's right of quiet enjoyment.

43. IF THE PROPERTY IS DESTROYED WILL THAT TERMINATE THE LEASE?

Destruction of the property would not terminate the tenancy at common law. Most states now have laws that if the property is entirely destroyed through no fault of the tenant, then the lease is terminated.

When the property is only damaged through no fault of the tenant, then most states will keep the lease in effect but reduce the rent the until the property is repaired.

Most lease have clauses that define the rights of the parties in the event the property is damages or destroyed.

44. IS THE LANDLORD LIMITED TO DAMAGES IF THE TENANT FAILS TO PERFORM THE CONDITIONS OF THE LEASE?

At common law, a landlord was not permitted to terminate a lease because the tenant failed to perform the conditions of the lease.

Today both by statute and the terms of most leases, a landlord is permitted to terminate a lease for the failure of the tenant to perform the conditions of the lease including the payment of rent.

After the breach has occurred, the landlord is required to give the tenant a short notice to perform the condition (usually pay rent) or quit the premises. If the tenant fails to do so, then an unlawful detainer action can be filed.

45. IF THE LEASED PROPERTY IS MORTGAGED AND THEN FORECLOSED HOW WILL THAT AFFECT THE LEASE?

If the leased property is mortgaged at the time the lease is made, then the the mortgage is superior to the lease. If the mortgage is subsequently foreclosed, the tenancy is destroyed because the lease was taken subject to, with knowledge of, the superior position of the mortgage.

As a result, foreclosing of the mortgage wipes out all of the rights of the tenant in the property. The tenant may sue the landlord for breach of the lease but given the fact that landlord has lost the property for failure for make payments, recovery might be doubtful.

46. IF THE PROPERTY IS MORTGAGED AFTER IT IS LEASED, HOW WILL THAT AFFECT THE LEASE?
If the lease is created before the mortgage is taken on the property, then the lease is superior to the mortgage. If the mortgage is foreclosed, that will not terminate the lease. The mortgage holder will simply become the new landlord. The tenant's estate in the property will still continue as it had.

Many lenders will not loan on property in which there are leases because for this reason.

47. WHAT REMEDIES ARE AVAILABLE WHEN THE LANDLORD FAILS TO DELIVER POSSESSION TO A NEW TENANT?
When the landlord is in possession of the property and fails to deliver it to the new tenant at the start of the lease term, the tenant has the following remedies:
1. the tenant may sue for possession and damages incurred, or
2. terminate the lease and sue for the damages suffered.

48. WHAT ARE THE REMEDIES AVAILABLE TO A NEW TENANT IF A THIRD PERSON IS IN POSSESSION WITH THE LANDLORD'S CONSENT?
When a third person is in possession of the property with the landlord's consent and refuses to deliver possession to the new tenant, the tenant may terminate the lease and sue the landlord for damages.

Whether the new tenant can sue to recover possession depends on whether the third party in possession has a superior lease to the new tenant. If the third party entered into a valid lease prior to the new tenant and it has not been terminated, then the new tenant may not sue for possession and is limited only to damages. If the new tenant's lease is superior, then the new tenant can sue both the landlord and the third party for possession and damages.

49. CAN A TENANT TERMINATE A LEASE IF A THIRD PARTY IS IN POSSESSION WITHOUT THE LANDLORD'S CONSENT?

Many states permit a tenant to terminate a lease if at the time the tenant is to take possession a third party is in possession of the lease and refuses to give it up to the new tenant. This is called the English Rule an imposes and absolute duty on the landlord to put the tenant into actual possession of the property.

The other states have adopted the American Rule. Under this rule, the landlord is not required to deliver actual possession. The new tenant is responsible for evicting the third party wrongfully in possession of the property.

50. IS EITHER PARTY TO A LEASE REQUIRED TO INSURE THE OTHER FOR DAMAGES TO THE PROPERTY?

Both landlord and tenant have insurable interest in the property. Unless the lease requires one party or the other to carry insurance, neither party has to carry it. If either party separately insures himself against damages caused by the disrepair or destruction of the property, that party alone is entitled to the proceeds of the insurance.

STORE LEASE

1. PARTIES. This Lease is entered into by an between _____(hereinafter referred to as the Landlord) and _____ (hereinafter referred to as the Tenant) on this day of _____ in the month of _____, in the year _____.

2. PREMISES. The Landlord hereby lease to the Tenant on the terms and conditions hereinafter set forth, which the Tenant hereby accepts, the real property and the building and other improvements located thereon situated in the City of _____, County of _____, State of _____ commonly referred to as _____ and described as follows: _____
_____
(said is hereafter called the "Premises").

3. TERM The term of this lease shall be for _____ commencing on _____ and ending on _____.

4. PURPOSE OF PREMISES. The Tenant shall only use the leased Premises for the following purpose: _____
_____ and no other use will be made of the Premises without the Landlord's written consent.

5. RENT. The Tenant shall pay the Landlord as rent for the Premises, the sum of _____ dollars per month, payable in advance on the first day of each month during the term thereof. Rent shall be payable without notice or demand and without any deduction, off-set, or abatement in lawful money of the United States to the Landlord at the address stated herein for notices or to such other persons or such other places as the Landlord may designate to the Tenant in writing.

6. SECURITY DEPOSIT Tenant shall deposit with Landlord the sum

of _____ dollars as a security deposit for the performance by Tenant of the provisions of this lease. Upon Tenant's default under this lease, Landlord may use the security deposit or any portion thereof to cure the default or to compensate the Landlord for all damage it incurs as a result of such default. In such event, Tenant shall immediately pay to Landlord a sum equal to the portion of the security deposit expended or applied by Landlord so as to maintain the security deposit in the sum initially deposited with Landlord. If Tenant is not in default at the expiration or ter termination of this Lease, Landlord shall return the security deposit to tenant. Landlord shall not be required to pay interest on the security deposit.

7. INDEMNIFICATION Tenant shall indemnify and hold Landlord harmless from and against any and all claims arising from Tenant 's use or occupancy of the Premises or from the conduct of its business or from any activity, work, or things which may be permitted or suffered by Tenant in or about the Premises including all damages, costs, attorney's fees, expenses and liabilities incurred in the defense of any claim or action or proceeding arising therefrom, Except for the Landlord's willful or grossly negligent conduct, Tenant hereby assumes all risk of damage to property or injury to persons in or about the premises.

8. UTILITIES Tenant shall make all arrangements and pay for all water, gas, light power, telephone and other utility services supplied to the Premises together with any taxes thereon and for all connection charges from _____.

9. INSURANCE. Tenant is to carry Bodily Injury and Property Damage Liability Insurance with a combined single limit for bodily and property damage of at least fifty thousand dollars ($50,000.00).

10. DEFAULT. It is agreed between the parties hereto that if any rent shall be due hereunder and unpaid, or if the Tenant sh all default and breach any other covenant or provision of the Lease, then Landlord, after giving the proper notice required by law, may re-enter the Premises and remove any property and any and all persons there-

from in the manner allowed by law. The Landlord may, at his option, either maintain this Lease in full force and effect and recover the rent and other charges as they become due or, in the alternative, terminate this Lease. In addition, the Landlord may recover all rentals and other damages and pursue any other rights and remedies which the Landlord may have against the Tenant by reason of such default as provided by law.

11. MAINTENANCE OF EQUIPMENT. Tenant is to be solely responsible for the maintenance and replacement of all equipment on the Premises.

12. RIGHT TO INSPECT Landlord reserves and shall at any and all times have the right to enter the Premises to inspect the same, to submit the Premises to prospective purchasers or tenants, to post notices of non-responsibility and "for lease" and "for sale "signs,and to alter, improve or repair the Premises and portion of the Building without abatement of rent. The business of the Tenant shall not be interfered with unreasonably. Tenant hereby waives any claim for damages for any injury or inconvenience to or interference with Tenant's business, any loss of occupancy or quiet enjoyment of the Premises, and any other loss occasioned thereby.

13. HOLDING OVER. If the Tenant, with the Landlord's consent remains in possession of the Premises after expiration or termination of the term of the Lease, such possession by the Tenant shall be deemed to be a tenancy from month to month at a rental in the amount of the last monthly rental plus all other charges payable hereunder, and upon the provisions of the Lease applicable to such month to month tenancy.

14. IMPROVEMENTS. The Tenant shall not without the prior written consent consent of the Landlord make any alterations, improvements or additions in or about the Premises.

15. ASSIGNMENTS OR SUBLETTING. The Tenant shall not voluntarily or by operation of law assign, transfer, sublet, mortgage, or

otherwise transfer or encumber all or any part of the Tenant's interest in the Lease without the Landlord's Prior written consent.

16. SUCCESSOR IN INTEREST. The terms and conditions of this Lease shall be binding upon and inure to the benefit of the heirs, personal representatives, successors and assigns of the parties.

17. NOTICES Whenever under this Lease a provision is made for any demand, notice or declaration of any kind, it shall be in writing and served personally or sent by mail either registered or certified, postage prepaid at the addresses set forth below:

Landlord: _____

_____

Tenant: _____

_____

Such notice shall be deemed to be received within forty eight hours of the time of mailing, if mailed as provided for in this paragraph.

18. TAXES. It is agreed that the Landlord shall pay all real property taxes and general assessments levied against the Premises during the term of the Lease. It is agreed that the Tenant shall pay all personal property assessed or levied against Trade Fixtures, Furnishings, Equipment and Other Personal Property of the Tenant contained in the Premises.

19. ENTIRE AGREEMENT. This Lease constitutes the entire agreement between the parties. This Lease can only be amended or modified in writing executed by both parties.

20. WAIVER. No covenant, term or condition, or breach of thereof shall be deemed waived, except by the written consent of the party

against whom the waiver is claimed and any waiver of the breach of any term, condition or covenant shall not be deemed to be a waiver of any preceding or succeeding breach of the same or any covenant, term, or condition. Acceptance by Landlord of any performance by Tenant after the same shall become due shall not constitute a waiver by Landlord of the breach or default of any covenant, term or condition unless expressly agreed by the Landlord in writing.

21. ATTORNEY FEES. In the event of litigation over the terms of this Lease, the prevailing party shall be entitled to reasonable attorney fees and costs.

The Parties have executed this Lease on the date first written above.

Landlord: _____

Tenant: _____

LANDLORD'S AND TENANT'S AGREEMENT

This Lease is entered into by an between _____
_____(hereinafter referred to as the Landlord) whose address is _____
_____and _____
_____ (hereinafter referred to as the Tenant) on this day of _____ in the month of _____, in the year _____ .

The Landlord hereby lease to the Tenant on the terms and conditions hereinafter set forth, which the Tenant hereby accepts, the real property and the building and other improvements located thereon situated in the City of _____, County of _____, State of _____ commonly referred to as _____ and described as follows: _____
_____
(said is hereafter called the "Premises").

The term of this lease shall be for _____ commencing on _____ and ending on_____ .

The Tenant shall pay the Landlord as rent for the Premises, the sum of _____ dollars per month, payable in advance on the first day of each month during the term thereof. Rent shall be payable without notice or demand and without any deduction, offset, or abatement in lawful money of the United States to the Landlord at the address stated herein for notices or to such other persons or such other places as the Landlord may designate to the Tenant in writing.

Tenant shall deposit with Landlord the sum of _____ dollars as a security deposit for the performance by Tenant of the provisions of this lease. Upon Tenant's default under this lease, Landlord may use the security deposit or any portion thereof to cure the default or to compensate the Landlord for all damage it incurs as a result of such default. In such event, Tenant shall immediately pay to Landlord a sum equal to the portion of the security deposit expended or applied by Landlord so as to maintain the security deposit in the sum initially deposited with Landlord. If Tenant is not in default at the expiration or termination of this Lease, Landlord shall return the security deposit to tenant. Landlord shall not be required to pay interest on the security deposit.

The Tenant hereby covenants and agrees with the Landlord as follows:

1. Tenant shall indemnify and hold Landlord harmless from and against any and all claims arising from Tenant's use or occupancy of the Premises including all damages, costs, attorney's fees, expenses and liabilities incurred in the defense of any claim or action or proceeding arising therefrom, Except for the Landlord's willful or grossly negligent conduct, Tenant hereby assumes all risk of damage to property or injury to persons in or about the premises.

2. Tenant shall make all arrangements and pay for all water, gas, light power, telephone and other utility services supplied to the Premises together with any taxes thereon and for all connection charges from _____.

3. It is agreed between the parties hereto that if any rent shall be due hereunder and unpaid, or if the Tenant shall default and breach any other covenant or provision of the Lease, then Landlord, after giving the proper notice required by law, may re-enter the Premises and remove any property and any and all persons therefrom in the manner allowed by law. The Landlord may, at his option, either maintain this Lease in full force and effect and recover the rent and other charges as they become due or, in the alternative, terminate this Lease. In addition, the Landlord may recover all rentals and other damages and pursue any other rights and remedies which the Landlord may have against the Tenant by reason of such default as provided by law.

4. Tenant is to be solely responsible for the maintenance of the

Premises. Tenant agrees to surrender possession of the Premises at the expiration of the term if the lease or any other sooner termination of the lease in good condition and repair, ordinary wear and tear and damage by the elements excepted.

5. If the Tenant, with the Landlord's consent remains in possession of the Premises after expiration or termination of the term of the Lease, such possession by the Tenant shall be deemed to be a tenancy from month to month at a rental in the amount of the last monthly rental plus all other charges payable hereunder, and upon the provisions of the Lease applicable to such month to month tenancy.

6. The Tenant shall not without the prior written consent consent of the Landlord make any alterations, improvements or additions in or about the Premises.

7. The Tenant shall not voluntarily or by operation of law assign, transfer, sublet, mortgage, or otherwise transfer or encumber all or any part of the Tenant's interest in the Lease without the Landlord's Prior written consent.

The terms and conditions of this Lease shall be binding upon and inure to the benefit of the heirs, personal representatives, successors and assigns of the parties.

In the event of litigation over the terms of this Lease, the prevailing party shall be entitled to reasonable attorney fees and costs.

This Lease constitutes the entire agreement between the parties. This Lease can only be amended or modified in writing executed by both parties.

No covenant, term or condition, or breach of thereof shall be deemed waived, except by the written consent of the party against whom the waiver is claimed and any waiver of the breach of any term, condition or covenant shall not be deemed to be a waiver of any preceding or succeeding breach of the same or any covenant, term, or condition. Acceptance by Landlord of any performance by Tenant after the same shall become due shall not constitute a waiver by Landlord of the breach or default of any covenant, term or condition unless expressly agreed by the Landlord in writing.

The Parties have executed this Lease on the date first written above.

Landlord: _____

Tenant: _____

SUMMONS
(CITACION JUDICIAL)

UNLAWFUL DETAINER—EVICTION
(PROCESO DE DESAHUCIO—EVICCION)

NOTICE TO DEFENDANT: *(Aviso a Acusado)*

JOHN SMITH

FOR COURT USE ONLY
(SOLO PARA USO DE LA CORTE)

YOU ARE BEING SUED BY PLAINTIFF:
(A Ud. le está demandando)

DOE ASSOCIATES

You have **5 CALENDAR DAYS** after this summons is served on you to file a typewritten response at this court.

A letter or phone call will not protect you; your typewritten response must be in proper legal form if you want the court to hear your case.

If you do not file your response on time, you may lose the case, you may be evicted, and your wages, money and property may be taken without further warning from the court.

There are other legal requirements. You may want to call an attorney right away. If you do not know an attorney, you may call an attorney referral service or a legal aid office (listed in the phone book).

Después de que le entreguen esta citación judicial usted tiene un plazo de **5 DIAS CALENDARIOS** para presentar una respuesta escrita a máquina en esta corte.

Una carta o una llamada telefónica no le ofrecerá protección; su respuesta escrita a máquina tiene que cumplir con las formalidades legales apropiadas si usted quiere que la corte escuche su caso.

Si usted no presenta su respuesta a tiempo, puede perder el caso, le pueden obligar a desalojar su casa, y le pueden quitar su salario, su dinero y otras cosas de su propiedad sin aviso adicional por parte de la corte.

Existen otros requisitos legales. Puede que usted quiera llamar a un abogado inmediatamente. Si no conoce a un abogado, puede llamar a un servicio de referencia de abogados o a una oficina de ayuda legal (vea el directorio telefónico).

The name and address of the court is: *(El nombre y dirección de la corte es)*

CENTRAL ORANGE COUNTY JUDICIAL DISTRICT
MUNICIPAL COURT
700 CIVIC CENTER DRIVE WEST, SANTA ANA, CA. 92701

CASE NUMBER: *(Número del Caso)*
XX678

The name, address, and telephone number of plaintiff's attorney, or plaintiff without an attorney, is:
(El nombre, la dirección y el número de teléfono del abogado del demandante, o del demandante que no tiene abogado, es)

MICHAEL LYNN GABRIEL
643 B SOUTH MAIN STREET
UKIAH, CA. 95482
(707) 468-0268

DATE:
(Fecha)

Clerk, by _____, Deputy
(Actuario)   *(Delegado)*

[SEAL]

NOTICE TO THE PERSON SERVED: You are served
1. ☐ as an individual defendant.
2. ☐ as the person sued under the fictitious name of *(specify)*:
3. ☐ on behalf of *(specify)*:

   under: ☐ CCP 416.10 (corporation)   ☐ CCP 416.60 (minor)
          ☐ CCP 416.20 (defunct corporation) ☐ CCP 416.70 (conservatee)
          ☐ CCP 416.40 (association or partnership) ☐ CCP 416.90 (individual)
          ☐ other:
4. ☐ by personal delivery on *(date)*:

Form Adopted by Rule 982
Judicial Council of California
2(a)(11) (Rev. January 1, 1984)

(See reverse for Proof of Service)
SUMMONS — UNLAWFUL DETAINER

CCP 412.20

PROOF OF SERVICE — SUMMONS – Unlawful Detainer
(Use separate proof of service for each person served)

1. I served the
   a. [XX] summons [XX] complaint [ ] amended summons [ ] amended complaint
      [ ] completed and blank Case Questionnaires [ ] Other *(specify)*:
   b. on defendant *(name)*: JOHN SMITH
   c. by serving [XX] defendant [ ] other *(name and title or relationship to person served)*:
   d. [XX] by delivery [XX] at home [ ] at business
      (1) date: OCTOBER 5, 1984
      (2) time: 5:30 p.m.
      (3) address: 5478 Blaine Apt.2, Santa Ana, CA. 92707
   e. [ ] by mailing
      (1) date:
      (2) place:

2. Manner of service *(check proper box)*:
   a. [X] **Personal service.** By personally delivering copies. (CCP 415.10)
   b. [ ] **Substituted service on corporation,** unincorporated association (including partnership), or public entity. By leaving during usual office hours, copies in the office of the person served with the person who apparently was in charge and thereafter mailing (by first-class mail, postage prepaid) copies to the person served at the place where the copies were left. (CCP 415.20(a))
   c. [ ] **Substituted service on natural person,** minor, conservatee, or candidate. By leaving copies at the dwelling house, usual place of abode, or usual place of business of the person served in the presence of a competent member of the household or a person apparently in charge of the office or place of business, at least 18 years of age, who was informed of the general nature of the papers, and thereafter mailing (by first-class mail, postage prepaid) copies to the person served at the place where the copies were left. (CCP 415.20(b)) *(Attach separate declaration or affidavit stating acts relied on to establish reasonable diligence in first attempting personal service.)*
   d. [ ] **Mail and acknowledgment service.** By mailing (by first-class mail or airmail, postage prepaid) copies to the person served, together with two copies of the form of notice and acknowledgment and a return envelope, postage prepaid, addressed to the sender. (CCP 415.30) *(Attach completed acknowledgment of receipt.)*
   e. [ ] **Certified or registered mail service.** By mailing to an address outside California (by first-class mail, postage prepaid, requiring a return receipt) copies to the person served. (CCP 415.40) *(Attach signed return receipt or other evidence of actual delivery to the person served.)*
   f. [ ] Other *(specify code section)*:
      [ ] additional page is attached.

3. The "Notice to the Person Served" (on the summons) was completed as follows (CCP 412.30, 415.10, and 474):
   a. [ ] as an individual defendant.
   b. [ ] as the person sued under the fictitious name of *(specify)*:
   c. [ ] on behalf of *(specify)*:
      under: [ ] CCP 416.10 (corporation) [ ] CCP 416.60 (minor) [ ] other:
             [ ] CCP 416.20 (defunct corporation) [ ] CCP 416.70 (conservatee)
             [ ] CCP 416.40 (association or partnership) [ ] CCP 416.90 (individual)
   d. [ ] by personal delivery on *(date)*:

4. At the time of service I was at least 18 years of age and not a party to this action.
5. Fee for service: $ 0.00
6. Person serving:
   a. [ ] California sheriff, marshal, or constable.
   b. [ ] Registered California process server.
   c. [ ] Employee or independent contractor of a registered California process server.
   d. [XX] Not a registered California process server.
   e. [ ] Exempt from registration under Bus. & Prof. Code 22350(b).

   f. Name, address and telephone number and, if applicable, county of registration and number:
   JOHN CLAY
   1546 Carlson
   Santa Ana, CA. 92707
   (213) 234-1267

I declare under penalty of perjury under the laws of the State of California that the foregoing is true and correct.

(For California sheriff, marshal, or constable use only)
I certify that the foregoing is true and correct.

Date: October 5, 1984

Date:

▶ _____ *(SIGNATURE)*

▶ _____ *(SIGNATURE)*

ATTORNEY OR PARTY WITHOUT ATTORNEY (NAME AND ADDRESS):	TELEPHONE:	FOR COURT USE ONLY
MICHAEL LYNN GABRIEL ATTORNEY AT LAW 643 B SOUTH MAIN STREET UKIAH, CA. 95482	(707) 468-0268	

ATTORNEY FOR (NAME): PLAINTIFF

Insert name of court, judicial district or branch court, if any, and post office and street address:

MUNICIPAL COURT OF CALIFORNIA COUNTY OF ORANGE
CENTRAL ORANGE COUNTY JUDICIAL DISTRICT
700 CIVIC CENTER DRIVE WEST
SANTA ANA, CA. 92701

PLAINTIFF: **DOE ASSOCIATES**

(THIS IS AN ACTUAL CASE WITH NAMES CHANGED TO PRESERVE THE PARTIES PRIVACY)

DEFENDANT:
JOHN SMITH

DOES 1 TO **5, INCLUSIVE**

COMPLAINT—Unlawful Detainer	CASE NUMBER: XX678

1. This pleading including attachments and exhibits consists of the following number of pages: **7**
2. a. Plaintiff is ☐ an individual over the age of 18 years. ☒ a partnership.
   ☐ a public agency. ☐ a corporation.
   ☐ other (specify):
   b. ☒ Plaintiff has complied with the fictitious business name laws and is doing business under the fictitious name of (specify): DOE ASSOCIATES
3. Defendants named above are in possession of the premises located at (street address, city and county):
   5428 Blaine, Apt. #2, Santa Ana, California 92707
4. Plaintiff's interest in the premises is ☒ as owner ☐ other (specify):
5. The true names and capacities of defendants sued as Does are unknown to plaintiff.
6. a. On or about (date): JUNE 28, 1983 defendants (names): JOHN SMITH
   agreed to rent the premises for a ☐ month-to-month tenancy ☒ other tenancy (specify): SIX MONTH TENANCY
   at a rent of $ 335.00 payable ☒ monthly ☐ other (specify frequency):
   due on the ☐ first of the month ☐ other day (specify):
   b. This ☒ written ☐ oral agreement was made with
   ☐ plaintiff ☐ plaintiff's predecessor in interest
   ☒ plaintiff's agent ☐ other (specify):
   c. ☐ The defendants not named in item 6.a. are
   ☐ subtenants ☐ assignees ☐ other (specify):
   d. ☒ The agreement was later changed as follows (specify):
   EFFECTIVE 3/2/84 RENT INCREASED FROM $335.00 TO $345.00
   e. ☒ A copy of the written agreement is attached and labeled Exhibit A.
7. Plaintiff has performed all conditions of the rental agreement.
8. ☒ a. The following notice was served on defendant (name):
   ☐ 3-day notice to pay rent or quit ☐ 3-day notice to quit
   ☐ 3-day notice to perform covenant or quit ☒ 30-day notice to quit
   ☐ other (specify):
   b. The period stated in the notice expired on (date): OCTOBER 3, 1984 and defendants failed to comply with the requirements of the notice by that date.
   c. All facts stated in the notice are true.
   d. ☐ The notice included an election of forfeiture.
   e. ☒ A copy of the notice is attached and labeled Exhibit B.
   (Continued)

Form Approved by the
Judicial Council of California
Effective January 1, 1982
Rule 982.1(90)

COMPLAINT—Unlawful Detainer

CCP 425.12

SHORT TITLE:	CASE NUMBER:
DOE VS. SMITH	XX678

COMPLAINT—Unlawful Detainer   Page tw

9. [X] a. The notice referred to in item 8 was served
   - [ ] by personally handing a copy to defendant on *(date)*: SEPTEMBER 4, 1984
   - [ ] by leaving a copy with *(name or description)*: _____, a person of suitable age or discretion, on *(date)*: _____ at defendant's [ ] residence [ ] business AND mailing a copy to defendant at his place of residence on *(date)*: _____ because defendant cannot be found at his residence or usual place of business.
   - [ ] by posting a copy on the premises on *(date)*: _____ ([ ] and giving a copy to a person residing at the premises) AND mailing a copy to defendant at the premises on *(date)*:
      - [ ] because defendant's residence and usual place of business cannot be ascertained OR
      - [ ] because no person of suitable age or discretion can there be found.
   - [ ] *(not for 3-day notice. See Civil Code section 1946 before using)* by sending a copy by certified or registered mail addressed to defendant on *(date)*.
   b. [ ] Information about service of the notice on the other defendants is contained in attachment 9.

10. [X] Plaintiff demands possession from each defendant because of expiration of a fixed term lease.
11. [ ] At the time the 3-day notice to pay rent or quit was served, the amount of rent due was $ _____
12. [X] The fair rental value of the premises is $ 11.50 per day.
13. Plaintiff is entitled to immediate possession of the premises.
14. [ ] Defendants' continued possession is malicious, and plaintiff is entitled to treble damages. *(State specific facts supporting this claim in attachment 14.)*
15. [X] A written agreement between the parties provides for attorney fees.
16. [ ] Defendants' tenancy is subject to the local rent control or eviction control ordinance of *(city or county, title of ordinance, and date of passage)*:

    Not Applicable

    Plaintiff has met all applicable requirements of the ordinances.
17. [ ] Other allegations are stated in attachment 17.
18. Plaintiff remits to the jurisdictional limit, if any, of the court.

19. PLAINTIFF REQUESTS
   a. possession of the premises.
   b. [XX] costs incurred in this proceeding.
   c. [XX] past due rent of $ 46.00 10/2/84 to 10/5/84
   d. [XX] damages at the rate of $ 11.50 per day.
   e. [ ] treble the amount of rent and damages found due.
   f. [XX] reasonable attorney fees. $350.00
   g. [XX] forfeiture of the agreement.
   h. [ ] other *(specify)*:

MICHAEL LYNN GABRIEL
....
(Type or print name)   (Signature of plaintiff or attorney)

VERIFICATION
(Use a different verification form if the verification is by an attorney or for a corporation or partnership.)
I am the plaintiff in this proceeding and have read this complaint. I declare under penalty of perjury under the laws of the State of California that this complaint is true and correct.
Date: SEE ATTACHMENT

....
(Type or print name)   (Signature of plaintiff)

VERIFICATION

State of California, Couty of Los Angeles

I am the <u>MANAGING PARTNER OF THE PARTNERSHIP DOE ASSOCIATES THE PLAINTIFF</u> in the above entitled action or proceeding. I have read the foregoing <u>COMPLAINT FOR UNLAWFUL DETAINER</u> and know the contents thereof; and I certify that the same is true of my own knowledge, except as to those matters which are therein stated upon my information or belief, and as to those matters, I believe it to be true.

Executed on <u>October 5, 1984</u> at <u>Sherman Oaks,</u> California.

JOHN DOE

EXHIBIT "A"
LEASE AGREEMENT
(SIX MONTH TENANCY)

THIS LEASE AGREEMENT MADE THIS <u>28th</u> day of <u>JUNE</u>, 1983 by and between DOE ASSOCIATES ("LANDLORD") and <u>JOHN SMITH</u> ("Tenant"). Landlord leases to Tenant and Tenant leases from Landlord for use as a residence only, Apartment 2, located at 5428 Blaine, Santa Ana, California 92707 for a period of six months commencing on the <u>2nd</u> day of <u>July</u> 1983. The lease rental for the six month term is payable in equal monthly installments of <u>Three hundred and thirty five dollars</u> ($335.00) in advance without demand on the <u>2nd</u> day of each and every month. This lease is subject to the following terms and conditions:

   1. The apartment shall be occupied by no more than <u>2</u> adults and <u>2</u> children and shall be used solely as a residence, no pets to be allowed on the premises. Tenant shall not sublet the premises or any part thereof or assign or transfer his interest in and under this Agreement. No other person shall reside in the premises. If any other person resides in the premises, at the Landlord's option, Landlord may terminate this Agreement and declare a forefeiture thereof.

   2. Tenant agrees not to commit, nor to suffer to be committed, the following: (a) any waste upon said premises, (b) any nuisance, (c) any other act which may disturb the quiet enjoyment of any other tenant in the building where the apartment is located, (d) any act which which increase the existing rate of insurance upon the apartment or any part thereof, (e) any alterations, additions, or improvements to the premises without the written consent of the Landlord. Any such additions, alterations or improvements shall remain upon and be surrendered to the Landlord with the premises at termination of the Agreement unless otherwise provided by written agreement between the parties.

   3. Tenant shall keep and maintain the premises in a clean and sanitary condition at all times and shall surrender the premises to the Landlord at termination of this tenancy in as good condition as when received, ordinary wear and tear excepted. Tenant agrees to be responsible for all broken windows, screens and furnishings and to promptly reimburse Landlord therefor upon demand.

   4. Tenant shall promptly notify the Landlord of any repairs required to be made and consents to entry by Landlord, its agents or representatives, to the premises at any time during reasonable hours to inspect and make repairs to the premises.

   5. No water beds shall be allowed in the premises. Drains and waste pipes are acknowledged to have been clear at commencement of this Agreement unless reported otherwise to Lessor within one week therefrom, and the cost of clearing any partial or complete stoppage occurring during the term of this Agreement shall be paid by Tenant.

6. Violation by Tenant of any city ordinance or state law regulating apartment houses in or about premises shall be sufficient cause for termination of this Agreement.

7. Any failure by Tenant to promptly perform any covenant required to be performed hereunder including any failure by Tenant to pay rent within THREE (3) days from the date due, shall terminate this tenancy at the election of the Landlord.

8. The waiver by Landlord of any breach of any term covenant or conditions of this Agreement shall not be deemed a waiver of such term, covenant or condition or of any subsequent breach of the same or any other term, covenant or condition of this Agreement and nothing contained in this Agreement shall be construed as waiving any of the Landlord's rights under the laws of the State of California.

9. If an action be brought for the recovery of rent or other monies due or to become due under this Agreement, or by reason of a breach of any covenant herein contained, or for the recovery of possession of the premises, or to compel the performance of anything agreed to be done by the Tenant, or to recover for damages to the premises, or to enjoin any act contrary to the provisions hereof, Tenant agrees to pat to Landlord all of the costs in connection therewith, including but not limited to reasonable attorney fees and court costs.

10. Landlord acknowledges receipt from tenant of the sum $100.00 as a security deposit, $45.00 as a cleaning fee and $5.00 as a key deposit, which deposits shall not bear interest, need not be kept separately, and shall be returned to Tenant after Tenant vacates the premises, less the costs of any repairs made necessary by acts of Tenant, the costs of preparing said premises for subsequent tenants, lost keys and unpaid rent due prior to the vacation of the premises.

11. Tenant shall not, nor permit to be done, any major repair work on automobiles in the parking areas.

12. A late charge of ten Dollars ($10.00) will be imposed on any installment for rent not received within five days of the due date, plus $1.00 per day for each day thereafter that payment is not received.

IF TENANT SHALL HOLD OVER AND CONTINUE IN POSSESSION OF SAID PREMISES AFTER THE EXPIRATION OF THE TERM HEREOF, SUCH HOLDING OVER SHALL BE CONSTRUED AS A TENANCY FROM MONTH TO MONTH. IN SUCH EVENT, ALL TERMS AND PROVISIONS HEREOF SHALL REMAIN THE SAME, SUBJECT TO MODIFICATION BY LANDLORD UPON THIRTY (30) DAYS ADVANCE WRITTEN NOTICE.

IN WITNESS WHEREOF, the parties hereto have executed this Agreement in duplicate the day and year first above written.

(Landlord) (Tenant)

EXHIBIT "A-1"

TENANT RENTAL RATE CHANGE

TENANT NAME: JOHN SMITH

TENANT ADDRESS: 5428 Blaine, Apt. 2, Santa Ana, CA. 92707

Old Rate $335.00   New Rate $345.00

Reason for Change: Effective 3-2-84

Date: 1-13-84

Delivered: 1-13-84

_____
Manager

EXHIBIT "B"

NOTICE TO QUIT

To **JOHN SMITH AND DOES 1 THROUGH 5, TENApT IN POSSESSION,**

TAKE NOTICE, that you are herby required to quit and deliver up to the undersigned the possession of the premises now held and occupied by you being the premises known as:

5428 BLAINE, APT 2, SANTA ANA, CALIFORNIA 92707.

at the expiration of **thirty (30) days**

commencing on the **4th** day of **SEPTEMBER 1984**

and ending on the **3rd** day of **OCTOBER 1984** .

THIS IS INTENDED as a **LEGAL 30 DAY** notice to quit for the purpose of terminating your tenancy aforesaid.

DATED this <u>4th</u> day of <u>SEPTEMBER 1984</u>.

DOE ASSOCIATES, LANDLORD

EXHIBIT "C"

PROOF OF SERVICE OF THIRTY DAY NOTICE

State of California

County of Orange

The undersigned hereby declares as follows:

I served the thirty day notice, a true copy of which is attached hereto on <u>JOHN SMITH</u> the Tenants on the <u>4th</u> day of <u>SEPTEMBER 1994</u> in the manner indicated below:

<u>XX</u> By personal delivery of a copy to the Tenant at

<u>5478 Blaine, Apt. 2, Santa Ana, CA. 92707</u>

___ *By leaving a copy with a responsible person over the age of 18 years at Tenant(s)' (home address or place of business) and mailing a copy of the notice on the same day addressed to the Tenant(s) at:

_____

___ *By affixing a copy of this notice in a conspicuous place on the property and mailing a copy on the same day addressed to the Tenant(s) at the place where the property is located:

_____

*(Substitute service was made because Tenant(s) could not be located at the home or usual place of business.)

At the time of service, I was at least 18 years of age.

I declare, under of perjury, that the foregoing is true and correct. Executed on <u>September 5, 1984</u> at <u>Santa Ana, California.</u>

_____
JOHN CLAY

NAME, ADDRESS AND TELEPHONE NUMBER
OF THE ATTORNEY

MICHAEL LYNN GABRIEL
643 B SOUTH MAIN
UKIAH, CA. 95482
(707) 468-0268

Default of Defendant entered

by _____
                              Deputy Clerk

ATTORNEY FOR: Plaintiff

IN THE MUNICIPAL COURT, CENTRAL ORANGE COUNTY JUDICIAL DISTRICT
700 Civic Center Drive West, Santa Ana, California 92701
COUNTY OF ORANGE, STATE OF CALIFORNIA

DOE ASSOCIATES
_____
              Plaintiff(s)

No. XX678

JOHN SMITH
_____
              Defendant(s)
       (ABBREVIATED TITLE)

**JUDGMENT BY DEFAULT
BY COURT
(UNLAWFUL DETAINER)**

Date _____ NOVEMBER 13, 1984, HONORABLE JACOB TYPER _____ Judge.

In this action the Defendant(s), **JOHN SMITH** having been regularly served with summons and copy of complaint, having failed to appear and answer the complaint of Plaintiff(s) within the time allowed by law, and the default of said Defendant(s) having been duly entered, upon application of Plaintiff(s) to the Court, and

( ) after having heard the testimony and considered the evidence,

(X) a declaration under C.C.P. 585.4, in lieu of testimony, having been considered, the Court ordered the following judgment:

That the amount of rent due Plaintiff(s) is $ **$471.50** _____, and assesses the damage for the unlawful detainer at **$471.50** _____.

WHEREFORE, IT IS ORDERED AND ADJUDGED that the Defendant(s) is _____ guilty of unlawful detainer of the premises described in the complaint, and that Plaintiff(s) be restored to the possession of said premises; that the lease or agreement under which said property is held be, and the same is hereby forfeited; that Plaintiff **DOE ASSOCIATES** _____

have and recover from said Defendant(s), **JOHN SMITH** _____

the sum of $ **471.50** _____ rent and damages, $ **225.00** _____ attorneys fees, together with costs taxed in the sum of $ **89.00** _____ ; that execution issue herein at the time and in the manner provided by law; that the said property is situated in the County of Orange, State of California, and is described as follows, to-wit:

5478 Blaine, Apt. Santa Ana, Ca. 92707

Done in open Court this date: **Nov. 13, 1984** _____.

I hereby certify this to be a true copy of the Judgment in the above case.
Entered in Minute Book No. _____   ROBERT B. KUHEL, Clerk of the above-entitled Court
Page _____
on _____   By _____, Deputy

NOV 13 1984

F0363-2493.2 (R10/82)   **JUDGMENT BY DEFAULT BY COURT – UNLAWFUL DETAINER**

ATTORNEY OR PARTY WITHOUT ATTORNEY (Name and Address):	TELEPHONE NO.:	FOR RECORDER'S USE ONLY
☐ Recording requested by and return to: MICHAEL LYNN GABRIEL 643 B SOUTH MAIN STREET UKIAH, CA 95482 [XX] ATTORNEY FOR [XX] JUDGMENT CREDITOR ☐ ASSIGNEE OF RECORD	(707) 468-0268	

NAME OF COURT:	MUNICIPAL COURT
STREET ADDRESS:	700 Civic Center Drive West,
MAILING ADDRESS:	
CITY AND ZIP CODE:	SANTA Ana, CA. 92701
BRANCH NAME:	CENTRAL ORANGE JUDICIAL DISTRICT
PLAINTIFF:	DOES ASSOCIATES
DEFENDANT:	JOHN SMITH AND DOES 1 THROUGH 5

WRIT OF	[x] EXECUTION (Money Judgment) [x] POSSESSION OF ☐ Personal Property 　　　　　　　　　　[x] Real Property ☐ SALE	CASE NUMBER: XX678
		FOR COURT USE ONLY

1. To the Sheriff or any Marshal or Constable of the County of: **ORANGE**

   You are directed to enforce the judgment described below with daily interest and your costs as provided by law.
2. To any registered process server: You are authorized to serve this writ only in accord with CCP 699.080 or CCP 715.040.
3. *(Name):* **DOES ASSOCIATES**
   is the [XX] judgment creditor ☐ assignee of record
   whose address is shown on this form above the court's name.
4. Judgment debtor *(name and last known address)*:

   JOHN SMITH
   5478 Blaine, Apt. 2
   Santa Ana, CA. 92707

   ☐ additional judgment debtors on reverse
5. Judgment entered on *(date)*: Nov 13, 1984
6. ☐ Judgment renewed on *(dates)*:
7. Notice of sale under this writ
   a. [X] has not been requested.
   b. ☐ has been requested *(see reverse)*.
8. ☐ Joint debtor information on reverse.

   (SEAL)

9. [x] See reverse for information on real or personal property to be delivered under a writ of possession or sold under a writ of sale.
10. ☐ This writ is issued on a sister-state judgment.
11. Total judgment . . . . $ 787.50
12. Costs after judgment (per filed order or memo CCP 685.090) . $
13. Subtotal *(add 11 and 12)* . . . . . $
14. Credits . . . . $
15. Subtotal *(subtract 14 from 13)* . $ 787.50
16. Interest after judgment (per filed affidavit CCP 685.050) . . . . . . $
17. Fee for issuance of writ . . . . . $ 3.50
18. Total *(add 15, 16, and 17)* . . . $ 789.00
19. Levying officer: Add daily interest from date of writ *(at the legal rate on 15)* of . . . . $ .21
20. ☐ The amounts called for in items 11-19 are different for each debtor. These amounts are stated for each debtor on Attachment 20.

Issued on *(date)*:	Clerk, by _____ , Deputy

— NOTICE TO PERSON SERVED: SEE REVERSE FOR IMPORTANT INFORMATION —

(Continued on reverse)

Form Approved by the
Judicial Council of California
EJ-130 (Rev. January 1, 1989)

WRIT OF EXECUTION

CCP 699.520, 712.010, 715.010

169

SHORT TITLE:	CASE NUMBER:

Items continued from the first page:
4. ☐ Additional judgment debtor *(name and last known address)*:

7. ☐ Notice of sale has been requested by *(name and address)*:

8. ☐ Joint debtor was declared bound by the judgment (CCP 989-994)
    a. on *(date)*:   a. on *(date)*:
    b. name and address of joint debtor: b. name and address of joint debtor:

    c. ☐ additional costs against certain joint debtors *(itemize)*:

9. ☒ *(Writ of Possession or Writ of Sale)* Judgment was entered for the following:
    a. ☒ Possession of real property. The complaint was filed on *(date)*: October 5, 1984
        (1) The court will hear objections to enforcement of the judgment under CCP 1174.3 on the following dates *(specify)*:
        (2) The daily rental value on the date the complaint was filed is *(specify)*: $
    b. ☐ Possession of personal property
        ☐ If delivery cannot be had, then for the value *(itemize in 9e)* specified in the judgment or supplemental order.
    c. ☐ Sale of personal property
    d. ☐ Sale of real property
    e. Description of property: 5478 BLAINE , Apt. 2, Santa Ana. CA. 92707

— NOTICE TO PERSON SERVED —

Writ of execution or sale. Your rights and duties are indicated on the accompanying Notice of Levy.

Writ of possession of personal property. If the levying officer is not able to take custody of the property, the levying officer will make a demand upon you for the property. If custody is not obtained following demand, the judgment may be enforced as a money judgment for the value of the property specified in the judgment or in a supplemental order.

Writ of possession of real property. If the premises are not vacated within five days after the date of service on the occupant or, if service is by posting, within five days after service on you, the levying officer will remove the occupants from the real property and place the judgment creditor in possession of the property. Personal property remaining on the premises will be sold or otherwise disposed of in accordance with CCP 1174 unless you or the owner of the property pays the judgment creditor the reasonable cost of storage and takes possession of the personal property not later than 15 days after the time the judgment creditor takes possession of the premises.
A Claim of Right to Possession form accompanies this writ.

EJ-130 (Rev. January 1, 1989)   **WRIT OF EXECUTION**

1-3a

ATTORNEY OR PARTY WITHOUT ATTORNEY (Name and Address):	TELEPHONE NO.	FOR RECORDER'S USE ONLY
[X] Recording requested by and return to: LAW OFFICE OF MICHAEL LYYN GABRIEL 643 B SOUTH MAIN STREET UKIAH, CA. 95482 [X] ATTORNEY FOR [X] JUDGMENT CREDITOR [ ] ASSIGNEE OF RECORD	(707) 468-0268	

NAME OF COURT: MUNICIPAL COURT OF CALIFORNIA
STREET ADDRESS: 700 CIVIC CENTER DRIVE WEST
MAILING ADDRESS:
CITY AND ZIP CODE: SANTA ANA, CA. 92707
BRANCH NAME: CENTRAL ORANGE COUNTY JUDICIAL DISTRICT

PLAINTIFF:
DOE ASSOCIATES

DEFENDANT:
JOHN SMITH

CASE NUMBER:

ABSTRACT OF JUDGMENT

FOR COURT USE ONLY

1. [XX] Judgment creditor [ ] Assignee of record
   applies for an abstract of judgment and represents the following:
   a. Judgment debtor's
      Name and last known address

   JOHN SMITH
   5478 BLAINE, APT.2
   SANTA ANA, CA. 92707

   b. Driver's license no. and state: [X] unknown.
   c. Social Security number: [X] unknown.
   d. Summons or notice of entry of sister state judgment was personally served or
      mailed to (address):

   [ ] Information regarding additional judgment debtors is shown on the reverse.
Date:

   MICHAEL LYNN GABRIEL
         (TYPE OR PRINT NAME)   ▶   (SIGNATURE OF APPLICANT OR ATTORNEY)

2. a. [X] I certify that the following is a true and correct abstract of the judgment entered in this action.
   b. [ ] A certified copy of the judgment is attached.
3. Judgment creditor (name and address):

   DOE ASSOCIATES
   5478 BLAINE
   SANTA ANA, CA. 92707

5. a. Judgment entered (date): NOV 13, 1984
   b. Renewal entered (date):
   c. Renewal entered (date):
6. Total amount of judgment as entered or last renewed:
   $ 787.50

4. Judgment debtor (full name as it appears in judgment):

   JOHN SMITH

   [SEAL]

7. [X] An [ ] execution [X] attachment lien is endorsed
      on the judgment as follows:
      a. amount: $ 789.00
      b. in favor of (name and address):
         DOE ASSOCIATES
         5478 BLAINE, SANTA ANA, CA.
8. A stay of enforcement has
   a. [X] not been ordered by the court.
   b. [ ] been ordered by the court effective until (date):
9. [ ] This is an installment judgment.

This abstract issued on
(date): NOV. 14, 1984   Clerk, by _____, Deputy

Form Adopted by the
Judicial Council of California
982(a)(1) (Rev July 1, 1983)

ABSTRACT OF JUDGMENT
(CIVIL)

CCP 488.480, 674
700.190

PLAINTIFF:	CASE NUMBER:
DEFENDANT:	

Information regarding additional judgment debtors:

). _____ Name and last known address

Driver's license no. & state: ☐ unknown.
Social Security no.: ☐ unknown.
Summons was personally served at or mailed to *(address)*:

14. _____ Name and last known address

Driver's license no. & state: ☐ unknown.
Social Security no.: ☐ unknown.
Summons was personally served at or mailed to *(address)*:

1. _____ Name and last known address

Driver's license no. & state: ☐ unknown.
Social Security no.: ☐ unknown.
Summons was personally served at or mailed to *(address)*:

15. _____ Name and last known address

Driver's license no. & state: ☐ unknown.
Social Security no.: ☐ unknown.
Summons was personally served at or mailed to *(address)*:

2. _____ Name and last known address

Driver's license no. & state: ☐ unknown.
Social Security no.: ☐ unknown.
Summons was personally served at or mailed to *(address)*:

16. _____ Name and last known address

Driver's license no. & state: ☐ unknown.
Social Security no.: ☐ unknown.
Summons was personally served at or mailed to *(address)*:

13. _____ Name and last known address

Driver's license no. & state: ☐ unknown.
Social Security no.: ☐ unknown.
Summons was personally served at or mailed to *(address)*:

17. _____ Name and last known address

Driver's license no. & state: ☐ unknown.
Social Security no.: ☐ unknown.
Summons was personally served at or mailed to *(address)*:

18. ☐ Continued on attachment 18.

ABSTRACT OF JUDGMENT (CIVIL)

ATTORNEY OR PARTY WITHOUT ATTORNEY (NAME AND ADDRESS):	TELEPHONE:	FOR COURT USE ONLY
ATTORNEY FOR (NAME):		

Insert name of court, judicial district or branch court, if any, and post office and street address:

PLAINTIFF:

DEFENDANT:

ANSWER—Unlawful Detainer

CASE NUMBER:

1. This pleading including attachments and exhibits consists of the following number of pages: _____
2. Defendants *(name):*

    answer the complaint as follows:
3. **Check ONLY ONE of the next two boxes:**
    a. ☐ Defendant generally denies each statement of the complaint. *(Do not check this box if the complaint demands more than $1,000.)*
    b. ☐ Defendant admits that all of the statements of the complaint are true EXCEPT:

      (1) Defendant claims the following statements of the complaint are false *(use paragraph numbers from the complaint or explain):*

      ☐ Continued on Attachment 3.b.(1).

      (2) Defendant has no information or belief that the following statements of the complaint are true, so defendant denies them *(use paragraph numbers from the complaint or explain):*

      ☐ Continued on Attachment 3.b.(2).
4. **AFFIRMATIVE DEFENSES**
    a. ☐ *(nonpayment of rent only)* Plaintiff has breached the warranty to provide habitable premises. *(Briefly state the facts below in item 4.k.)*
    b. ☐ Plaintiff waived, changed, or canceled the notice to quit. *(Briefly state the facts below in item 4.k.)*
    c. ☐ Plaintiff served defendant with the notice to quit or filed the complaint to retaliate against defendant. *(Briefly state the facts below in item 4.k.)*
    d. ☐ Plaintiff has failed to perform his obligations under the rental agreement. *(Briefly state the facts below in item 4.k.)*
    e. ☐ By serving defendant with the notice to quit or filing the complaint, plaintiff is arbitrarily discriminating against the defendant in violation of the constitution or laws of the United States or California. *(Briefly state the facts below in item 4.k.)*
    f. ☐ Plaintiff's demand for possession violates the local rent control or eviction control ordinance of *(city or county, title of ordinance, and date of passage):*

      (Briefly state the facts showing violation of the ordinance in item 4.k.)
      (Continued)

Form Approved by the
Judicial Council of California
Effective January 1, 1982
Rule 982.1(95)

ANSWER—Unlawful Detainer

CCP 425.12

SHORT TITLE:	CASE NUMBER:

ANSWER—Unlawful Detainer — Page two

g. ☐ Plaintiff accepted rent from defendant to cover a period of time after the date stated in paragraph 8.b. of the complaint.
h. ☐ *(nonpayment of rent only)* On *(date):* _____ defendant offered the rent due but plaintiff would not accept it.
i. ☐ Defendant made needed repairs and properly deducted the cost from the rent, and plaintiff did not give proper credit.
j. ☐ Other affirmative defenses. *(Briefly state below in item 4.k.)*
k. FACTS SUPPORTING AFFIRMATIVE DEFENSES CHECKED ABOVE *(Identify each item separately.)*

☐ Continued on Attachment 4.k.

5. OTHER STATEMENTS
   a. ☐ Defendant vacated the premises on *(date):*
   b. ☐ Defendant claims a credit for deposits of $_____
   c. ☐ The fair rental value of the premises in item 12 of the complaint is excessive *(explain):*

   d. ☐ Other *(specify):*

6. DEFENDANT REQUESTS
   a. that plaintiff take nothing requested in the complaint.
   b. costs incurred in this proceeding.
   c. ☐ reasonable attorney fees.
   d. ☐ other *(specify):*

_____   _____
(Type or print name)   (Signature of defendant or attorney)

_____   _____
(Type or print name)   (Signature of defendant or attorney)

(Each defendant for whom this answer is filed must be named in item 2 and must sign this answer unless represented by an attorney.)

VERIFICATION
(Use a different verification form if the verification is by an attorney or for a corporation or partnership.)
I am the defendant in this proceeding and have read this answer. I declare under penalty of perjury under the laws of the State of California that this answer is true and correct.

Date:

_____   _____
(Type or print name)   (Signature of defendant)

8
REAL PROPERTY

8. REAL PROPERTY

It is the American Dream for a person to strive to own his own property. When the United States was first formed only persons of property could vote. Wealth, land and happiness have always been viewed as the same in America.

This chapter is intended to cover the basic tenets of real property law. It will attempt to do that by answering the various questions that are most frequently propounded concerning real estate. These questions, as questions often do, engender even more questions that are also answered in striving to develop the reader's understanding of the law.

Real estate law covers more than just the land itself. It also covers the rights and duties owed by the landowner to neighbors and even, under certain circumstances, to trespassers. In the not so dim past, an owner could do virtually anything that he or she wished on or with the property. Today, however, such unbridled control over owns property is past. Land use is now strictly controlled and regulated by zoning and environmental laws.

The rights and duties of landowners form a rich and diverse body of law. Every state has its own body of real property law and the best this chapter can accomplish is to point the majority and minority views when they are not unanimous. In those situations, the reader must consult applicable state statutes to determine which view is followed in the user's home state

1. WHAT IS FEE SIMPLE TITLE TO REAL PROPERTY?
A fee simple is the total ownership rights recognized by law. It is capable of full and complete alienability. In addition, it passes by inheritance to both lineal and collateral heirs of the owner. The duration of time for which a fee simple will last is forever provided it is a fee simple absolute. If it is a fee simple defeasible, the ownership rights may be altered on the happening on certain conditions.

2. WHAT IS MEANT BY A TITLE TAKEN
IN FEE SIMPLE ABSOLUTE?
A fee simple absolute is the most complete and absolute ownership of real property permitted by law. A fee simple absolute is limited only by

governmental powers such as zoning and eminent domain. A fee simple absolute lasts forever. It will not terminate in the future based on time or the happening of any event.

At common law, a fee simple absolute had to be expressly created. It was necessary to use the language "and his or her heirs" to create a fee simple absolute. For example the deed had to read, "To George and his heirs," in order to create a fee simple absolute. The language "and heirs" did not create an estate in the heirs but was still needed to show that a fee simple absolute had been granted.

Today, only South Carolina requires that the language "and heirs" still be on the deed to prove that a fee simple absolute was granted. All of the other states now, either by law or judicial decision, hold that unless a grantor states otherwise on the deed a fee simple absolute is presumed to have been granted.

3. WHAT IS A DEFEASIBLE FEE IN REAL PROPERTY?

A fee simple defeasible in real property refers to three main of fee simple in which an owner's otherwise infinite possession of the property could be terminated under certain circumstances. These types of defeasible fees are:

1. Fee Simple Determinable. Under this type of defeasible fee, the estate lasts only so long as the property is used in certain manner. The words "for so long as", "until" or "while" are used. The example is, "For A as long as it used for a farm." If the land is not farmed, then it reverts back automatically to the grantor or the grantor's heirs.

2. Fee Simple With Condition Subsequent. Under this type of defeasible fee, upon the happening a certain event, the grantor has a right to take the property back. It isn't automatic. Courts prefer this over a determinable fee.

3. Fee Simple with Executory Interest. This defeasible fee is similar to the fee simple determinable except that on the happening of the event the title passes automatically to another. For example, "To A so long as he farms the property, if not to B."

4. WHAT IS A LIFE ESTATE?

A life estate is an estate in real property that lasts only as long as a person or persons lives. It does not terminate on the based on a certain length of time.

A conventional life estate comes into being as a result of the stated intent of the grantor to create it. For example, "To A for life," means that A is entitled to complete possession of the property for his or her life. The right to possess the property ends on his or her death. Another example is, "For A as long as B lives". A's right to possess the property ends when B dies not when A dies.

5. WHAT IS COVERTURE?

Coverture is a legal life estate of a husband in the real property owned or seized during the marriage. Under common law, the husband had the to exclusively use, occupy, posses, control and collect all rents and profits from the wife's property. Coverture ended on the death of the wife or divorce.

Coverture has been abolished in nearly all jurisdictions.

6. WHAT IS JOINT TENANCY?

Joint tenancy is the concurrent ownership of real property by two or more persons with the right of survivorship. When a joint tenant dies, his or her interest in the property passes automatically to the surviving joint tenant or joint tenants.

An owner's joint tenancy interest in the joint tenancy property passes without a probate is is not effected by the terms of the owner's Will.

A joint tenancy must be expressly created. The deed must have language similar to this, "To A and B as Joint Tenants." Anyone can be a joint tenant with anyone else. Usually spouses or the children are joint tenants so as to avoid probate of the property.

A joint tenant owns an equal interest in the property regardless of whether that interest was purchased or acquired by a gift. As such, each joint tenant's interest can be attached by that joint tenant's creditors.

7. CAN A JOINT TENANCY BE TERMINATED?

A joint tenancy can be terminated and turned into a tenancy at common by the following acts:
1. Conveyance by one joint tenant of part or all of his or her interest. Any conveyance will terminate the joint tenancy because the other joint

tenants did not agree to give to the new co-tenant in the property a right of survivorship in their interest in the property.

2. Mortgaging by one joint tenant of his share of the joint tenancy property without the consent of the other joint tenants.

3. Leasing by one joint tenant of the joint tenancy property without the consent of the other joint tenants.

4. A few states permit the termination of a joint tenancy in a Will. This is a minority view.

8. WHAT IS A TENANCY IN COMMON?

A tenancy in common is ownership among two or more persons of an undivided interest without a right of survivorship. The interest in the real property is entirely transferable and subject only to the claims of the owner's creditors.

A tenant in common has the right to possess and use all of the property subject only to the equal right of the co-tenants to do likewise. Such right to equal possession exists even though the tenants may own unequal percentage rights.

9. WHAT IS TENANCY IN THE ENTIRETY?

Only about twenty states recognize tenancy in the entirety. It is a special joint tenancy estate between a husband and wife.

Neither spouse may can obtain a partition of the estate or defeat the right of survivorship of the other spouse. It can not be terminated by the unilateral act of one spouse.

A tenancy in the entirety is terminated only by:

1. Divorce which changes the tenancy into that of a tenants in common.
2. Mutual agreement whereby they agree to terminate the tenancy.
3. Execution against the property by a joint creditor of both spouses. A creditor of just one spouse can not execution against property held in a tenancy in the entirety.

10. WHAT IS AN EASEMENT?

An easement is a liberty, privilege, or advantage which one may hold in then lands of another. It is a non-possessory interest. The holder of an easement has the right to use the real property for a certain use but has no general right use to possess or occupy the land.

The owner of the servient estate, the land subject to the easement, continues to have the right to full possession and enjoyment of his property subject only to the limitation that he can not interfere with the special use of the property by the easement holder.

11. WHAT IS AN EASEMENT APPURTENANT?

An easement appurtenant is an easement in one piece of land, the servient estate, that benefits another piece of land, the dominant estate.

The easement appurtenant becomes an incident of possession of the dominant estate. All of the successors in interest, those who buy or inherit or otherwise succeed in ownership to the dominant estate, are entitled to ownership and benefit of the easement. There can be no transfer of the easement apart from the dominant estate. The easement goes with the dominant estate.

12. WHAT IS AN EASEMENT IN GROSS ?

An easement is gross is a personal easement owned by the easement holder. The easement does not benefit a dominant estate. For example, giving an easement to a person to hunt birds on the real property is an easement in gross, it does not benefit any other land.

13. WHAT IS AN EASEMENT BY RESERVATION?

A easement by reservation exists when the owner of a piece of property conveys it but reserves the right to continue to use the real property for a special purpose after he conveyance. In essence, the owner gave himself an easement on the property at the time of conveyance.

An easement by reservation was required, under common law, to specifically contain language stating that the easement was intended to pass to the grantor's heirs. Without such language, the easement terminated on the death of the grantor. The modern view is for courts to presume that easements by reservation run with the land.

14. WHAT IS AN EASEMENT BY NECESSITY?

When a tract of land is sold that has no outlet to a public road except over the remaining lands of the seller, a right of way is created by the implied grant over the remaining lands of the seller. This easement based on absolute necessity is for access to the property and, in some states, utilities also.

15. HOW ARE EASEMENTS TERMINATED?
Easements are terminated by the following:
1. The express terms of the easement can state on what conditions, if any, the easement will terminate.
2. Excessive or misuse of the easement can terminate an easement.
3. The easement holder can abandon the easement by actions that manifest an intent to permanently abandon the easement and never use it again.
4. The parties may agree in writing to release the easement.
5. An easement may be ended by adverse possession of the easement by the owner of the servient estate.
6. When the easement owner acquires the servient easement, there is a merger of interest which terminates the easement. An owner can not have an easement in his own property.

16. WHAT IS ADVERSE POSSESSION?
Title to real property of another can be acquired by adverse possession if the possession of the land is:
1. Open and Notorious. The possession is sufficient to put the owner of the real property interest be acquired on notice, either the owner or the land or easement.
2. Hostile. The possession must be without the owner's consent.
3. Claim of Right. The person seeking to acquire the property by adverse possession must assert his claim of ownership to the world. The majority of states hold that the good or bad faith belief of the person is not a factor in determining adverse possession. The person just has to assert that he or she is the true owner.
4. Continuous. The property must be held for a statutory period, usually 20 years. In California, a person holding the property for 5 years and pays the taxes on the property has acquired the property by adverse possession. When all of the elements are met, then title passes to the persons performing the acts by virtue of adverse possession.

17. WHAT IS A PRESCRIPTIVE EASEMENT?
An easement in real property can be acquired by adverse possession.

A person who fulfills the requirements for adverse possession by using the real property for the required period of time, in an open and notorious manner and without the consent of the owner will acquire a prescriptive easement to continue using the property in that manner.

A prescriptive easement is personal to the holder unless it was acquired by the public under state law. Public use of the property may result in an implied dedication for public use.

An easement acquired by prescription may be terminated in the same manner as ordinary easements.

18. WHAT IS A QUIET TITLE ACTION?
When title to real property is in dispute, such as by an assertion of adverse possession or prescripted easement, the remedy is to file a complaint in court for quiet title.

The court will determine the rights on the parties in the property in the quiet title action. Such an action is required to perfect the legal interest of the parties.

When there are conflicting claims of ownership, no lending institution will loan on the property until a court has adjudicated the claims of the true ownership interest of the parties.

19. WHAT IS A COVENANT?
A covenant is an agreement by the owner of the real property to do or refrain from doing some action. A covenant runs with the land when the burdens, benefits or both pertaining to the covenant pass to the succeeding holders of the property.

An enforceable covenant requires:
1. A writing which satisfies the Statute of Frauds.
2. The parties must intend the covenant to run with the land.
3. The covenant must touch and concern the land. The covenant must affect the parties as landowners not just as members of the community.
4. There must be privity of estate between the parties. There must be a direct relationship connecting the parties to the covenant. If the following conditions are not met, the covenant would not be found to run with the land and thus be unenforceable for successors of the parties.

20. WHAT IS AN EQUITABLE SERVITUDE?

An equitable servitude is similar to a covenant. It is a restriction on the use of the land adopted by the owner of the land. The basic behind the enforcement of an equitable servitude is that a person who takes property with notice that the property's use is restricted by the equitable servitude should be bound by the restriction.

An equitable servitudes requires:
1. A writing which satisfies the Statute of Frauds.
2. The owner must intend the servitude to run with the land.
3. The servitude must touch and concern the land. The servitude must affect the parties as landowners not just as members of the community. The majority of states do not require privity of contract between the owner and the person seeking to enforce the servitude. Anyone can seek to enforce an equitable servitude in these states.

If the following conditions are not met, the servitude would not be found to run with the land and thus be unenforceable after the original grantor dies or divests himself of the property.

21. HOW ARE COVENANTS AND EQUITABLE SERVITUDES ENFORCED?

Covenants and equitable servitudes are enforced by the courts. The party seeking enforcement asks for a court order, such as an injunction, to require the owner to perform the covenant or refrain from violating the servitude.

Damages may also be awarded for injuries suffered as a result of any breach of the covenant or servitude that the owner committed.

22. WHEN ARE COVENANTS AND SERVITUDES TERMINATED?

Covenants and servitudes terminate when:
1. When all the parties release them.
2. Adverse possession destroys them.
3. Enforcement is waived by not timely objecting to the breaches.
4. Enforcement would violate public policy such as violating zoning requirements or be illegal discrimination.
5. The terms of the agreement state the conditions by which they terminate.

23. WHAT IS A RECORDING ACT?

All states have statutes called recording acts to determine the legal ownership of real property when two or more persons claim ownership of the same property.

These acts vary from state to state but fall into three separate categories, Notice, Race and Race-Notice Statutes. The rights of the parties in the real property is determined by who filed recorded their deed first and if they they knew of the claims by the other parties.

A person who purchased the property may still be denied title to the property under a state's recording act. It is important that anyone purchasing property be aware of their state's recording acts and perform a comprehensive title search to be sure that the seller has a valid title to the property.

24. WHAT IS RECORDATION?

Most states require that all deeds, mortgages, powers of attorney and other instruments relating to affecting the title to real property to be recorded. The recordation is done in the Recorder's Office of the County where the real property is located.

Most County Recorder Offices use two indexes to aid in title search of the property, the Grantor and Grantee indexes. Every transaction relating to the real estate is listed in a chronological order according to the respective names of the grantor and grantee.

A few states use a Tract Index which list all of the transactions involving particular piece of property. Searches in Tract Indexes are easiest to perform since all of the transactions affecting the title are listed in one document.

The purpose of recordation is to give notice to the world of the buyer's ownership interest in the real property. Recording gives constructive notice of the person's claimed ownership to the world from the date of recordation forward.

Recording gives the court a basis to determine the conflicting claims of ownership in real property where there are multiple sales or conveyances of the property.

25. WHAT IS A NOTICE RECORDING ACT?

About half of the states have a pure notice recording act. Under this statute, a good faith purchaser, also called a bona fide purchaser, without notice of the conflicting claims of others will acquire the property free of all conflicting claims regardless of whether he or she is the first to record. The important issue under this statute is when the purchaser acquired notice of the other conflicting claims not when the deed was recorded.

For example, A sells a farm to B and later sells it again to C who had no knowledge of the earlier sale. Under this act, C gets the title to the farm and B must sue George for his damages.

26. WHAT IS A RACE RECORDING ACT?

Two states, North Carolina and Louisiana, have this recording act. Under this act, the first purchaser who records wins. Notice of the conflicting claims is irrelevant. The first purchaser that records his or her deed cuts off all rights in the property of anyone recording later.

In the above example, if C knew of the sale to B and recorded his deed first, he would still acquire title to the farm.

27. WHAT IS A RACE-NOTICE RECORDING ACT?

Most states have a race-notice recording act. Under this act the first good faith purchaser that records will be recognized as the owner of the property. This requires that the purchaser both buy the property without knowledge of the conflicting claims of others and then be the first one to record his deed.

A person who acquires his or her interest in a manner other than a sale, such as a gift, is not a purchaser and therefore can have his or her interest in the property terminated by the subsequent recordation of a deed by a good faith purchaser.

For example, A sells the property first to B and then to C and finally to D. C records first followed by B and then D. Under this act, the property goes to C because he bought it in good faith, without knowledge of the earlier sale and recorded first.

28. WHAT IS THE STATUTE OF FRAUDS?

All states have laws that require that any contract for the sale of land or that affects any interest that will touch and concern the land for over a year, such as a lease, easement, condition, covenant or restriction, must be in writing to be enforceable.

A court may order specific performance of a contract involving real property that is not in writing if it can be proven that a contract did exist between the parties along with one or more of the following acts:
1. The purchaser has taken possession of the land,
2. The purchaser has made substantial improvements to the real property, or
3. The purchaser has paid for the property.

29. WHAT IS MARKETABLE TITLE?

All contracts for the sale of land contain an implied warranty of marketable title unless expressly stated otherwise. The warranty of marketable title requires that the property be delivered free from reasonable doubt either in law or fact regarding the title.

The warranty of marketable title does nor require perfect title be delivered. It does require that the real property not have any clouds on the title that poses an unreasonable risk of litigation. Title is marketable if a reasonably prudent buyer would accept it after exercising ordinary diligence and prudence.

30. WHAT ARE THE REMEDIES FOR BREACH OF A SALES CONTRACT?

The remedies for breach of the contract for sale of real property are:

1. Damages. The non-breaching party may sue the breaching party for the damages suffered as a result of the breach. The measure of the damages is the difference between the fair market value of the property and the sale price. In addition, consequential damages, damages reasonably foreseeable to be suffered from a breach, are also recoverable. Examples of consequential damages are replacement rents, costs of title searches, etc.

2. Specific Performance. Land is considered unique. For that reason, courts will always force the seller to honor the contract and complete the sale. Courts will sometimes force the buyer to purchase the

property if the seller can not reasonably sell it to someone else for the contract price. If the seller sells for less than the contract price, the buyer will have to pay the difference.

31. WHO BEARS THE LOSS IF THE PROPERTY IS DESTROYED DURING ESCROW?
The majority of states hold that the risk of loss for destruction of the property is with the buyer after the sales contract is signed even though the buyer may not have taken taken possession of the property. Unless the contract says otherwise, if the property is destroyed after the contract to sale is executed the risk, the buyer must still pay for it. An important exception exists when the destruction is a result of the seller's negligence.

Twelve states have adopted the Uniform Vendor and Purchaser's Risk Act which places the risk of loss on the buyer only after the buyer has taken possession of the property.

32. WHAT ARE COVENANTS OF TITLE?
A grant deed is a deed contains the following covenants of title by implication:
1. Covenant of Seisin: This covenant is that the grantor has both title and possession of the property.
2. Right to Convey: This is a covenant that the grantor has the right and authority to make a conveyance.
3. Encumbrances: This covenant is that the property is not encumbered by liens, or mortgages not previously disclosed.
4. Quiet Enjoyment: That the purchaser will not have his or her possession of the property interrupted by any lawful claim against title by a third party.
5. Warranty: The seller will defend the title against claims by third parties.
6. Further Assurances: The seller will do all acts necessary to perfect the buyer's title in the property.

33. WHAT IS A QUIT-CLAIM DEED?
A quit claim deed is a written instrument that transfers all of a person's right title and interest, if any, to another. A quitclaim deed is not a

statement that person actually owns the property but that if the person did have an interest in the property then he has transferred it by the quit claim deed.

A quitclaim deed is usually used to perfect a person's title in real property by having persons holding potential conflicting claims release their contingent interest in the property.

A person can not be sued for issuing a quit claim deed because there is no warranty that the person actually has an interest in the property. A sample form for a quitclaim deed follows this chapter.

34. WHAT IS THE DOCTRINE OF AFTER ACQUIRED TITLE?

The Doctrine of After Acquired Title is also called Estoppel on the Deed. If a person sells, by a warranty deed, real property that he or she does not own and subsequently acquires title to the property, then under this doctrine the title to the property will pass automatically to the person to whom the property had been previously sold.

For example if Mary sold a farm which she did not own, by a warranty deed, to George and then inherited the farm from her mother, the title will immediately vest in George's name. Under this legal theory, the the seller, Mary, becomes just a conduit to pass the title to George if an when she ever receives it. This doctrine only works for a grant deed with a warranty and future assurance covenant. The doctrine does not work for a quitclaim deed .

35. WHAT IS A MORTGAGE?

A mortgage is a security interest in real property given by the owner to secure payment of a loan. The borrower is called the mortgagor and the lender is the mortgagee.

In the event of a mortgagor's default on the mortgage, the only remedy available for the mortgagee is a lawsuit seeking a judicial foreclosure on the property.

At trial if the court finds the mortgagor is in default, the court will order the property sold in a judicial sale. Most states allow the mortgagor to redeem the property within a year by paying the buyer of the property at the judicial sale the amount actually paid by him not the amount originally owed.

If the sale proceeds do not satisfy the amount owed, a deficiency judgment for the balance may be obtained against the debtor if permitted under state law.

36. WHAT IS A DEED OF TRUST?
A deed of trust is a security interest in real property to secure payment of a loan or some other obligation. The borrower is called the trustor and the lender is the beneficiary. The trustor executes a promissory note for the amount of the loan. The payment of the loan is secured by a trust deed on the property for the benefit of the lender referred therein as the beneficiary.

In the event of a trustor's default on the payment of the promissory note, the beneficiary notifies the trustee of the breach. The trustee then gives the trustor (the lender) notice that unless the default is cured within a statutorily mandated period of time the property will be sold.

If the default is not cured (back payments made), the property will be sold at a public auction. The advantages of a deed of trust are twofold: (1) there is no power of redemption after the property is sold and (2) the lender does not have to go through the long expense and delay of a judicial foreclosure.

A trustee usually has the option of selling the property at a private sale under the terms of the deed of trust or filing a lawsuit for judicial foreclosure. The only real advantage of filing a judicial foreclosure action (sue in court) is that a deficiency judgment might be obtainable. However, many states have enacted antideficient legislation which precludes a lender getting a deficiency judgment on any purchase money loan on residential real property.

37. WHAT IS THE DIFFERENCE BETWEEN A LONG FORM AND SHORT FORM DEED DEED OF TRUST?
In a long form deed of trust all of the terms and conditions of the trust deed are specifically stated, spelled out and recited. As such, document runs between five to ten pages.

Many institutional lenders do not use a long form deed of trust. Instead, they record a standard list of clause for their trust deeds in each county. Then, the lender simply refers to those clauses in their abbreviated short form deed of trust and incorporate the clauses therein by reference. The reason for doing this is to save money by not having to record as many pages. A County Recorder charges on the average $5.00 for each page of a document that is recorded. Incorporating by reference the standard clauses of a pre-recorded master in a short form deed of trust will save around $30.00 in unnecessary recordation fees. The important clauses are, of course, still listed in the short form deed of trust i.e. the payment and acceleration clauses. A copy of the recorded clauses is given to the borrower. The total loan agreement then consists of the short form trust deed and the incorporated clauses.

38. CAN A HOLDER OF DEED OF A TRUST SELL IT?

A deed of trust is an interest in real property like any other. It can be sold, given away, attached or encumbered just like any other interest in real property. For all purposes, it is the same.

The method for transferring an interest in a deed of trust is for the beneficiary of the deed of trust, who also is the holder of the promissory note on the property, to execute an assignment of the deed of trust and then to have it recorded.

Recordation of the assignment of the deed of trust transfers the deed of trust. It acts as the same as a bill of sale for personal property or a grant deed for real estate. A sample form for an assignment of a deed of trust follows this chapter.

39. WHAT IS A DEED OF RECONVEYANCE?

When a promissory note secured by a deed of trust is paid off, in order to have the trust deed encumbering the property removed from the title to the property, a deed of reconveyance must be recorded. The recording takes the deed of trust off the title to the property and gives the title to the property solely in the name of the owner.

The trustee listed on the deed of trust or any successor trustee must sign a deed of reconveyance and then record it. The mechanics of this procedure is as follows:
1. The lender marks the original promissory note paid in full.
2. The note is then sent to the trustee. The trustee will prepare and execute a Deed of Reconveyance.
3. The Deed of Reconveyance is recorded.

Trustees tend to charge between $100 and $500 for signing and recording a Deed of Reconveyance. A copy of a Deed of Reconveyance is at the end of this chapter.

40. CAN A TRUSTEE BE REPLACED IN A DEED OF TRUST?

A trustee can always be replaced by the beneficiary of the deed of trust. The cheapest way to get a Deed of Reconveyance is to have the beneficiary sign a substitution of trustee statement. The beneficiary appoints himself the new substituted trustee.

As the new trustee, the beneficiary executes and records the deed of reconveyance. A copy of a joint Substitution of Trustee and Deed of Reconveyance is an the end of this chapter.

41. WHAT IS A DEFICIENCY JUDGMENT?

In the case of a mortgage debt, if the judicial sale does not pay off the debt, the mortgagee can sue the mortgagor for the balance remaining which is called the deficiency.

A number of states have limited the judgment in such cases to the difference between the debt and the foreclosure price. Some states, including California, have anti-deficiency legislation that prohibit deficiency judgments on purchase money mortgages. A purchase money mortgage is one used to buy the property rather than improve it.

Many states do not permit deficiency judgments in the case of a deed of trust where the property was sold under a the trust deed's power of sale. If a deed of trust is foreclosed using a judicial foreclosure (suing in court for a judgment rather than selling the property under a power of sale in the trust deed), then a deficiency judgment may be possible provided there is no anti-deficiency legislation barring them.

42. WHAT IS THE EFFECT OF A FORECLOSURE ON OTHER LIENHOLDERS?

Any foreclosure, either judicial in nature or by deed of trust, wipes out all junior liens and encumbrances. It does not affect in any way a superior lien or encumbrance.

For example, George purchases a piece of property at a foreclosure sale on a second mortgage. The property had a first mortgage of $100,000 and a third mortgage of $50,000. The first mortgage still stays on the property but the third mortgage is wiped out. The holder of the third mortgage can sue the mortgagee personally for the balance owed on the third mortgage but can not go against the new buyer of the property.

43. WHAT IS AN INSTALLMENT LAND CONTRACT?
An installment sales contract is one is which legal title stays with the seller until the contract is paid off. In the event of the buyer's breach, this type of contract results in the forfeiture of the buyer's interest rather than foreclosure on the property.

Because of the harshness of the forfeiture, some states treat installment sales contracts as mortgages. These states require the seller to judicially foreclose on the property in order to clear his title on the land.

If the seller elects to treats the property as a forfeiture then the seller is prevented by law from suing for damages or specific performance. The seller can not keep the property and yet still demand payment for it.

44. WHAT IS A COOPERATIVE?
One form of common housing ownership is that of cooperatives. A cooperative is a corporation which owns the title to the land and buildings thereon. The cooperative leases apartments in its buildings to its shareholders.

The residents in a cooperative are thus tenants by virtue of their leases and owners of the cooperative by virtue of their stock interests.

The residents are not direct owners of their apartments. They are entitled to reside there only as long as they pay the rent and obey the terms of the leases that they execute with their corporation.

45. WHAT IS A CONDOMINIUM?
Another form of common ownership of housing units are condominiums. In a condominium, each person owns the interior of his or her unit plus an undivided interest in the exterior and common areas. Usually the condominium owners get together to form an association or corporation to manage the condominium.

Each owner finances the purchase of his or her unit by a separate mortgage on that unit. The condominium association has authority to levy assessments against the owners for maintenance, taxes and other proper purposes. Failure to pay the assessments, gives the association the right to lien the property and, if necessary, to sue in court to collect payment.

46. WHAT IS A MECHANIC'S LIEN ON REAL PROPERTY?

Nearly all states permit licensed contractor that perform improvements on real property to record a lien on the property to protect their interest prior to filing a lawsuit to collect on their bill. Often the mere filing of the lien is sufficient to force payment of the debt without having to sue.

A mechanic's lien can only be for work performed or supplies furnished on the real property. The lien must be filed within a fixed statutory period of time following the work. A lawsuit must be filed within a period of time to keep the lien in effect, usually six months after recording the lien, in order to keep the lien in effect until the trial.

47. WHAT IS A HOMESTEAD?

Most states permit an owner of real property which is his or her primary residence to claim a certain amount of equity, usually $40,000, in the property as exempt from attachment by creditors.

In such states, creditors can not attach a debtor's home if a homestead declaration was recorded and the debtor's equity does not exceed the statutory amount. If the equity does exceed the statutory amount, then on the sale, the statutory amount is returned to the debtor even if the debt is not paid off.

A declaration of homestead must be recorded in the County Recorder's Office of the County where the home is located prior to any lawsuit by a creditor being filed. Recording the homestead declaration of homestead after the lawsuit is filed does not perfect the homestead or afford any protection from creditors.

48. IS THERE AN IMPLIED WARRANTY OF FITNESS FOR USE IN THE SALE OF REAL PROPERTY?

At common law, there was no implied warranty of implied fitness for use in the sale of real property. The major exception, at common law, existed for a building under construction or to be constructed based on the rationale that the buyer had no ability or opportunity to inspect the building.

A majority of states now hold that there is an implied warranty for fitness in the sale of a new house by the builder. The warranty implied, by these states, is that the house is designed and constructed in a reasonably workmanlike manner and is suitable for human occupation.

49. WHAT ARE THE REMEDIES IF A SELLER MADE FALSE STATEMENTS OR CONCEALED RELEVANT CONDITIONS?

If the seller knowingly made false statements to the buyer on a fact that materially affects the value of the real estate which the buyer relied upon in purchasing, then the buyer has the following remedies:

1. The buyer may rescind the contract and demand return of the money purchase price plus damages incurred in performing the sale.
2. The buyer can affirm the contract and sue for damages. The damages are the difference in value between the purchase price and the true value of the property. Additional damages may be recovered for incidental expenses incurred because of the false statements and if appropriate punitive damages may be obtained. The seller is just as liable for defects that he actually conceals from the buyer as he is if he makes false statements about them. The common law view is that the seller is under no duty to disclose defects as long as he does not lie about them or conceal them. Many states, including California, now require an owner to disclose all known defects where the defect is not readily discoverable by the buyer.

50. WHAT IS A DUE ON SALE CLAUSE IN A MORTGAGE OR DEED OF TRUST?

Many mortgages and deeds of trust contain clauses that state if the property is sold or conveyed in any manner, the entire balance then becomes immediately due and payable.

The purpose of these clauses are to protect the lender from risky sales or assignments. These clauses have the effect of preventing the sale of the property without the lender's approval unless the lender's loan is paid off.

Federal law will enforce a due on sale clause if the loan is from a federally insured lender. Some states, such as California, have adopted legislation that prevent private lenders or state charted lenders from enforcing due on sale clauses if the value of the property exceeds the amount owed.

51. WHAT IS ZONING?

Every state has the authority to enact all laws reasonably necessary for the health, safety and welfare of its citizens. this is known as the the state's police power.

Zoning is the term given to the laws enacted by a city, county or state that regulate the develop of land within its boundaries according to a general plan of development.

The implementation of any zoning plan must comply with the constitutional provisions of due process or equal protection. If as a result of zoning, private property is taken for public use, this is called eminent domain, the owner must be paid the fair market value of the property.

52. WHAT IS INVERSE CONDEMNATION?

The government can so restrict the development of private property that no reasonable use of the property remains. In that event, the United States Supreme Court has held that inverse condemnation has occurred. Inverse condemnation is a violation of the U. S. Constitution's Fifth Amendment as a taking without just compensation.

A taking for public purposes can occur if the government requires dedication of easements or transfers of portions of the property in order to get building permits when such easements or dedications have no relationship to the project sought to be built. This is the hottest area of contention in zoning law. Many regulatory agencies routinely demand public easements across private property or dedications of land in order to grant building permits.

53. WHAT ARE MINERAL RIGHTS?

Mineral rights are the ownership rights of all the minerals on a designated piece of real property. Mineral rights can be segregated and split off from land.

Mineral rights carry with them a right to enter upon the real property to search for an develop the minerals contained there on. This right of entry is called a profit a prendre and is a nonpossessory interest in the land.

A profit a prende is in essence an easement to enter upon and develop the minerals on the property. It can be terminated for the same reasons as an easement.

54. WHAT ARE WATER RIGHTS?

A riparian right is the right of the owner of land bordering a stream to use all of the water necessary for the domestic purposes. The owner also has the right to use a reasonable amount of the water for other non-domestic, business, purposes provided he returns the water to the stream in an unpolluted state.

The water from the stream may not be diverted beyond the watershed of the stream. A subterranean stream is treated the same as a surface stream.

The owner has an absolute right to use as much water as he or she wants from water percolating on the surface. Many states, especially in the West, now hold that such use must be reasonable and that there may not be careless waste or pollution.

Some other states hold that all of the water belongs to the state and the owner of the land must perfect his or her rights to legally use the water on the property by application to the state.

55. WHAT IS THE TORRENS TITLE SYSTEM?

In a very few jurisdictions, the ancient Torrens Title System is used to clear title. In the few places where it is used, a buyer will petition a court for a hearing.

At the hearing, the court will direct the issuance of a certificate of title after giving creditors with liens or security interests on the property a chance to assert their liens or security interest. The court may order the creditor's obligation paid off as a condition of passing title.

With a few exceptions, the court's certificate is conclusive on the title of the landowner.

RECORDING REQUESTED BY: _____

AND WHEN RECORDED MAIL TO

_____
(SPACE ABOVE FOR RECORDER'S USE)

DECLARATION OF HOMESTEAD
(by a single person not a head of household)

I, _____ do hereby certify and declare as follows:

1. I am now residing on the land located in the City _____ _____, County of _____, State of _____ and more particular described as follows:

and commonly referred or addressed as follows: _____ _____.

2. I claim the land and premises, hereinabove described, together with the dwelling house, and its appurtenances, as a Homestead.

3. No former declaration of homestead has been made by me except as follows: _____ _____.

4. The character of said property so sought to be homesteaded and the improvements which have been affixed thereto, may generally be described as follows:_____
_____.

IN WITNESS WHEREOF, I have hereunto set my hand this ____ day of _____, 199

_____

STATE OF _____ COUNTY OF _____

On _____, before the undersigned personally appeared _____
personally known to me or proved to me on the basis of satisfactory evidence to be the person(s) whose name(s) is/are subscribed to the within instrument and acknowledged to me that he/she/they executed the same in his/her/their authorized capacities and that by his/her/their signature(s) on the instrument the person(s) or the entity upon behalf of which the person(s) acted, executed the within instrument.

WITNESS MY HAND AND OFFICIAL SEAL.

_____

RECORDING REQUESTED BY:

AND WHEN RECORDED MAIL TO

_____
(SPACE ABOVE FOR RECORDER'S USE)

AFFIDAVIT OF DEATH OF JOINT TENANT

STATE OF

COUNTY OF

_____ being of legal age and duly sworn, deposes and states:

That _____, the decedent mentioned in the attached Certificate of Death, is the same person as _____ _____ _____ named as one of the parties in that certain dated _____ and executed by _____ to _____ _____as joint tenants recorded in Book _____ Page _____ as Instrument number _____ on _____ of the Official Records of _____ _____ County, State of _____ covering the following described property situated in the County of _____ State of _____:

That the value of all real and personal property owned by said decendent at the time of death, including the full value of the above described property did not exceed the sum of _____.

Dated: _____

_____

SUBSCRIBED AND SWORN TO BEFORE ME

this _____ day of _____

_____

RECORDING REQUESTED BY:

AND WHEN RECORDED MAIL TO

___

(SPACE ABOVE FOR RECORDER'S USE)

QUITCLAIM DEED

Documentary Transfer Tax $ _____ ___ Computed on Full Value of Property, or ___ Computed on Full Value Less Liens and Encumbrances Remaining Thereon At Time of Sale
___ Unincorporated Area ___ City of _____
Tax Parcel Number _____

JOHN A. DOE,
TRUSTEE OF THE JOHN A. DOE REVOCABLE TRUST

FOR VALUABLE CONSIDERATION, HEREBY REMISE, RELEASE AND FOREVER QUITCLAIMS ALL RIGHT, TITLE AND INTEREST TO:

SAMUEL S. BUYER

in the real property in the County of _____, State of California described as:
1245 Skyplace Drive, Willits, California as described in Book 1, Page 1487 of the County Recorder's Office, Assessor's Parcel Number 1-14-782.

Dated: _____

_____

JOHN A. DOE,
TRUSTEE OF THE JOHN A. DOE REVOCABLE TRUST

STATE OF _____ COUNTY OF _____

On _____, before the undersigned personally appeared
_____
personally known to me or proved to me on the basis of satisfactory evidence to be the person(s) whose name(s) is/are subscribed to the within instrument and acknowledged to me that he/she/they executed the same in his/her/their authorized capacities and that by his/her/their signature(s) on the instrument the person(s) or the entity upon behalf of which the person(s) acted, executed the within instrument.

WITNESS MY HAND AND OFFICIAL SEAL.

_____

RECORDING REQUESTED BY:

AND WHEN RECORDED MAIL TO

(SPACE ABOVE FOR RECORDER'S USE)

INDIVIDUAL GRANT DEED

Documentary Transfer Tax $ _____ ___ Computed on Full Value of Property, or ___ Computed on Full Value Less Liens and Encumbrances Remaining Thereon At Time of Sale
___ Unincorporated Area ___ City of _____
Tax Parcel Number _____

For Valuable Consideration, the receipt of which is hereby acknowledged:

JOHN A. DOE,
TRUSTEE OF THE JOHN A. DOE REVOCABLE TRUST

hereby GRANTS TO

SAMUEL S. BUYER

the real property in the County of _____, State of California described as:

1245 Skyplace Drive, Willits, California as described in Book 1, Page 1487 of the County Recorder's Office, Assessor's Parcel Number 1-14-782.

Dated: _____

_____

JOHN A. DOE,
TRUSTEE OF THE JOHN A. DOE REVOCABLE TRUST

STATE OF _____ COUNTY OF _____

On _____, before the undersigned personally appeared _____

personally known to me or proved to me on the basis of satisfactory evidence to be the person(s) whose name(s) is/are subscribed to the within instrument and acknowledged to me that he/she/they executed the same in his/her/their authorized capacities and that by his/her/their signature(s) on the instrument the person(s) or the entity upon behalf of which the person(s) acted, executed the within instrument.

WITNESS MY HAND AND OFFICIAL SEAL.

_____

RECORDING REQUESTED BY:

AND WHEN RECORDED MAIL TO

_____
(SPACE ABOVE FOR RECORDER'S USE)

ASSIGNMENT OF DEED OF TRUST

For Value received, the undersigned hereby grants, assigns and transfers to _____ all beneficial interest under that DEED OF TRUST date_____ executed by_____ _____, Trustor to _____ and recorded as Instrument Number _____ on ___ _____ in Book _____ Page _____ of the Official Records of the County Recorder's Office of _____ County, State of _____ _____ describing land therein as:

Together with the note or notes therein described or referred to the money due and to become due thereon with interest, and all rights accrued or to accrue under said DEED OF TRUST.

Dated: _____

_____

_____

STATE OF _____

COUNTY OF _____

On _____, before the undersigned personally appeared _____

personally known to me or proved to me on the basis of satisfactory evidence to be the person(s) whose name(s) is/are subscribed to the within instrument and acknowledged to me that he/she/they executed the same in his/her/their authorized capacities and that by his/her/their signature(s) on the instrument the person(s) or the entity upon behalf of which the person(s) acted, executed the within instrument.

WITNESS MY HAND AND OFFICIAL SEAL.

_____

RECORDING REQUESTED BY:

AND WHEN RECORDED MAIL TO

(SPACE ABOVE FOR RECORDER'S USE)

DEED OF FULL RECONVEYANCE

_____, as the duly appointed Trustee under the DEED OF TRUST hereinafter referred to, having received from the beneficiary and the holder of the promissory note thereunder a written request to reconvey stating that all of the sums secured by the DEED OF TRUST have been fully paid, and the DEED OF TRUST along with the note or notes secured thereby having been surrendered to the Trustee for cancellation, do hereby RECONVEY, without warranty, to the persons legally entitled thereto, the estate now held by the Trustee thereunder. Said Deed of Trust was executed by _____
_____,
Trustor and recorded in the Official Records of _____,
County _____ in Book _____, Page _____.

The property is described as follows:

Dated: _____

_____

STATE OF _____ COUNTY OF _____

On _____, before the undersigned personally appeared _____

personally known to me or proved to me on the basis of satisfactory evidence to be the person(s) whose name(s) is/are subscribed to the within instrument and acknowledged to me that he/she/they executed the same in his/her/their authorized capacities and that by his/her/their signature(s) on the instrument the person(s) or the entity upon behalf of which the person(s) acted, executed the within instrument.

WITNESS MY HAND AND OFFICIAL SEAL.

_____

RECORDING REQUESTED BY:

AND WHEN RECORDED MAIL TO

(SPACE ABOVE FOR RECORDER'S USE)

SUBSTITUTION OF TRUSTEE AND DEED OF FULL RECONVEYANCE

THE UNDERSIGNED, BEING THE PRESENT BENEFICIARY, under the DEED OF TRUST EXECUTED BY _____ _____, as Trustor with _____, as the Original Trustee and recorded in Book _____ _____, Page _____ as Instrument Number _____ in the Official Records of the County Recorder's Office of _____ County, State of _____ hereby appoints and substitutes as the Beneficiary as the new and substituted Trustee for the DEED OF TRUST in accordance with the terms and provisions therein.

As the Duly appointed Substituted Trustee, the Beneficiary DOES HEREBY RECONVEY WITHOUT WARRANTY to the person or persons legally entitled entitled thereto all of the estate, rights, title and interest ACQUIRED BY THE Original Trustee and by the Beneficiary as the Substituted Trustee under the DEED OF TRUST.

DATED: _____

BENEFICIARY AND SUBSTITUTED TRUSTEE

_____

STATE OF _____

COUNTY OF _____

On _____, before the undersigned personally appeared
_____
personally known to me or proved to me on the basis of satisfactory evidence to be the person(s) whose name(s) is/are subscribed to the within instrument and acknowledged to me that he/she/they executed the same in his/her/their authorized capacities and that by his/her/their signature(s) on the instrument the person(s) or the entity upon behalf of which the person(s) acted, executed the within instrument.

WITNESS MY HAND AND OFFICIAL SEAL.

_____

RECORDING REQUESTED BY:

AND WHEN RECORDED MAIL TO

(SPACE ABOVE FOR RECORDER'S USE)

PARTIAL DEED OF RECONVEYANCE

_____, as the duly appointed Trustee under the DEED OF TRUST hereinafter referred to, having received from the Beneficiary in accordance with the terms of the DEED OF TRUST a written request to reconvey all interest held by the Trustee under said DEED OF TRUST in and to the hereinafter described property, said Beneficiary having presented said DEED OF TRUST and note or notes secured thereby for indorsement-said Deed of Trust having been executed by _____, Trustor and recorded in the Official Records of _____, County, State of _____ in Book _____, Page _____; Now therefore, in accordance with the request and the provisions of the DEED OF TRUST, _____ ___ as Trustee do hereby RECONVEY, without warranty, to the persons legally entitled thereto, all interest held by the Trustee in the following described property in the County of _____ State of _____:

The remaining property described in the DEED OF TRUST shall continue to be held by said Trustee under the terms thereof. This Partial Reconveyance is made without affecting the personal liability of any person for payment of the indebtedness secured by Deed of Trust

Dated: _____

_____

STATE OF _____ COUNTY OF _____

On _____, before the undersigned personally appeared _____ personally known to me or proved to me on the basis of satisfactory evidence to be the person(s) whose name(s) is/are subscribed to the within instrument and acknowledged to me that he/she/they executed the same in his/her/their authorized capacities and that by his/her/their signature(s) on the instrument the person(s) or the entity upon behalf of which the person(s) acted, executed the within instrument.

WITNESS MY HAND AND OFFICIAL SEAL.

_____

9
ESCROW

9. ESCROW

One of the most daunting problems facing any buyer or seller of real estate faces is the procedure for actually transferring the title and closing the transaction. When viewed from the prospective of the party, it seems unnecessarily cumbersome and convoluted to use a third party to act as an intermediary. However, such is always required where an institutional lender is involved in the sale. This third party is called the escrow holder and the actions undertaken in performing the duties as the escrow holder are referred to collectively as the escrow.

This chapter attempts to clarify as much as possible the various roles of the buyer, seller and escrow holder in this play called escrow. Today, most contracts for sale of real property also contain the clauses establishing the escrow. This merger of the two contracts intertwine them to a greater degree than ever in the past. As a result, a breach of the escrow conditions will almost always result in a breach of the sales agreement.

This chapter has attempted to answer the most common questions regarding escrows as completely as possible. It is intended that through this chapter the user will understand that which is required under an escrow and not be overawed by the complexity of the process.

1. WHAT IS AN ESCROW?
An escrow is a temporary trust arrangement. The general definition as stated in the California Financial Code is as follows:

"Escrow means any transaction whereon one person for the purpose of effecting the sale, transfer, encumbering or leasing real or personal property to another person, delivers any written instrument, money, evidence of title to real or personal property, or other thing of value to a third person to be held by such third person until the happening of a specified event or the performance of a prescribed condition, when it is then to be delivered by the third person to a grantee, grantor, promisor, promisee, obligee, obligor, bailee, bailor, or any agent of the latter."

Briefly, an escrow is an arrangement whereby an independent third party agrees to hold the deed and money for the sale of real property. When the terms of the sale have been met, the escrow holder delivers the deed to the buyer and the money to the seller.

2. WHAT IS NEEDED FOR VALID ESCROW?
The two essential elements needed for a valid escrow are:
1. A valid contract between the buyer and seller which specifically outlines the duties and obligations of the escrow holder, and
2. The conditional delivery of the property to be held in the escrow. The escrow instructions to the escrow holder may be joint or separate instructions. Separate instructions are those furnished by the buyer and seller in separate sets to the escrow holder. Joint escrow instructions is just one set of instructions signed by the the buyer and seller and furnished to the escrow holder.

3. WHAT ARE ESCROW INSTRUCTIONS?
Escrow instructions are specific directions to the escrow holder as to how the escrow is to be operated, managed and administrated. Escrow instructions set forth the following:
1. the purchase price,
2. agreements as to mortgages,
3. how the buyer will take the title,
4. matters of record subject to which the buyer is to acquire title,
5. the title policy,
6. the date of closing,
7. inspection reports to be delivered in to escrow,
8. proration adjustments,
9. date of possession by the buyer,
10. documents to be delivered into escrow, signed by the parties and recorded by the escrow holder,
11. disbursements to be made;
12. costs and charges and who pays them.

Escrow instructions can also include any special agreement or term among the parties. The closing of the escrow can be made contingent on the performance or happening of the special term or agreement.

4. WHY ARE ESCROWS USED?
The purpose of escrows are to insure the concurrent performance of the parties. Concurrent performance means that the purchase price for the

property is paid at the same time that the title is recorded. Use of an escrow prevents both the buyer and seller from getting the title or money for the property without first performing their part of the contract.

An escrow provides a means, through the use of a disinterested third party, to assure that all conditions of the sale are met before title and money changes hands. This provides protection to both parties and minimizes the opportunity for fraud or breach of the sales agreement.

5. WHAT ARE THE DUTIES OF THE ESCROW HOLDER?

The escrow holder is contractually required to perform the obligations imposed on him by the terms of the escrow instructions. The escrow holder is not an agent of either party but is instead an impartial party to the sale. The escrow holder must perform all clerical duties needed to close the escrow.

Some of the normal duties of the escrow holder are:
1. Ordering a preliminary title report and title insurance,
2. Proration of taxes, interest, rent, insurance and assessments,
3. Receiving all loan documents from the lender,
4. Paying off all existing lenders, if required,
5. Recording the necessary deeds and other documents to transfer title,
6. Making all payments to the proper parties,
7. Preparing closing statements.

6. WHO PAYS THE ESCROW HOLDER?

Usually the escrow holder charges a single fee for an escrow based on the size of the sale. Extraordinary services could result in additional fees being charged depending on the terms of the escrow agreement.

The buyer and seller have to decide who pays the escrow fees. Customarily, the fees are split between the buyer and seller although in many parts of the country the fees are paid entirely by one party or the other. There is no law requiring how the parties agree to pay the fees. The payment of the escrow fees is determined by the agreement of the parties.

7. HOW IS THE ESCROW HOLDER SELECTED?

The selection of an escrow holder depends quite often on whether there will be a loan taken on the property to help pay for it. If so, the lender will usually chose the escrow holder.

When the lender does not dictate who will be the escrow holder, the parties should look at the following factors in choosing an escrow holder:
1. The experience the escrow holder has had in the past in handling escrows,
2. The reputation of the escrow holder,
3. The location of the escrow holder,
4. The fees to be charged,
5. What the escrow holder will do in the escrow without charging extra fees.

8. WHAT INFORMATION DOES AN ESCROW HOLDER NEED?
In the escrow agreement, the buyer and seller must provide the escrow holder with the following information so that the escrow holder can perform its duties under the escrow:
1. Most important are the purchase price and legal description of the property being sold;
2. The names, addresses and phone numbers of the buyer and seller;
3. The inspections reports to be order;
4. The Real Estate Agents to be paid;
5. Who are to receive copies of the title reports;
6. Special information or instructions regarding the sale;
7. Closing date for the escrow, and
8. Proration and closing instructions.

9. WHAT DOES THE ESCROW HOLDER DO AFTER THE ESTATE IS OPENED?
After the escrow is officially opened, the escrow holder will commence a title check on the property to be sold or exchanged. The purpose of the title search is to trace the seller's title through public records to a point where the title is insurable.

The title search determines if the seller of the property actually has the legal right to sell the property. Furthermore, a title search will disclose if there are any "defects" or "clouds" on the title. Defects or clouds on the title are loans, liens, encumbrances, covenants, equitable servitudes or other matters of public record that affect the transferability or value for the property.

10. HOW IS A TITLE SEARCH DONE?
A title search is performed either by a title company or by an attorney. In some states, title companies do not exist and title searches must be done by the attorney.

The title examiner searches all of the public records available that pertain to the property. A title search should specific ally investigate the County Recorder's Office, County Assessor's Office and school assessment districts where the real property is located.

County Recorders' Offices use a Grantor and Grantee Indexes. All transactions by an owner of the property or anyone else that otherwise affect the owner's real property are indexed and cross referenced to the book and page where the document is recorded.

Title companies use a tract method of title search. The title companies keep all of the public records relating to a particular piece of property together in a file. A title search then consists of simply pulling the file and checking everything contained in the file for the property.

11. WHAT IS AN ATTORNEY'S CERTIFICATE OF TITLE?
As mentioned above, some states, mostly in the East, do have title companies. A title search is therefore done by attorneys.

The attorney's report on the status of the title of the property is called a certificate of title. The certificate of title specifies what documents were reviewed and what liens and encumbrances are on the property. As with title companies, the attorney's search is usually limited to public records unless expanded by agreement of the parties.

An attorney can be sued for damages suffered as a result of a negligently performed title search. Liability is conclusive when the attorney missed a defect on the title of the property that was contained in a public record.

12. WHAT IS THE PRELIMINARY REPORT?
The results of the title search are contained in a written report. The report is called a "Preliminary Report" in most states. In other states, such as Florida, it is called a "Commitment of Title" while others call

it an "Abstract of Title".

Whatever the report is called, it shows the conditions of the title of the property as of a certain date. Specifically, it shows:

    1. The name of the legal owner as shown on public records.
    2. The current status of taxes on the property.
    3. The legal description of the property.
    4. Outstanding liens and encumbrances of record on the property including easements, covenants and servitudes.
5. A copy of the official map on file with the Recorder's Office.

13. WHO PAYS FOR THE TITLE REPORT?

The buyer and seller have to decide who pays the fees for the title report. Customarily, the fees are split between the seller although in many parts of the country the fees are paid entirely by buyer or sometimes by the seller. There is no law requiring how the parties agree to pay the fees, it is all determined by the agreement of the parties.

14. WHAT SHOULD THE PARTIES DO AFTER THE TITLE REPORT IS ISSUED?

After the title report is received the parties should immediately read it carefully so as to discover any mistakes. The legal description should be minutely checked to ascertain that it is correct. Any map or survey should be checked to make such it accurately reflects the boundaries.

The seller's interest in the property must be verified and it must be affirmed that the seller can sell, transfer and convey title to the property.

Any disclosed liens, encumbrances, easements or servitudes shown in the title report must be researched. If they are not removed from the title, the buyer can cancel the sales contract and terminate the escrow.

15. WHAT IS CLEARING A TITLE?

Clearing a title is the term given for the process of the removal of defects or clouds on a title so that a sale can occur. Outstanding loans on the property are either paid or subordinated to the new buyer's interest in the property. Easements, restrictions and conditions are released or the buyer accepts them.

If the clouds on the title are not cleared, the buyer either can terminate the sale or complete the sale with those defects on his title.

16. WHAT ARE CC & R'S?
CC & R's is an abbreviation for conditions, covenants and restrictions. These are the uses and limitations placed upon the property by owner or one of the owner's predecessors in title.

CC & R's are usually agreements among neighbors in a real estate development that the property will only be used in a certain way so as to create an uniformity in style and value.

Zoning requirements are public restrictions used to promote the general health, safety and welfare of the community. CC & R's can be enforced in Court by any neighbor whose property was originally benefited by the CC & R's. CC & R's are clouds on a title of property. A buyer must accept them, clear them from his title or terminate the sale. Termination of CC & R's are difficult. Courts will enforce them unless they violate public policy or are illegal.

17. WHAT IS AN EASEMENT?
An easement is the right acquired by one person to use another's person's property in a particular manner. An easement is not an ownership interest but rather a nonpossessory interest which allows the easement owner to use the property. The owner of the property can use it in any manner that he wishes as long as he does not interfere with the easement owner's special use of the property.

Because the easement affects the use of the property by the owner, it is a cloud on its title. When the preliminary report discloses the existence of the easement, the buyer may terminate the sale, get the easement removed (cleared) or complete the sale and accept the title with the easement on the property.

For example, an easement which permits a road across the property would prevent building on the land where the easement runs. As such, this could prevent the owner of the property from having a home or garage build on the land.

The effects easement have on the value of property are great. Restrictions on the use of the property diminish the value of it by limiting the possible development of the land.

18. WHAT IS A LIEN?

A lien is a defect of title that is often a kiss of death to a sale and an escrow. By definition a lien is a security interest in the property given by the owner or operation of law to secure payment of some obligation.

A lien stays on the property until paid, released or executed upon. A lien follows the property. Therefore, if the owner sells property which has a lien on it, the buyer must pay off the lien or risk having the property seized and sold to pay the lien.

A voluntary lien is a mortgage or deed of trust. It is usually given to secure payment of the loan on the property. There are four types of involuntary liens:

1. Property Tax Liens. A taxing agency records a statement of unpaid taxes. If these taxes are not paid in accordance with state law, the agency can seize and sell the property. These tax sales will terminate an owner's interest in the property. Therefore it is important for a buyer know that if liens exist for unpaid taxes.

2. Judgment liens. A person who was awarded a judgment against another may record an Abstract of Judgment. Recordation of the Abstract of Judgment immediately places a lien on all real property owed by the debtor. No real property can be sold, by the debtor, without the lien following it.

3. Mechanic's lien. A licensed contractor is permitted to record a lien, in most states, for services and goods furnished improving real property. A lawsuit must be initiated within a fixed period of time, usually 180 days, after the lien is recorded or the lien is terminated.

4. Tax Liens. Both the IRS and the States can place liens on the real property of the owner for back taxes of all types. Like all other liens, they follow the property therefore a buyer of the property could have it encumbered by a previous seller's tax lien.

19. WHAT IS AN ENCUMBRANCE?

An encumbrance is a defect of title disclosed in the escrow that can kill the sale. Encumbrances by definition are anything that limits or affects the title of the property in any way. CC & R's are specialized forms of encumbrances designed to promote uniformity of development.

A fee simple defeasible creates an encumbrance in the seller's title because the stated condition may occur that divests the owner of all title in the property.

Easements, mineral leases, real estate leases are all encumbrances that affect the owner's development of the property and thus its value. Encumbrances may become significant enough that a buyer may not wish to purchase the property unless the defects are cleared from the title.

20. CAN A BUYER TAKE TITLE SUBJECT TO THE CLOUDS ON THE TITLE?

The clouds on the title which are disclosed in the title report are called exceptions. A title insurance policy will insure the title of the property against all claims of record except those particular defects disclosed in the title report. These disclosed defects are "excepted" from the insurance coverage.

A buyer can agree to purchase the property with full knowledge of the exceptions. This is known as the buyer taking the property "Subject to" the exceptions.

The buyer will not be personally obligated by any lien or encumbrance on the property. However, the property will still remain bound by the lien or encumbrances on it.

The escrow holder usually requires that the buyer agree in writing to take the property subject to the exceptions before the closing the escrow.

21. IS A TERMITE INSPECTION A REQUIREMENT OF ESCROW?

In some states, a termite inspection is required on all homes sales. Furthermore, most lenders tend to require a termite or pest report as a requirement for lending. Most purchasers nowadays require a termite or pest inspection as an ordinary caution regardless of whether a lender requires it.

The requirement for a termite inspection may be in the sales contract or in the escrow instruction. In either case, when there is such a clause, it becomes an express condition of the escrow. Therefore, until the inspection occurs the escrow will not close unless expressly waived by the parties.

22. WHAT HAPPENS AFTER A TERMITE REPORT IS OBTAINED?

When a pest or termite report is required, it is submitted by the owner into the escrow and treated in the same manner as a title report. A pest report lists corrective work to remedy current pest damage and preventive work to be done in the future.

Pest damage is treated as a exception. The buyer may take the property subject to the disclosed pest damage, require that the pest damage be corrected or terminate the sale.

As with the title report, the escrow holder will usually want written approval of the pest report before closing the escrow.

23. HOW DOES THE BUYER TAKE TITLE TO THE PROPERTY AT THE CLOSE OF ESCROW?

The purpose of a sale is to transfer title to the property to another for a price. The transfer of title is performed by the delivery of a deed to the buyer.

The deed will state what warranties of title (discussed in the Chapter Real Property) the seller is making on the property and in what capacity the buyer is receiving the property.

A buyer can take title to property in his or her own name, in joint tenancy with other persons, in a tenancy in the entirety with a spouse, in community property with a spouse or as a tenant in common with others.

The title from the seller reflects status of the title of the property at the time it is passed to the buyer. The status of the title is important because for not only determining ownership rights but for tax purposes in determining the basis of the property for resale purposes.

24. CAN A BUYER CHANGE THE TITLE TO THE PROPERTY AFTER ESCROW?

A buyer can always change his or her title in real property. It is one of the prime incidents of ownership that the owner can sell, convey or otherwise change title to the property.

Merely by recording a new deed, an owner can sell, give or encumber the property. Quitclaim and Grant Deeds are frequently used by an owner to place the property in a revocable trust for the owner's estate planning. The trust then becomes the legal owner while the original owner keeps full control over it by virtue of his total control of the trust.

25. CAN OTHER INSPECTIONS BE ORDERED IN THE ESCROW?
Most lenders tend to require a building inspection in addition to a pest inspection as a requirement for lending. Also, most buyers will have a house or building inspected out of an ordinary caution regardless of whether a lender requires it.

There have developed businesses that do nothing but inspect buildings for potential buyers. The inspectors are usually licensed contractors and check between 100 to 300 items for a fee. The requirement for a building inspection may be in the sales contract or in the escrow instruction. In either case, when there is such a clause it becomes an express condition of the escrow. Therefore, until the inspection occurs, the escrow will not close unless expressly waived by the parties.

26. WHAT HAPPENS AFTER A BUILDING REPORT IS OBTAINED?
When a passing building inspection report is required, it is submitted by the owner into the escrow and treated in the same manner as a title report. A report lists corrective work to remedy current structural or cosmetic damage and preventive work to be done in the future.
Damage listed in the inspection report is treated as an exception. The buyer may take the property subject to the disclosed damage or require that the damage be corrected or terminate the sale.

As with the title report, the escrow holder will usually want written approval of the building report before closing the escrow.

27. WHAT HAPPENS IF THE NEITHER THE CONTRACT OR ESCROW INSTRUCTIONS MENTIONED A BUILDING INSPECTION?
If there is no requirement in either the contract or escrow instructions about having a building inspection done, then it need not be done. If it is done anyway, the seller might not be under any obligation to repair any damages that it discloses. The exception to this is that under some state laws, the sale of new home must have certain warranties of plumbing, electrical, or sewer. In these states, if the new building fails a building inspection on those protected items, the seller must fix

them.

Absent statutory requirements, once a contract is signed the duties of both parties under the contract are fixed. Neither party may unilaterally change the contract or force the other party to do something that he or she had not previously agreed to do. If passing the inspection was not a condition for the sale, it can not be added as a condition later by the buyer.

If the contract does not condition the sale on the property passing a building inspection, the buyer can not, unless state law says otherwise, refuse to purchase the property based upon the failure of the building to pass an inspection.

28. CAN A HOME WARRANTY POLICY BE ORDERED IN THE ESCROW?

A home warranty policy is an insurance policy sold by some companies that warrants the good performance of the home and appliances contained therein for a fixed period time, usually a year. It can cover the electrical, plumbing, roof and other items depending on cost.

A common condition in many escrows is the requirement that the seller purchase such a home warranty policy for the buyer. This operates to protect the buyer from potential liability for missed defects and give peace of mind to the buyer.

29. WHAT ARE PRORATIONS?

Until the escrow closes, the seller still has the rights and duties incident to ownership. After the close of escrow, the buyer becomes the new owner of the property.

From the date that the buyer becomes the owner, or at any other time that the parties agree, the buyer becomes responsible for the maintaining the property and paying all taxes or debts that accrue on it after that date.

Therefore, there must be an adjustment between the obligations that accrued when the seller owned the property and those that belong to the buyer. These adjustments are called prorations. They are the division of the expenses between the buyer and seller in relationship to who actually owned the property when they were incurred.

30. IS INTEREST ON AN ASSUMED LOAN PRORATABLE?

If a loan is assumed or taken subject to, then there should be a proration of the interest in the escrow. Interest is not generally paid in advance. Therefore, the first monthly payment after the close of escrow will reflect interest on the loan for the period of time when the seller owned the property.

Interest should be prorated for the number of days of the month of closing that the seller owned the property. In other words, if the escrow closed on the thirteenth day of the month, then thirteen days of interest should be credited to the buyer.

31. IF RENTAL PROPERTY IS SOLD, THEN HOW IS THE RENT PRORATED?

If rent is received from rental property covering a period both before and after the close of escrow, then there should be a proration of the rent in the escrow. Rent is generally paid in advance. For that reason, it covers a period in which both the buyer and seller own the property. Therefore, the rent payment covering the time when the escrow closes will reflect tenancy when both the buyer and seller each owned the property.

Rent should be prorated for the number of days of the month of closing that the seller and buyer each owned the property. In other words, if the escrow closed on the thirteenth day of the month, then thirteen days of the rent should be prorated to the seller and seventeen days of the rent should be prorated to the buyer.

32. IF A FIRE INSURANCE POLICY IS ASSUMED, HOW IS IT PRORATED?

A fire insurance policy is paid in advance. Sometimes a buyer assumes the coverage of the old policy rather than buying a new policy. In such an event, the seller is entitled to a proration for the value of the unused fire insurance policy payment that was paid.

The fire insurance premium should be prorated for the number of unused days remaining on the policy. In other words, if a year remains on a two year policy that cost $4,000.00, then the seller is entitled to a $2,000.00 proration.

33. HOW ARE MAINTENANCE, CONDO OR CO-OP FEES PRORATED?

A homeowner's association in a planned development, condominium project or co-operative functions by assessing its members fees for the maintenance of the common areas and for the payment of taxes and insurance.

The association's dues or fees are paid monthly. Therefore they cover a period when the buyer and seller will each own the property. As such there must be a proration of the dues or fees to reflect the change of ownership in the escrow.

If the escrow closes on the 15 day of a month, then one half of the fees should be paid by the buyer and the other half by the seller (when the month has thirty days.)

34. WHAT IS AN IMPOUND ACCOUNT?

Some lenders collect an amount from the borrower in advance to be applied towards certain fixed expenses such as property taxes and fire insurance.

The balance of the account is refunded when the loan is paid. However, when there is an assumption of the loan or when it taken "subject" to there must be an adjustment because the buyer is now assuming the obligation to pay the taxes and insurance.

The seller is credited with the money in the impound account and the buyer is debited for it. The escrow holder had already prorated the property taxes and fire insurance so the money in the account should credited to the seller.

35. WHAT IS AN ASSUMPTION?

An assumption exists when a buyer assumes all of the rights and duties of the seller in a loan on the property. The assumption replaces the seller with the buyer and releases the seller from all obligations on the loan. The seller cannot thereafter be sued or have a deficiency judgment taken against him. The buyer, however, can be sued for nonpayment on the loan and be subject to a deficiency judgment, if appropriate under state law.

A loan can only be assumed by the written agreement of the lender. If the lender does not consent, then the seller still remains on the loan and is responsible for the payment of the loan.

36. WHAT IS SUBJECT TO FINANCING?
An assumption of a loan releases the seller from all liabilities under the loan. When the loan is not assumed or paid off at the close of escrow, it stays on the property and the buyer takes the property subject to it.

The seller still remains personally liable for the loan. If it is not paid, then the property will be foreclosed and the seller may be found personally liable for a deficiency judgment if appropriate under state law.

A deficiency judgment can not be obtained against a buyer who took the property subject to the loan and did not assume the obligation to pay the loan.

Letting a buyer purchase property by taking it subject to an existing loan rather than assuming the loan can have terrible consequences to the seller. The seller may be sued years later on the loan if the buyer fails to make the payment. Furthermore, since the seller is still obligated to pay the loan, it will still appear on his credit history and may prevent future loans.

37. WHAT EFFECT DOES A DUE ON SALE CLAUSE IN A MORTGAGE OR DEED OF TRUST HAVE ON THE ESCROW?
In any escrow covering real property that is encumbered by a pre-existing loan that will not be paid off, the parties must carefully read the loan documents to determine if there is a due on sale clause. Many mortgages and deeds of trusts contain clauses that state if the property is sold or conveyed in any manner, then the entire balance becomes immediately due and payable. These clauses have the effect of preventing the sale of the property without the lender's approval unless the loan is paid off.

Federal law will enforce a due on sale clause if the loan is from a federally insured lender. Some states, such as California, have adopted legislation that prevent private lenders or state charted lenders from enforcing due on sale clauses if the value of the property exceeds the amount owed.

Technically, a due on clause contained in a loan encumbering the property does not directly affect the escrow. However once the escrow closes, the buyer might have a nasty surprise when the lender makes a demand for full payment of the loan.

Some of the larger lenders have arrangements with title companies whereby they are informed of any transfers of property in which they have a security interest. In this manner, they are able to demand full payment whenever there is a transfer.

38. WHAT IS AN INSTALLMENT LAND CONTRACT?

Normally, the buyer who is purchasing property by making payments will execute, in the escrow, a mortgage or promissory note secured by a deed of trust. In some cases, the parties agree to enter into an installment land sales contract. In such a case, the buyer does not receive a deed to the property until the full sales price is paid. Only after the seller has received the full sales price with all interest will the buyer be given the deed to the property. Until the buyer pays the entire purchase price for the property, even if it takes decades, the buyer has only the sales contract to protect his rights.

Except for not giving the buyer a deed, an escrow for a land sales contract is conducted in the same manner as a regular escrow involving a mortgage or deed of trust.

39. HOW IS THE ESCROW FOR A COOPERATIVE? HANDLED

A cooperative is a corporation which owns the title to the land and buildings thereon. The cooperative leases apartments in its buildings to its shareholders. The residents in a cooperative are thus tenants by virtue of their leases and owners of the cooperative by virtue of their stock interests.

Because the owners of the cooperative do not directly own the buildings or their apartments, they can only sell their ownership interest in the cooperative. To do that they sell their stock in the cooperative.

Therefore instead of placing a deed in the escrow, as is done in the normal escrow, the seller places his stock certificate in the cooperative made out for transfer to the buyer.

Upon the close of escrow, the escrow holder has the cooperative's secretary change the stock register to reflect the new ownership of the shares of stock by the buyer.

40. WHY DOES THE ESCROW HOLDER RECORD THE DEEDS AND OTHER DOCUMENTS?

The escrow holder is required by the terms of the escrow to record the deeds and any mortgages or deeds of trust given to secure the financing of the property.

The purpose of the recording is two fold:
1. To transfer legal title from the seller to the buyer in the property.
2. To perfect the security rights on the lender in the property.

The date of recordation is important in determining a person's claim of interest in real property. All states have laws for determining the priority of conflicting claims in real property. All of these laws revolve around the date of recording a person's claimed interest in the property (see the Real Property chapter for greater discussion.)

41. CAN AN EXCHANGE OF REAL PROPERTY OCCUR THROUGH AN ESCROW?

Generally speaking, the Internal Revenue Code permits the tax free exchange of like kind property without having to recognize a gain or loss.

In a tax-free exchange, the basis of the new property received is the same as for the property traded. For example, A and B each own commercial buildings and want to trade them with each other. The fair market value of the buildings are $200,000 each. A's basis (investment in the building) is $34,000. B's basis is $56,000.00. After the trade, A's basis in what used to be B's property is $34,000 and B's basis in A's former property is $ 56,000.00.

The escrow holder in a tax free exchange trades deeds in place of money in the escrow. Except for the exchange of deeds instead of money, the escrow for a tax-free exchange is handled the same as an ordinary escrow.

42. CAN THERE BE A DELAYED TAX-FREE EXCHANGE?

As long as the escrow is properly structured, there can be a delayed tax-free exchange. A delayed tax-free exchange is called a Starker Exchange for the first case in which it was done.

In a delayed exchange, the buyer pays cash into the escrow. At the close of the escrow, the escrow holder records the buyers' deed and loan documents. The escrow holder then holds the proceeds of the sale until the seller directs the escrow holder to apply those proceeds to the purchase price of replacement like kind property.

The seller has 45 days after the close of escrow to identify the replacement property and 180 days after the close of escrow to acquire it. The buyer and seller must agree to the tax free exchange in writing prior to the close of escrow.

Because of the tax complexity in a tax-free exchange, a tax professional should be consulted before any such contracts are executed.

43. WHAT IS THE DOCUMENTARY TRANSFER TAX AND WHO PAYS IT IN ESCROW?

Many states require that a seller pay a tax for the privilege of selling his or her real property. The payment of this tax was once evidenced by stamps placed on the deed.

Today stamps are no longer used to prove the payment of the transfer taxes although the term documentary stamps is still used to denote the obligation to pay the tax.

The usual transfer tax is based on a percentage of the sales price. The tax varies widely from county to county. The seller normally pays the tax but the parties can agree otherwise.

44. WHEN IS THE REAL ESTATE COMMISSION PAID?

Real estate commissions are not owed by a seller unless there was an agreement in writing hiring the agent to sell the real property. There are several types of contracts called listings. The most common listings are:
1. An Exclusive Right to Sell Listing. This listing gives the agent the sole right to sell the property. This means if the seller finds a buyer, he must still pay the commission to the agent.
2. An Exclusive Agency Listing. This listing gives the agent the exclusive right to sell the property but the seller reserves the right to sell it itself. If the seller finds the buyer himself, then he will not have to pay a commission.
3. An Open Listing. This listing is not an exclusive listing and permits the seller to have several different agents selling his property. A commission is not earned until an agent finds a person that actually purchases the property. If there was a written listing agreement, the real

estate commission becomes owed when the agent has found a ready, willing and able buyer who will purchase the property on the exact terms that the seller wishes to sell.

The seller's obligation to pay the agent is conditioned only upon the buyer completing the sale. If the buyer does not purchase the property then obviously the seller is not obligated to pay the commissions.

The commissions are paid directly out of the escrow from the proceeds that the seller is to receive.

45. WHEN DOES AN ESCROW TERMINATE?
Escrows are either fully performed by the parties or terminated. All conditions required by the escrow instructions must be performed within the time limit set forth in the escrow agreement. The escrow holder does not have any authority to accept performance after the date provided for the close of escrow.

When the time limit provided for the close of escrow has expired and performance by either party has not fully occurred, then the parties may agree to cancel the escrow and receive back their property which they previously placed into the escrow.

The escrow may terminate automatically if certain stated conditions are not met. For example, the escrow may have a clause stating that it terminates if the buyer does not obtain financing by the close of escrow.

Even if the escrow is terminated for failure of one party to perform the conditions under the escrow contract that does not prevent the other party from suing for breach of contract. For example, if the escrow is terminated because the seller failed to provide a termite report required in the sales contract, the buyer can still sue for specific performance of the contract. The existence of an escrow is not a requirement for a valid contract.

46. WHAT IS SETTLEMENT OF THE ESCROW?
Settlement of an escrow means the accounting that the escrow holder does prior to calling for the funds for the buyer. In the settlement statement the escrow holder makes all of the prorations and adjustments as instructed by the parties. In preparing the settlement statement, the escrow holder uses the date for the close of escrow, the date

of the buyer's possession or other date assigned by the parties as the control date.

When all of the the above is done, the escrow holder notifies the buyer of the escrow's readiness to continue when the buyer's funds are deposited.

47. WHAT DOES IT MEAN WHEN AN ESCROW HOLDER ASKS FOR CLOSING FUNDS?

Sometimes additional funds are needed to pay for the services required to be performed in the escrow. For example, the buyer may be required to pay for the documentary transfer tax. If so, additional funds will have to added to cover this expense.

The necessity of requiring the payment into escrow of the closing funds is to assure that the escrow will not close short, that is with money being owed to the buyer, the seller or escrow holder.

48. WHAT HAPPENS AT THE CLOSE OF ESCROW?

After confirming the recordation of the deeds, loan agreements and other transaction documents, the escrow holder closes the escrow by preparing settlement documents for both the buyer and seller. After the buyer and seller have approved and accepted the closing documents, the escrow holder disburses all funds to the designated parties and delivers the documents in the possession of the escrow holder to the proper parties.

The seller is given a check from the escrow holder for the net proceeds of the sale and the appropriate documents for which he or she is entitled.

The buyer receives the recorded deed, the title policy and any other items required to be delivered under the terms of the escrow.

49. WHAT IS RESPA?

RESPA is short for Federal Real Estate Settlement Procedures Act. It requires that all closings of home sales and other transactions covered by this law use a uniform settlement statement. The law also requires that the lender or party performing the closing give the buyer and seller advance information and estimates of closing costs.

Among its provisions. RESPA limits the amount which a lender may collect for establishing new insurance and tax reserves and requires advance cost estimates be furnished prior to closing.

RESPA applies to transactions involving federally related first mortgages for one to four family dwellings. It also applies to the VA, FHA and lenders whose reserves are federally insured.

50. WHAT SHOULD THE BUYER CHECK PRIOR TO CLOSING?
The buyer should both check and verify that the following information is correct prior to closing:
1. Is the purchase price right?
2. Are all the notes properly filled out? Are all of the terms of any new loans such as interest rate, due date, interest, prepayment terms correct?
3. Are the prorations correct?
4. Is the legal description correct?
5. Is the buyer's name spelled correctly?
6. Was the title cleared of defects to the buyer's satisfaction?
7. Has proper credit been given for all sums paid into the escrow?
8. Is the buyer being given a bill of sale for any personal property in the sale?
9. Are any payments for taxes or insurance premiums correct?
10. Is the date for close of escrow correct?

51. WHAT SHOULD THE SELLER CHECK PRIOR TO CLOSING?
The seller should both check and verify that the following information is correct prior to closing:
1. Is the purchase price right?
2. Are all the notes properly being paid off or assumed?
3. Are the prorations correct?
4. Is the deed correct?
5. If the seller is financing, are the the notes and mortgage or deed of trust properly filled out?
6. Was credit given for any impound account?
7. Has proper credit been given for all sums paid into the escrow?
8. Does a bill of sale for any personal property in the sale cover all of the personal property being sold?
9. Are any payments for taxes or insurance premiums correct?

10. Is the date for close of escrow correct?

52. WHAT HAPPENS IN THE ESCROW IF THE SELLER IS A NON-RESIDENT ALIEN?

When real property owned by a foreign investor is sold, a withholding tax is imposed on the proceeds. Generally, the buyer is required to withhold and deduct a tax equal to ten (10%) of the amount realized by the foreign seller.

The escrow holder usually handles the withholding on behalf of the buyer and pay the money as required to the IRS.

53. ARE ESCROW FEES DEDUCTIBLE BY THE SELLER?

The escrow fees paid by the seller in marketing his or her real property are deductible as selling expenses. The escrow fees are deducted along with the other selling expenses along with the adjusted basis of the property from the sales price. The remaining balance is then the amount subject to taxation by the government unless it is rolled over into a new home or otherwise eligible for the one time $125,000 tax credit for the sale of a home by a person over 55 years of age.

54. HOW ARE ESCROW FEES TREATED BY THE BUYER?

Escrow fees paid by a buyer are treated as a capital expenditure. The amount of the escrow fees are added to the buyer cost of the house. Therefore, when the house is resold the escrow fees previously paid by the seller will be used to reduce the capital gain if any. For example, the buyer pays $1,000.00 escrow fees on a $50,000.00 house. Two years later he sells it for $60,000.00. The buyer will have $9,000.00 in capital gain ($50,000 cost plus $1,000 in escrow fees).

10
TORTS

10. TORTS

Torts are the terms given for civil wrongs. When a person is sued for the damages caused by a wrongful act, the person is sued for having a committed a tort. Almost all criminal acts are torts but not all torts sink to the status of a crime.

This chapter is intended to familiarize the reader with the most common torts and their defenses and with the remedies available to victims of tortious acts.

Generally, if a reasonable person feels that some type of conduct is wrong, then quite likely that conduct is tortious and the courts will stop it. Most people are unaware of the various types of torts that exist. Conduct that many people would take for granted and ignore as petty annoyances may actually be tortious in nature and actually expose the perpetrator to civil suits. A painful example is sexual harassment. Jokes and conduct acceptable to most men may be considered sexual harassment when said or done around women. In such event, the person committing the act may find himself a defendant in a sexual harassment action.

It is important, in today's litigious society, for people to understand as much as possible about their legal rights which are constantly changing in today's society. In addition, it is important to understand what conduct is legally considered tortious so that a person can protect himself, his property and his family.

1. WHAT IS A TORT?
A tort is the term given to a civil wrong rather than a criminal wrong or breach of a contract. Nearly every criminal act is also a tort.

A tort is by definition is a legal wrong committed upon the person or property of another without justification or privilege that makes the perpetrator liable for damages occurring as a result of the conduct.

2. WHAT ARE PUNITIVE DAMAGES?
Punitive damages are also called exemplary or special damages. Punitive damages is an additional damage award given to the Plaintiff in an action and over and above the amount necessary to compensate the Plaintiff for his actual damages.

Punitive damages are awarded where the wrong done to the Plaintiff was aggravated by circumstances of violence, oppression, malice, fraud, or wanton and wicked conduct on the part of the defendant. Punitive damages are intended to afford solace to the innocent Plaintiff for the undeserved mental anguish, shame, degradation suffered or to punish the defendant for his evil behavior or to make an example of him.

Punitive damages can be awarded by the court for any intentional tort. Intentional torts for which punitive damages can be awarded are assault, battery, false imprisonment, and defamation. Punitive damages can also be awarded in negligence cases where the negligent act is so gross and unreasonable that it becomes almost intentional, for example shooting a gun in an open area which results in someone being hit by the bullet.

3. WHAT IS ASSAULT?

An assault is tort whereby a person creates a well-founded fear of immediate physical harm in another. Merely threatening an other is not an assault but a threat coupled with the reasonable belief by the victim that it will be carried out is an assault.

Damages can be recovered by the person assaulted for the compensation of the emotional distress and other injuries suffered as a direct and reasonable result of the assault. Punitive damages may also be recovered for an assault.

4. WHAT IS A BATTERY?

A battery, at common law, is defined as a harmful and offensive touching of another without consent or privilege. To have committed a battery there must be these elements:
1. An act which brings about the harmful or offensive touching committed by the defendant,
2. An intent to bring about the harmful or offensive touching. Merely bumping into someone is not a battery, pinching them could be,
3. The harmful or offensive touching must derive from the direct or indirect contact arranged by the defendant, setting a trap that injures a person is still a battery. Rape is referred to as sexual battery. Such is a modern term to demote the severity of the offense. Under common law,

rape was treated as any other tortious battery.

5. WHAT IS FALSE IMPRISONMENT?
The tort of false imprisonment is the unlawful arrest or detention of another. The person falsely detained is entitled to compensation for his or her loss of time, for physical discomfort or inconvenience suffered as the result of the of the confinement, and for any resulting physical injury or illness to his or her health. The falsely imprisoned person is also entitled to his or her damages for mental suffering and humiliation.

Because of the malevolent intentions or reckless disregard for the victim's rights that often accompany false imprisonment, punitive damages are frequently awarded.

False imprisonment may exist where a person is detained by virtue of the fact that personal property is being held. A woman that has her purse taken may be falsely imprisoned because she won't leave without it.

6. CAN A SHOPKEEPER DETAIN A SUSPECTED THIEF?
Most states permit a shopkeeper to detain a person suspected of shoplifting for an investigation an be immune for a suit against false imprisonment. In order for this privilege to apply, the following conditions must be met:
1. There must a reasonable belief that a theft occurred,
2. The detention must be conducted in a reasonable manner and only non-deadly force can be used,
3. The period of detention can only be for a reasonable period of time and only for the purposes of making an investigation. When any of the foregoing conditions are not met, the shopkeeper can be sued for false imprisonment and punitive damages are awardable.

7. WHAT IS CONVERSION?
The tort of conversion is the intentional interference with the property of another which is serious enough in nature to warrant the defendant paying full value for it.
    Example of conversion are:
1. Wrongful acquisition-theft or embezzlement,

2. Wrongful transfer-selling, taking loans on,
3. Wrongful detention- refusing to deliver or return
4. Severely damaging or destroying the property. The intent to take the property does not have to be a matter of conscious wrongdoing. A mistaken belief in the right to take the property is no defense. An innocent purchaser of stolen goods is still a converter.

The damages awarded to a person who property is converted is the value of the goods when converted along with the damages suffered as a result of the conversion. The award of punitive damages depends on whether the person committing the conversion knew that he or she was converting the property.

Return of the converted property does not bar a suit a suit for damages but merely reduces the amount that can be awarded.

8. WHAT IS TRESPASS?

Trespass in the unlawful entry onto the property of another. A continuing trespass is one that is a permanent invasion of the property of another. An example of a continuing trespass is the building of a house on the land of another. A permanent trespass is a repeated trespass that occurs in a series of acts that when taken together constitute one act.

Trespass can take place both above and below the ground. A mine or well can trespass by crossing onto the land of another. Damages are presumed for a trespass. Actual damages need not be proven before recovering punitive damages. The trespasser is liable for all damages to the property that arise as a result of the trespass. If the trespass is intentional or reckless, then punitive damages may be awarded as well.

Anyone in actual or constructive possession of the land may maintain an action for trespass. A tenant or lessee can file a lawsuit for trespass or if none then the owner can do so.

9. WHAT IS TRESPASS TO CHATTELS?

Trespass to chattels is the interference with a person's right of possession of his property not amounting to a conversion. The elements of Trespass to Chattels are:
1. An act of the defendant to interfere with the plaintiff's right of possession or use of his property,
2. The intent to deliberately interfere with the property

of another, for example breaking a window.
3. Damages suffered by the plaintiff. for example replacing the window. Punitive damages are awardable for trespass to chattels.

10. WHAT IS DEFAMATION?

Defamation is a false statement, written or oral, which injures a person's reputation so as to lower him in the estimation of the community or to defer third persons from associating or dealing with him.

To create liability for defamation there must be (1) a false defamatory statement concerning another (2) an unprivileged publication to a third party and (3) the statement must be made intentionally or at least negligently.

If the defamation is written, then it is libel. If the defamation is oral, then it is slander.

11. WHAT IS SLANDER?

Slander is the malicious defamation of a person in his reputation, profession or business by spoken words. The essential element of slander is that the defamation be spoken in the presence of someone other than the person being slandered. Therefore, a slanderous statement only heard by the slandered person is not actionable.

Some states require proof of damages as a result of the slander before recovery of punitive damages. In such cases, a suit for slander could not be maintained and no recovery for punitive damages would lie unless there was some direct damage suffered as a result of the defamation.

The harsh slander rule requiring the proof of damages before recovering punitive damages does not apply to defamatory acts constituting slander per se.

Slander per se are defamatory statements that:
1. falsely accuse a person of committing a crime,
2. falsely impute the existence of a loathsome disease,
3. falsely impute the fitness of the person to conduct business, trade or profession, or
4. falsely accuse a woman of unchastity.

In slander per se damage is presumed. Therefore, punitive damages may be awarded without proof of actual damages.

12. WHAT IS LIBEL?

Libel is a false and malicious defamatory writing which tends to degrade a person in the eyes of his community, or tends to hold him up to ridicule or tends to injure his property or business. Libel may consist of a writing, effigy, picture or the like. There must be publication of the libel which means it must be communicated to a third person. A defamatory statement read over a radio is libel.

Unlike slander, actual damages need not be proven before recovery for a published statement libelous on its face. In addition, no actual damages have to be proven prior to recovery of punitive damages for libel per se.

Libels per se are defamatory statements that:
1. falsely accuse a person of committing a crime,
2. falsely impute the existence of a loathsome disease,
3. falsely impute the fitness of the person to conduct business, trade or profession, or
4. falsely accuse a woman of unchastity.

In libel per se, as in slander per se, damage is presumed. Therefore, punitive damages may be awarded without proof of actual damages.

Libel that needs extrinsic evidence to prove its falsity or defamatory nature requires, in most states, actual proof of damages, before there can be a recovery of punitive damages.

13. WHAT ARE THE DEFENSES TO DEFAMATION?

The following are the main defenses to defamation:
1. Consent of the party being defamed is a defense as with an intentional torts as discussed above.
2. Truth is an absolute defense for defamation. A person cannot be defamed by the truth. However, statement while true may nonetheless expose the person telling it to liability under the theory of infliction of emotional distress or invasion of privacy.
3. There are absolute privileges for defamatory statements made in court, for judges, attorneys and witnesses.
4. Qualified privileges exist, meaning there can be no recovery unless actual malice (knowledge of the falsity or reckless disregard of its truthfulness) is proven in:
a. Reports of Public Proceedings;

b. Statements made to those taking public action;
c. Statements made to someone having an interest in the information. An example is a potential employer speaking to a former employer about an applicant; anything said therein without malicious intent is privileged from a lawsuit for defamation.

14. WHEN IS CONSENT A DEFENSE TO A TORT?
When the plaintiff expressly consented to the defendant's conduct, the defendant normally will not be liable for the defendant's conduct.

Where the plaintiff had consented to the defendant's conduct by mistake, the consent is still valid unless the defendant knows of the mistake on the part of the plaintiff and takes advantage of it.

A consent induced by fraud will not constitute a defense. Likewise, a consent obtained by force, threats or duress is invalid.

In the professional setting, especially medical, the lack of informed consent invalidates the consent given to the defendant. Some courts have declared that the failure to disclose risks is a breach of the standard of care and therefore treats the tort as negligence rather than an intentional tort. For example, a doctor that performs an operation and failed to disclose all risks could be sued for negligence, not assault or battery.

Consent may also be implied by the apparent conduct of the plaintiff which would lead a reasonable person to infer that consent was given for the defendant's conduct. An example of implied consent is an owner letting a person drive his car in the past without asking permission. This might create the impression that he would be given permission to drive it at any time.

Most jurisdictions hold that a person cannot consent to a criminal act. A minority view does permit consent to commit a criminal act to be a defense in a civil case.

15. WHAT CONSTITUTES SELF-DEFENSE?
A person, with reasonable grounds to believe that he or she is about to be attacked, may use whatever force as is reasonably necessary for protection against the anticipated injury.

Self-defense requires:
1. A reasonable belief that the other party intends to attack. A reason-

able mistake as to the existence of the danger does not invalidate the defense, if the initial belief was reasonable;

2. A majority of courts hold that a person does not have to first attempt to flee and escape before attempting to defend himself or herself. A few courts hold that the victim must first attempt to retreat safely before deadly force can be used. An exception to the retreat rule in some states is that a person does not have to retreat in his own home before using deadly force;

3. Retaliation is not self-defense. Excessive force or force used after the threat is over does not constitute self-defense. If a third party is injured in the course of a person defending himself, self-defense can be argued to protect the person from liability. However, there may still be liability to a third person accidentally injured in the self-defense on a negligence theory of the facts support it.

16. WHAT IS THE DEFENSE OF OTHERS?

Most jurisdictions permit a person going to the aid of another to use as much force as the person being defended could have used for protection. The person coming to the defense of another is held to have stepped in the shoes of the person being defended.

If the person being aided has no defense (if that person is found to have been the aggressor and instigator of the situation) then anyone coming to his aid, under the majority view, likewise has no defense for injuries caused by intervening in the dispute.

A small minority view permits a person to use the force that he reasonably believes the person being defended has the right to use in self-defense. In such an event, the person coming to the defense of another would be immune for any injuries that might be caused by his use of force that he believed was reasonably necessary.

17. WHAT IS THE DEFENSE OF PROPERTY?

It is the view of all jurisdictions that a person may use reasonable force to prevent the commission of a tort against property. The defense has the following elements:

1. A requirement that a request to stop be made before the use of force. Such a request to stop is not required if under the circumstances it would be futile or expose the defender to danger;

2. The majority view is that force can only be used to prevent the commission of the tort against the property. Once the tort is accomplished, force can no longer be used. For example, force can be used to prevent theft of property but once stolen, force cannot be used to retrieve or recapture it. An exception exists for hot pursuit of a thief. In such an event, force can used to recapture the property because the theft is still is progress.

3. The right to defend land is superseded by the privileges of another who has the right to enter the property in self-defense, to defend others, to recapture property or out of necessity. Injuries caused in opposing such entries are not protected and are tortious.

18. WHAT IS THE DEFENSE OF NECESSITY?

The defense of necessity permits a person to interfere with the real personal property of another:

1. when it is reasonably and apparently necessary to avoid a probable injury from a threatening force; and
2. where the threatened injury is substantially more serious than the action taken to prevent it. When the action is for public necessity, it is absolutely privileged. A public necessity is an act for the public good. For example, the shooting of a rabid dog would be a public necessity.

When the action is for a private necessity, the defense is qualified meaning the person must pay for the damages that he caused but is not liable for punitive damages. A private necessity is one for solely for the benefit of any person or to protect any property from destruction.

19. WHAT IS THE TORT OF INTENTIONAL INFLICTION OF EMOTIONAL DISTRESS?

The tort of intentional infliction of emotional distress consists of:

1. An act or conduct of a defendant that is considered by a reasonable person as outrageous and extreme;
2. The defendant manifested by his words or conduct an intent to cause the victim severe emotional distress;
3. The acts of the defendant caused the victim emotional distress; and
4. Actual damages must have been incurred by the victim as the result of the defendant's outrageous conduct. This tort covers the situation where it is not physical injury or threat by the defendant which causes

the victim's injuries but rather the shocking actions of the defendant.

This tort requires conduct designed to designed to shock the victim with the purpose of injuring the victim. It is also necessary to prove damages directly related to injuries suffered by the defendant's conduct.

20. WHAT IS A NUISANCE?
A nuisance is not a tort in and of itself. It is subject to its own rules. Nuisances are types of damages that are tortious because they derive from activities that annoy, harm, inconvenient or damage people or property. There are two types of nuisances, a public nuisance and private nuisance.

A nuisance is different from a trespass to land. A trespass to land is an interference with exclusive possession of the land wherein a nuisance is an interference with the use and enjoyment of the land.

The remedies for a nuisance are:
1. For a private nuisance or a public nuisance where the plaintiff has suffered some unique injury, the usual remedy is a court action for damages.
2. Injunctive relief is available where the legal remedy of damages is inadequate or unavailable. Where the nuisance will cause irreparable injury or is a continuing wrong, the award for damages may be inadequate to cure the harm caused by the nuisance.

21. WHAT IS A PRIVATE NUISANCE?
A private nuisance is a substantial, unreasonable interference with another's person's use and enjoyment of his or her property.

To constitute substantial interference, the conduct must be considered by a reasonable person to be offensive, inconvenient or annoying to the average person in the community. Special sensitivity of the complaining person is not substantial interference if a reasonable person would not complain.

Unreasonable interference requires the injury suffered by the plaintiff to be greater than the advantage to the defendant derived by his conduct. The courts must balance the respective rights and injuries to the parties.

22. WHAT IS A PUBLIC NUISANCE?

A public nuisance is an act which unreasonably interferes with the health, safety and welfare of the community. A continuing ongoing pattern of criminal activity can constitute a public nuisance such as drug dealing, book making, prostitution, etc.

A private person can recover for damages suffered as a result of a public nuisance only if those damages are unique and in addition to the damages suffered by the public at large.

An example of a public nuisance is dangerous air pollution emitted by a plant, illegal water pollution, illegally blocking a street, etc. If any of these or other public nuisances cause special damages beyond those suffered generally by the community, a suit for those special damages can be maintained.

23. WHAT IS VICARIOUS LIABILITY?

Vicarious liability is liability imposed on someone for the torts committed by another. Generally, this means that a third party may be liable and have to pay damages for the torts committed by another which he or she did not commit.

The basis for this liability rests on the special relationship between the person committing the tort and the person to whom the liability is imputed or assessed.

Vicarious liability is substituted or indirect liability imposed on one persons entity for the actions of another.

24. IS AN EMPLOYER LIABLE FOR THE ACTIONS OF EMPLOYEES?

An employer will be vicariously liable for all torts committed by an employee within the scope of the employee's employment.

The liability is founded on the principle that a duty rests upon every employer in the management of his affairs, whether by himself or by agents, to conduct them so as not to injure others.

The liability for the employer for an employee's act is referred to as "Respondeat-Superior". As long as the employee was acting within the scope of his employment, then the employer is liable for the damages resulting therefrom.

Generally, intentional torts by an employee are not within the scope of employment. However, courts have found intentional tortious

conduct to be within the scope of employment when:
1. Force is authorized by employment,
2. Friction is generated by employment;
3. The servant is furthering the business of the employer.

25. IS A PRINCIPAL RESPONSIBLE FOR AN INDEPENDENT CONTRACTOR?

A person hiring an independent contractor will not be liable for the torts of an independent contractor except when:
1. The independent contractor is engaged in especially hazardous activities such as blasting. In such instances, the principal, the person hiring the services of the independent contractor is liable for the damages caused by the independent contractor.
2. The duty, because of public policy considerations, is not delegable that is transferrable to another. An example is the duty of due care in building a fence around a dangerous area. A principal may be liable for the damages caused by the independent contractor under the theory of negligent selection.

Under such a theory, if the reasonable person would not have used the services of the independent contractor the principal may be liable for the torts caused by the independent contractor.

26. IS A PARTNER LIABLE FOR THE TORTS OF THE OTHER PARTNERS?

Every partner is jointly and severally liable for the torts committed by the other partners committed in the scope and course of affairs of the partnership.

27. IS AN OWNER OF AN AUTOMOBILE LIABLE FOR THE DRIVER?

Most jurisdictions hold that the owner of an automobile is not liable for the torts committed by the driver of the automobile, if not the owner. However, some states have adopted special laws making the owner liable for the torts committed by a family member driving with the express or implied permission of the owner. Other states have gone further to extend liability to the owner of the vehicle for the torts of any driver operating it with the permission of the owner.

The owner may still be liable for the torts of the driver under the theory of negligent entrustment of the vehicle to the driver. An owner giving a car to an obviously drunk driver may be sued for negligent entrustment in all states.

28. IS A PARENT LIABLE FOR THE TORTS OF A CHILD?
Most jurisdictions hold that a parent is not liable for the torts committed by a child. However, some states have adopted special laws making the parent liable for the torts committed by a child while acting as an agent of the family or with the express or implied permission of the parent. Other states have gone further to extend liability to a parent for a serious tort by a child up to a fixed amount usually $15,000..

The parent may still be liable for the torts of the child under the theory of negligent entrustment or supervision if the parent failed to adequately supervise or train the child in the use of an item that caused the injury.

29. WHAT IS MALICIOUS PROSECUTION?
The tort of malicious prosecution is a tort based upon the fact that the plaintiff was wrongfully and maliciously accused of a crime and thereby suffered damage. The elements of the tort are:
1. The institution of criminal proceedings against the plaintiff;
2. A conclusion of the criminal proceeding favorable to the plaintiff;
3. Absence of probable cause for the prosecution;
4. Improper purpose of the defendant;
5. Damages to the plaintiff.

The defendant must initiates the criminal proceeding by filing a complaint. The criminal case terminates in such a manner that the innocence of the accused is demonstrated.

There must have been no probable cause for the defendant's activities in instituting the criminal prosecution. The defendant must have known that there were insufficient facts to believe the plaintiff was guilty or did not actually believe the accused to be guilty.

The defendant must have had the primary purpose in initiating the false criminal proceeding the intent to injure the plaintiff and not to bring a person to justice.

Many jurisdictions extend the tort of malicious prosecution to improperly brought civil actions. A civil suit for malicious prosecution must prove the same elements as a criminal malicious prosecution action.

30. WHAT IS THE TORT OF ABUSE OF PROCESS?

It is a tort to misuse the judicial process to accomplish a result which the proceeding or process was not intended to accomplish. An example is an attachment of wages on a debt that is known not to be owed. The gist of this tort is the wrongful use of the judicial process and not the motive in doing so.

If the process is used in the manner it was designed to be used, it does not matter that the intent was to injure a person. No liability will exist for damages caused as the result of properly executed judicial process. For example, an attachment of wages to satisfy a judgment is proper even though it is designed to injure a person and done while an appeal is pending which the attaching party knows will be granted.

Abuse of process is different from malicious prosecution because the merits of the case are irrelevant. All that is needed to be proven is that the judicial process was misused causing damages to the other party.

31. WHAT IS WRONGFUL DEATH?

Wrongful death is a tort permitting recovery of pecuniary damages to the next of kin of a person wrongfully killed by another.

The action for wrongful death may be brought by the personal representative and in some states by the spouse or next of kin.

The measure of damages in a wrongful death case is the pecuniary injury resulting to the surviving spouse and next of kin from the wrongful death. The recovery is limited to loss of consortium, loss of support etc. There is no recovery under wrongful death for the pain and suffering of the decedent.

Creditors of the decedent have no claim against the judgment awarded in a wrongful death action. A defendant in a wrongful death action can raise any defense it had against the decedent such as assumption of the risk, contributory negligence, etc.

32. WHAT IS INVASION OF PRIVACY?

Everyone has the right against the unreasonable interference with his

or her solitude. The right of privacy has been held to include protection against personal rights as well the right of solitude. In essence the right to privacy includes:
1. Protection against the appropriation of a person's name picture or voice for commercial use;
2. Protection from intrusion into a person's private affairs and seclusion;
3. Protection from publication of facts that places a person in a false light, that is something a reasonable person would find objectionable;
4. Protection against the public disclosures of private facts. The defenses for invasion of privacy are the same as for defamation. The same privileges exist for this tort as exist for defamation.

33. WHAT IS FRAUD?

Fraud is also known as intentional misrepresentation and deceit. It is the intentional misrepresentation of fact to another upon which the other person relies and suffers damages.

The misrepresentation must be of a material fact. A material fact is one that a reasonable person would have relied on in making a decision. There is no general duty to disclose information. However when a person stands in a fiduciary relationship with another or when his words or actions serve to deceive a person then there is a duty to disclose the material facts.

It must be proven that the person making the misrepresentation knew that it was false. This is known as scienter. If the person did not actually know that the statement was false, he may still be liable for negligent misrepresentation.

The statement must be made with the intent to induce reliance. The statement must be intended to get a person to do something.

The plaintiff must have justifiable relied on the misrepresentation. Justifiable reliance means that a reasonable person would have accepted the statement and acted on it the same as the plaintiff. Opinions are usually sufficient statements which can not be justifiably relied upon. In fraud actions, the statements can be relied on by persons other than the ones to whom they were made and liability will still exist.

The remedies for fraud are:

1. recision of any contract entered into,
2. reaffirmation of any contract but damages to compensate the plaintiff for injuries sustained, and
3. punitive damages for the fraud.

34. WHAT IS NEGLIGENT MISREPRESENTATION?
Negligent misrepresentation is similar to fraud except that:
1. the misrepresentation was made without knowledge of its falsity,
2. the misrepresentation was made by the defendant in a business or professional capacity, and
3. the misrepresentation can only be relied on by the person to whom it was actually made. Except for these changes, negligent misrepresentation is treated the same as fraud. There must still be the elements of justifiable reliance, causation of injury and damages in order to recover an award.

As with fraud, the remedies are either rescinding a contract or affirming the contract an suing for damages. Punitive damages are rarely awarded except in situations of such extreme gross negligence that they border upon intentional conduct.

35. WHAT IS NEGLIGENCE?
Negligence is the most common tort. It is the breach of the normal standard of care owed to the world in performing an act which causes the actual and proximate injury to another.

By duty of care it is meant that everyone owes the duty to everyone else to conduct himself in such a way as to not injure anyone else or their property. That duty of care is breached when a perform acts in such a manner as to result in another person being injured.

The requirement of the breach causing the actual injury of another is met when as a result of the defendant's actions another person is injured.

The issue in negligence for many cases is whether the defendant's actions proximately caused the injury. Was the breach sufficiently connected to the plaintiff's injuries so that the defendant should beheld accountable? If not, then there is no liability. Actions by third parties may intervene and cut off liability to a defendant or a long delay between the time of the breach and the injury may cut off the liability.

These are issues for the court or jury to decide.

36. WHAT IS CONTRIBUTORY NEGLIGENCE?

Contributory negligence is a defense to a charge of negligence against a defendant. Every person is held by law to owe himself a duty of care that is to conduct himself in such a way as to not injure himself. Therefore a person who violates that duty and contributes to his own injury because of another person's negligence has committed contributory negligence. For example if both drivers are speeding and have an accident, then one driver sues another then the contributory negligence of the plaintiff for speeding is a defense for the other driver.

Contributory negligence is not a defense to an intentional tort. If a driver had intentionally crashed his car into the other driver's car, the fact that the other driver was speeding is no defense whatsoever.

In some states, contributory negligence is a complete bar to recovery of damages. In such a state neither driver would be able to sue the other for damages if both drivers negligently got into an accident.

Acts that may constitute contributing negligence are:
1. failure to discover or appreciate a risk which would be apparent to a reasonable man,
2. an inadvertent mistake in dealing with a recognized risk, or
3. recognizing the danger or risk and still exposing oneself to it. For example, a person that gets in a car with an obviously drunk driver may be found to be contributorily negligent for any injuries suffered in an accident. In such as instance, the person's conduct may be such as to indicate the consent or willingness to accept the danger posed by the defendant's conduct. As such, the contributory negligence defense and the defense of assumption of the risk overlap.

While contributory negligence is a defense against the ordinary negligence of the defendant, it is not a defense when the defendant actually intended to inflict harm. The defense of contributory negligence has never been applied to intentional torts such a s assault and battery or false imprisonment.

Just as the defense of contributory negligence is not available for an intentional tort, it is also not available when the defendant's negligence was so great as to be characterized as "wanton", "reckless" or "willful". In these instances, the defendant's is so grossly negligent and such a departure from ordinary standards of conduct that the possibility of causing an injury is so great that the act is almost intentional.

Most states permit recovery in case where there was contributory negligence provided that the defendant was over 50% at fault.

37. WHAT IS COMPARATIVE NEGLIGENCE?

In a few states, including California, a defense of comparative negligence exists to reduce the award of damages recoverable where the plaintiff was also negligent.

In such states, the plaintiff's damages are calculated and then the defendant's percentage of blame is assessed. The defendant is then assessed his percentage of liability for the plaintiff's injuries. In the case where two speeding drivers have an accident, if the plaintiff suffers $60,000 damages and is 40% at fault the defendant's liability is 60% or $36,000.00.

38. WHAT IS ASSUMPTION OF THE RISK?

Assumption of the risk is the defense whereby the plaintiff is denied recovery for his injuries if he knowingly assumed the risk of the danger of the defendant's acts. This assumption may be expressed or implied. To have assumed the risk, the plaintiff must have known of it and voluntarily assumed it.

If the plaintiff had no other alternative but to accept the risk then the assumption is not voluntary. Knowledge of the risk may be implied form the circumstances if the risk is obvious to a reasonable person. A person entering a construction site with signs clearly posted calling for hardhats has assumed the risk for injuries easily prevented had he or she worn a hardhat.

39. WHAT IS STRICT LIABILITY?

Strict liability is the legal theory that persons engaged in certain conduct have an absolute duty to perform that duty in a safe manner and if that duty is breached the person is liable for the damages proximately caused.

Strict liability surrounds possession of dangerous or wild animals. The owner of such animals is strictly liable for the damages they cause unless the injured person did nothing to bring on the attack.

Strict liability does not exist for domestic animals unless an owner knows of the dangerous propensities of the animal. In most states this means a dog is allowed one free bite before the owner is held liable for the dog's bite. Some states make an owner totally liable for all unprovoked attacks of a dog.

A person engaging in an especially hazardous activity such as blasting, is strictly responsible for the damages he causes regardless of how careful he is. Even though a reasonable person would have said a person did everything possible, if the activity results in damage to another, then the person is liable.

Assumption of the risk is a defense and contributory negligence may be a defense if the plaintiff actually knew of the danger in the defendant's conduct.

40. WHAT IS PRODUCTS LIABILITY?

Generally, a manufacturer is liable for the damages caused by a product that has a defect making it unreasonably dangerous when used in the manner that it was made to be used, such as a television that shocks when simply plugged into an electrical outlet.

The theories for products liability are
1. Breach of warranties both express and implied. The implied warranties are fitness for use and merchantability (that it is generally fit for ordinary purposes,)
2. Negligence in the manner it was designed or manufactured, and
3. Strict liability.

The defenses are assumption of the risk, contributory negligence and lack of privity (that the person injured was not the purchaser or a member of the purchaser's family). In some states, some or all of the these defenses are available to some or all of the theories of product liability. However, if the injuries were caused by a defect in the product rather than a foreseeable misuse of the product, a defect recovery of damages usually occurs.

41. IS THE OWNER OF REAL PROPERTY LIABLE FOR INJURIES SUFFERED BY A TRESPASSER?

The majority of states hold that a property is not liable for injuries suffered by an unknown or undiscovered trespasser. A trespasser is someone who has entered upon the property without permission or privilege.

Once an owner has discovered the presence of the trespasser, then the owner is under a duty to exercise ordinary care to warn the trespasser of artificial conditions on the property which pose a risk of serious bodily harm.

Most states treat anticipated trespassers the same as discovered trespassers. An anticipated trespasser situation arises when the owner knows or should know of the presence of trespassers on the land.

42. WHAT IS AN ATTRACTIVE NUISANCE?

Most courts require landowners to use ordinary care to avoid reasonably foreseeable risks of harm to children by artificial conditions on the property. The requirements for liability are:
1. There is a dangerous condition on the property, such as a swimming pool or a large pile of debris.
2. The owner knows or should know that children frequent the property.
3. The condition of the property is dangerous because of the children's ability to appreciate the danger.
4. The expense of remedying the situation is slight compared to the risk of injury to the children.

43. CAN THE FEDERAL GOVERNMENT BE SUED FOR TORTS?

The federal government has complete immunity from lawsuits unless it waives that immunity. The Congress has waived immunities for unintentional torts when it implemented the Federal Torts Claims Act.

The Act makes the U.S. liable under the local laws of the state where the tort occurs, for the negligent or wrongful acts or omissions of federal employees committed in the scope of their employment "in the same manner and to the same extent as a private individual under like circumstances."

The federal government has expressly refused to waive liability for an intentional tort committed by a federal employee.

44. WHAT IS RES IPSA LOQUITOR?

Res ipsa loquitor is Latin for "The thing speaks for itself." It is a legal doctrine sometimes evoked in negligence actions to support liability. Under this doctrine, no proof of negligence need be proven beyond the incident itself. The injury suffered is presumed to have been caused by the negligence of the defendant when the following conditions are met:

1. The event causing the injury, such as an airplane crash, does not usually occur in the absence of negligence,
2. Other causes of the event are eliminated by the evidence,
3. The indicated negligence is within the scope of the defendant's duty to the plaintiff, operate the airplane safely. In short liability is presumed in those circumstances where it is the only explanation for the injury.

45. WHAT IS ADULTERY?

Adultery is the voluntary sexual intercourse of a married person other than his or her spouse. It was, at one time, a crime throughout the United States. It still remains an absolute ground for divorce.

In some states, the spouse of an adulterous spouse may still sue the person committing the sexual intercourse for criminal conversion. The adulterous spouse's consent is not a defense by the third party.

11
PROBATE

11. PROBATE

Probate is the legal term given to the process used to determine who will inherit the estate of deceased person when the decedent did not engage in any probate avoiding estate planning. Probate law is, in fact, the only area of law that is gradually fading out of existence. Revocable trusts have been steadily eliminating the need for probates. If all of person's estate is placed into a revocable trust, then there is nothing left for the heirs to have to probate upon the owner's death.

A revocable trust has the advantages over a probate of:
1 cost-it is much cheaper
2 time - the property passes immediately upon the owner's death rather than waiting up to a year for a probate and
3 secrecy - a trust is not a public proceeding.

As a general rule, anyone with an estate over $60,000 in value should consider using a revocable trust in place of a Will.

This chapter was written to assist the heirs of people who died without adequate estate planning. This chapter covers the basic questions concerning probate law and procedure. Using this chapter, the reader will be able to better understand and address those problems to be faced in any probate.

Probate Law is one of the most technically precise of all areas of law. Everything done in a probate is under the strict scrutiny of the court. For that reason, it is imperative that everyone involved in a probate understand exactly what is required and how the probate will be managed and conducted.

1. WHAT IS PROBATE?

Probate is the legal proceeding instituted in a probate court to determine how the estate of a deceased person is to be distributed. Probate is the legal mechanism whereby a court states who gets the estate of a deceased person.

A probate of a deceased person's estate is made necessary when the decedent did not do any estate planning beyond preparing a Will. Through appropriate estate planning, it is possible to avoid a probate altogether while providing for the immediate transfer of a decedent's estate to the designated heirs.

Probate proceeding are long, cumbersome, expensive and almost always totally avoidable if the proper estate planning is done. In recognition of the difficulties and expense in probating an estate, many states have enacted laws waiving probates or stream lining their procedures for small estates (usually under $60,000.) Usually, these summary probates involve nothing more than filing petitions with the court stating that the estate is too small to be effectively managed and that it should be distributed without administration to the heirs. Summary probate procedure, while fast, is only available for small estates. Above a certain amount in value, usually around $60,000, a regular full blown probate is required.

It is to avoid probate and all of its costs and hassles that a person should consider adopting an estate plan when his or her estate exceeds $60,000.

2. WHAT ARE THE FUNCTIONS OF A PROBATE COURT?

The probate of a deceased person's estate is handled through a probate court. It is a special court or department of a court of general jurisdiction and oversees the administration of the probate estate of a decedent.

The probate court is responsible for:
1. appointing the legal representative of the estate,
2. supervising the representative,
3. receiving and evaluating the inventories, accountings and other reports of the representative,
4. assuring that all bills, taxes and claims against the estate are paid by the representative,
5. overseeing the distribution to the the heirs,
6. closing the estate and releasing the representative from further responsibility. Until the probate court issues the final order of distribution, the estate remains under the control of the personal representative. It can take years for an estate to be closed and the assets distributed to the heirs.

3. WHAT IS A WILL?

A Will is the final testament of a person as to how that person wishes his or her to be distributed after death. A Will is totally revocable during the person's life.

A Will usually must be in writing and witnessed by two or more adult persons. The witnesses usually can not be heirs under the Will.

In some states, an oral Will made in immediate contemplation of death may be valid so as to direct distribution of the estate.

To be valid, the testator or creator of the Will must be legally competent to make a Will. That means the testator must be old enough to make the Will and not be insane or otherwise mentally impaired.

Unless a clause of the testator's Last Will specifically revokes all prior Wills, all of the Wills of the testator will be read together, by the probate court, in determining how the estate will be distributed. To avoid this problem, all Wills should have a simple clause revoking all of the testator's prior Wills.

A Will must be signed, dated and unless typed, it must be written entirely in the handwriting of the testator or an approved Statutory Will (a pre-printed Will authorized by statute in the testator's state of residence.)

4. WHAT IS A STATUTORY WILL?

In order to aid its citizens, many states have created statutory Wills. These statutory Wills comply with all of the terms for a valid Will in the state. They are pre-printed blank Wills in which the testators simply fill in, sign and then have notarized. Nearly all states have approved statutory Wills for their citizens. These statutory Wills are usually sold in stationery and office supply store.

A statutory Will still has to be probated the same as any other Will. It is important that whenever a pre-printed, do-it-yourself Will is used that the person pay particular attention to detail. A telling example of this is an actual case where a woman used a pre-printed Will. She was unmarried and had lived for thirty years with a man. She had a child whom she had not seen for over thirty years. In her Will, she left everything to her male companion. Unfortunately, the Will she had bought and used had a title Single Without Children. As a result, her son filed a claim as a pretermitted heir and was awarded her entire estate. The man, who had been with the decedent for thirty years, received nothing all because the woman chose the wrong pre-printed Will. Following this chapter is the Statutory Will used in California.

5. WHAT ARE THE TESTS FOR COMPETENCY FOR MAKING A WILL?

To be legally competent to make a Will, the following tests must be met:
1. the testator must be an adult or emancipated minor,
2. the testator must know the nature and quality of his or her estate,
3. the testator must know those who are the natural objects of his bounty (must know his or her family.)
4. the testator must mentally competent and not suffering from any insane delusions as pertains to the members of his or her family,
5. the testator must not be on mind altering drugs or alcohol when the Will was executed, and
6. the testator must know that he or she is making a Will.

If these elements are not met, then the Will is invalid no matter how many witnesses were present when it was executed. Competency is interesting because it does not have to be permanent. A person can be insane, have a temporary return to insanity, sign the Will and then a relapse into insanity. In such a case, the Will would still be valid.

The issue of competency most commonly arises when an elderly person creates a Will close to the time of death or while under some type of medical treatment that might cloud their judgment. Almost all Will contests arise under these circumstances whereby someone claims that the decedent was tricked or overreached in some way in order to get a Will signed.

6. WHAT IS A HOLOGRAPHIC WILL?

A holographic Will is a Will that is written entirely in the handwriting of the testator. Some states, such as Colorado and California, do not require a holographic Will to be witnessed. Most states require an holographic Will to be witnessed.

Most states will not accept a holographic Will as valid if there are any pre-printed or typed portions of the Will. Some states will permit pre-printed language in the Will if the material provisions are entirely in the testator's own handwriting.

To be as safe as possible, a holographic Will should have two more witnesses. However that means that it is no longer a holographic Will but an ordinary Will.

Generally, holographic Wills should not be used because they raise the potential issue of forgery. A case in point was the alleged holographic Will of Howard Hughes. The distribution of his estate of several billion dollars hinged on a purported unwitnessed holographic Will. After years of legal wrangling, the court ruled that the Will was a forgery but there are still some experts who believe it was not. (However, if it was real the issue of competency then exists because most sane people would not give away millions, if not billions to strangers.)

7. WHAT IS MEANT WHEN IT IS SAID A PERSON DIED INTESTATE?

A person is said to have died intestate if that person died without having executed a valid Will. The estate of a decedent, who had his or her Will declared invalid, will be treated as though the person died without a Will.

An unemancipated deceased minor's estate will be treated as though the minor died intestate, without a Will. Such minors can not write a valid Will.

If a Will of a decedent is declared invalid for any reason such as failure to be witnessed, having improper witnesses, being under age or lacking mental capacity, then the decedent's estate will be distributed as though the decedent died without ever having created a Will.

8. WHEN IS A WILL DECLARED INVALID?

A court will declare a person's Will invalid when:
1. the testator was an unemancipated minor, usually under eighteen years of age;
2. the testator did not sign it or have enough witnesses, the witnesses were heirs and those disqualified or the witnesses were minors. In most states, people named in Will as receiving property can not be witnesses and that will invalidate any of their signatures. As such, if there are not two, and in some states three, good witnesses then the Will is declared invalid;
3. the testator was mentally incompetent at the time the Will was executed, or
4. the testator was forced to make the Will as a result of fraud, duress or undue influence of another;
5. the oral Will was found invalid because it exceeded the statutory amount that can be passed by an oral Will, or

6. a holographic Will was not entirely in the handwriting of the testator or not signed or dated. When a Will is declared invalid, the last valid Will of the decedent will be admitted into probate. If there is no valid previous Will, then the decedent's estate will be distributed in accordance with the decedent's state's intestancy laws.

9. HOW IS AN INTESTATE ESTATE DISTRIBUTED?
Generally, when a person dies intestate the estate is divided among the immediate family as follows:
1. If there is a spouse and a child, then the estate is divided evenly between the two.
2. If there is a spouse and more than one child, one third of the estate usually goes to the spouse and the rest divided among the children.
3. If there are no children but a spouse and parents, the estate is usually split between the spouse and parents.
4. If there is no spouse or children, it goes to the parents.
5. If there is no parents, spouse or children, then the estate goes to any brothers and sisters. The Probate Court will keep searching for heirs until it finds someone to give the estate. An example of how intestancy works is how far back the courts had to go to find an heir to the Howard Hughes' estate. The estate ultimately went to a distant cousin, by adoption, several times removed. A Table of Consanquinity which defines the degree of relationship to a decedent (next of kin to inherit under the law of intestancy) follows this chapter.

10. WHAT IS COMMUNITY PROPERTY?
A small minority of states, California, Arizona, Idaho, Louisiana, New Mexico, Texas, Nevada, Washington, Wisconsin and to an extent Oklahoma have laws that make all property acquired by either spouse during a marriage, except by gift, devise or bequest to be jointly and equally owned by both spouses. Earnings by both spouses for their work during the marriage along with retirement benefits earned during the marriage also belong equally to both spouses. Upon death only one half of the community property is placed in the deceased spouse's estate. The only half remains the sole property of the surviving spouse.

When a spouse dies intestate, in some community property states, such as California, the surviving spouse automatically acquires title in the community property without the necessity of a probate.

11. HOW IS COMMUNITY PROPERTY PROBATED?
Since community property is considered by law to be owned equally by both spouses, a spouse's estate consists of only one half of the community property.

Either spouse can, through a Will, direct how his or her half of the community property would be distributed. A surviving spouse is not automatically entitled to the deceased spouse's share of the community property. For example, if Chet and Eileen are married in a community property state, say California, Chet could give his half of the community property and all of his separate property, by Will, to anyone, such as his children, and not his wife.

If the deceased spouse did not have Will, then the deceased spouse's half of the community property will be distributed by the state's laws of intestacy.

California has a special provision which holds that in the event a spouse dies intestate, all of the community property automatically passes to the surviving spouse. In the example above, if Chet died without a Will, then Eileen would inherit automatically, without the necessity of a probate, all of Chet's interest in the community property. A probate would still be needed for all of Chet's separate, non-community, property.

12. WHO IS AN HEIR?
An heir is someone who succeeds by operation of law to the estate of a person who died intestate. Each state identifies those persons that can be heirs under its laws of intestacy. A living person has no heirs, only "heirs apparent". Heirs must survive a decedent.

Generally, heirs are the spouse, parents, children and brothers and sisters (immediate family) of the decedent. In the event, none of the above survive the decedent, the laws of intestacy will extend heirship to the next of kin closest in relationship to the decedent.

13. WHO IS A PERSONAL REPRESENTATIVE OF AN ESTATE?
The person appointed by the court to act for the estate of a deceased person is the personal representative. There are two types of personal

representatives: the executor and the administrator.

The executor is a man and the executrix is a woman who is appointed by the court to represent the estate when the decedent created a Will. A person nominates an executor or executrix in the Will but it is the Court which does the actual appointment. If the Court is not satisfied with the decedent's chosen representative, it will appoint another.

An administrator is a man and an administratrix is a woman appointed by a court to administer an estate of a decedent who died intestate.

The personal representative is given statutory powers to handle the affairs of the estate in most transactions without court approval. The decedent can, through the Will, give the executor more powers and authority to act than are normally contained in the statutory powers conferred by the court.

Normally court approval must be sought before real estate can be sold. However, a testator may require that the real property be sold in the Will. In such a case, court approval is not necessary.

14. WHAT ARE LETTERS IN A PROBATE?

In a probate, the court appoints a personal representative. The appointment of a representative is manifested by a court document. The court order appointing an executor in an estate where there is a Will is called Letters Testamentary. The court order appointing an administrator in an estate where there is no Will (Intestacy) is called Letters of Administration.

The Letters are the official appointment of the personal representative to act for the estate. Once the Letters have been issued, the personal representative is legally entitled and indeed obligated to undertake the management of the affairs of the probate estate.

No one should ever deal with a person claiming to be the personal representative of an estate without first seeing the Letters of appointment.

15. WHAT IS DOWER?

Some states still have the ancient common law right of Dower. Dower is the wife's interest in the real property of the husband owned by him at any time during the marriage. The wife's right (Dower) was contingent on her surviving him and it became an absolute right after she did so.

The dower interest was a life estate in one-third of the real property in which the husband owned during the marriage. The wife's dower right could not be defeated by the husband during his life or by his Will and her interest was not subject to the claims of her husband's creditors.

Many states have abolished dower and replaced it with statutory shares in the deceased husband's estate.

16. WHAT IS CURTESY?

Some states still have the ancient common law doctrine of Curtesy governing the husband's statutory share in his wife's estate. Curtesy grants the husband an interest in the real property of the wife owned by her during the time of the marriage. The husband's right of curtesy was contingent on him surviving her and it became an absolute right when he did so provided a child was born during the marriage.

Curtesy entitled the husband to a life state in all of the wife's real property owned by her during the marriage. The husband's curtesy rights could not be defeated by the wife during her life or by her Will and was not subject to the claims of her creditors.

Most states have replaced the doctrine of curtesy with statutory shares for the surviving husband (between one-third and one-half), in the deceased wife's estate.

17. WHAT ARE THE COMMON LAW STATES?

Forty-one of the states and the District of Columbia follow the common law marital property rules. In these states, a person owns separately and apart from the spouse everything titled solely in his or her name and everything purchased with his or her own property, income or salary. In short, title to the property, if it has a title, controls who actually owns it. This is different from the law in community property states that hold that all property acquired during a marriage is owned equally except property acquired by gift, devise or bequest.

All except the following nine states are Common law states: Arizona, California, Idaho, Louisiana, Nevada, New Mexico, Texas, Washington, and Wisconsin.

18. WHAT IS THE STATUTORY SHARE
IN A COMMON LAW STATE?

Each state has its own laws determining the statutory share that a surviving spouse receives from a deceased spouse's estate.

In the following states, Connecticut, District of Columbia, Kentucky, Ohio and Rhode Island, the surviving spouse receives a one-third life estate. This is the right to use the property to obtain income but not the right to sell it

In the following states, the surviving spouse receives a fixed percentage of the deceased spouse's estate regardless of the number of the deceased's children:

Alabama	1/3 of augmented estate
Alaska	1/3 of augmented estate
Colorado	1/2 of augmented estate
Florida	30% of estate
Hawaii	1/3 of estate
Iowa	1/3 of estate
Maine	1/3 of augmented estate
Minnesota	1/3 of estate
Montana	1/3 of augmented estate
Nebraska	1/3 of augmented estate
New Jersey	1/3 of augmented estate
North Dakota	1/3 of augmented estate
Oregon	1/4 of estate
Pennsylvania	1/3 of estate
South Carolina	1/3 of estate
South Dakota	1/3 of augmented estate
Tennessee	1/3 of estate
Utah	1/3 of estate

In the following states, the percentage varies depending on whether the deceased had children:

Illinois
Indiana
Kansas
Maryland
Massachusetts
Michigan
Mississippi
Missouri
New Hampshire
New York
North Carolina
Ohio
Oklahoma
Vermont
Virginia
West Virginia
Wyoming

Usually, in such an event, the surviving spouse gets one-half of the estate if there are no children and one-third if there are children.

Georgia is a unique state that instead of a fixed share requires the deceased spouse's estate to support the surviving spouse for one year. This might or might not exceed the one-third of the estate usually given in other states.

19. HOW IS THE STATUTORY SHARE CALCULATED?

Most states base the statutory share on the AUGMENTED ESTATE of the deceased spouse. The augmented estate consists of everything owned by the decedent such as joint tenancy property, trust property etc. It is from the augmented estate that the amount of the statutory share is calculated. The probate court has the power to cancel joint tenancies and trusts created by the deceased spouse in order to give the surviving spouse his or her statutory share.

The purpose of using the augmented estate is to prevent the

deceased spouse from not passing to the surviving spouse his or her statutory share of the estate. However, not all states use the augmented estate and instead simply rely upon the property actually undergoing the probate.

20. IS AN ATTORNEY REQUIRED TO PROBATE AN ESTATE?

An attorney is not required to be employed in order to probate an estate. In a simple probate, a representative with normal intelligence and desire can handle the probate procedures quite well. There are a number of do-it-yourself probate manuals on the market which can assist a non-lawyer in the probate.

Notwithstanding the above, an attorney will be needed if there is any type of lawsuit against the estate by third parties, for example a creditor's claim or a Will-contest.

Most states have laws stating that only attorneys can bring or defend a lawsuit in court for another. Therefore, the personal representative, while the legal representative of the estate, would not be able to act as an attorney in court unless the personal representative was, in fact, a licensed attorney.

21. WHAT MUST A PERSONAL REPRESENTATIVE DO IN A PROBATE?

The personal representative, whether the executor or the administrator is responsible for performing the following duties in the probate:
1. Marshalling, which means assembling and inventorying, the assets of the estate,
2. Setting up a checking account in the name of the estate,
3. Arranges for appraisal of the asset of the estate both real and personal property,
4. Seeks payment on any insurance policies owed on the life of the deceased person,
5. Substitutes, as the representative of the deceased person, in any litigation pending at the time of death,
6. Files any litigation needed to collect debts owed to the estate or to maintain and preserve the estate,
7. Pays all bills including funeral bills and the medical bills for the last illness,

8. Prepare tax returns and pay all taxes both state and federal for the estate and the decedent,
9. Submits accounting to the court for review,
10. Petitions the court for authority to distribute to heirs,
11. Distributes to heirs, and
12. Applies to Court for final discharge terminating his authority to act and releasing him from liability. It takes usually a minimum of six months for a personal representative to do all of the above. It can take significantly longer. Some estates have been open for years. This is the prime factor in favor of revocable trust which can transfer property immediately subject only to the payment of appropriate estate and income taxes.

22. WHAT HAPPENS IF A WILL CAN NOT BE FOUND?
If a deceased person's Will can not be found, the general presumption by law is that the person destroyed it. In such a case, the estate will be distributed in accordance with the state's law of intestancy.

It is next to impossible to prove the existence of missing Will and what was in it to the satisfaction of a court. If an heir can do so and also the convince the court that the Will was inadvertently destroyed, then it might possibly distribute the estate as intended.

For example, if George made a Will and gave a copy to a friend and placed the original Will in his son's house which was destroyed by fire, then the court might distribute the estate as intended.

The evidence needed to prove to the Court that the deceased did not destroy a missing Will are so great that it is almost impossible to produce.

The better tactic is for the person to sign duplicate Wills with a general provision stating, "I have executed this Last Will and Testament in duplicate with one copy being held by my attorney. On my death if the Will in my possession can not be found, it is not to be presumed that I revoked it. The Will in the possession of my attorney can be admitted in probate and treated as though it was the Will in my possession."

23. CAN A COPY OF WILL BE PROBATED?
A Court will not accept a copy of a Will into probate unless it can be

shown to the satisfaction of the Court that the original Will was not destroyed by the deceased. The general presumption is that when a Will is missing it is to be presumed that the decedent revoked it.

Producing a copy of the Will proves what was in it but does not prove that the deceased did not revoke it. For that reason, it is better planning to execute the Will in duplicate with a clause that if the the Will in the deceased person's possession is not found it is not to be presumed to have been destroyed.

24. DOES PROBATE AVOID ESTATE TAX?

A common misconception is that probate exists as a means for the state or government to collect taxes. That is not the case.

Estate and inheritance taxes rates are based on the size of the estate and the relationship of the heirs to the deceased. It is irrelevant to the taxing entities whether a probate is conducted when determining the tax liability.

For example, if a person was giving $800,000 to his children, at his death, it makes no difference if the $800,000 came to t he children from a probate or through a revocable trust. There would be greater costs if the the estate was probated rather than passing it through a trust but the tax rates would be the same.

The tax is on the money distributed after death not whether or not it came from probate.

25. IS A JOINT WILL ENFORCEABLE?

Joint Wills are trouble and to be avoided. The problems are obvious. A married couple make a joint Will, then after one spouse dies the survivor wishes to change the Will, the ultimate beneficiaries, usually the children, object.

Whether the surviving spouse can alter a joint Will depends both on the language of the Will and the state law where the Will is probated. If the Will states that the after the death of one spouse the survivor can not amend or revoke it, most states would enforce that provision on contractual grounds. Those states take the position that the deceased spouse would not have executed the joint Will had he or she known that it could or would be changed after death.

If the Joint Will does not have the language that it is not revocable or amendable, then the Court will try to ascertain the intent of the parties when it was originally drafted and base its decision on that determination.

There simply isn't any real justification for running this type of risk. Individual Wills are relatively cheap, especially the statutory Wills, so cost should not be the determinative factor in deciding upon use of a Joint Will.

26. WHAT IS A CODICIL?

A Codicil is an amendment to a Will. It does not revoke the entire Will but it does changes certain provisions in the Will. The probate court will read the Will and all Codicils together so as to determine the final intent of the deceased on the disposition of his or her estate.

A Codicil is in essence a mini-Will. It is prepared, signed and witnessed in the same manner as an ordinary Will. Particular care must be taken in writing a Codicil so as to spell out just what changes are to be made in a Will. If an heir is to be removed or added, for example, it must be clearly stated.

A Codicil should be kept together with the Will to assure that it will not be overlooked when the estate is probated. A Codicil is governed by the same rules as a Will. Therefore, if a Codicil is missing, it will be presumed to have been previously revoked unless conclusively proven otherwise.

27. CAN A PERSON CHANGE HIS WILL BY SIMPLY WRITING THE CHANGES ON THE WILL?

All changes to the Will must comply to the same formalities used in making a Codicil or new Will. A person who simply crosses out old provisions or writes in new clauses, draws into question the validity of the Will.

A person can revoke his or her Will at any time by another Will or simple destruction of the old Will. Some states would consider the writing of the new clauses as an effective revocation of the old Will yet ineffectual in creating a new Will.

A person should never write on a Will. All changes to a Will should be by a valid codicil or a new Will in accordance with the requirements of the state of domicile.

Given the ease in which new Wills can be created, especially Statutory Wills, there is no reason to risk invalidation of an existing Will and dying intestate, by writing on it, rather than just doing a new Will or Codicil.

28. CAN A PARENT DISINHERIT A CHILD?

Most states permit a parent to disinherit a child, that means prevent the child from receiving anything from the parent's estate. While possible, the intent to specifically disinherit a child must be spelled out. The law of all states presumes that a parent does not intend to disinherit a child unless specifically stated so in the Will. If a child is simply not mentioned in the Will, the Court will presume it was an error and award the child his or her intestate share of the estate.

Louisiana has several probate laws different from the rest of the nation. The reason is that while the rest of the nation derived its basic law from English Common Law, Louisiana derived its law from the French Napoleonic Code. Therefore in certain areas of law, it differs from the rest of the nation. Louisiana permits the disinheriting of a child only on one of twelve different grounds. Therefore, in Louisiana, a parent can not disinherit a child, no matter how specifically the intent to do so is stated in the Will unless one of the twelve grounds are met. These grounds run from a minor marrying without consent, to planning to murder a parent.

29. WHAT IS A PRETERMITTED HEIR?

A Probate Court will presume that a parent did not intend to disinherit a child unless it is specifically stated so in the Will. This comes into play in the pretermitted heir situation.

A pretermitted heir is an heir, usually a child, who is not mentioned in the Will but who would have inherited under the laws of intestancy if there had been no Will. When the Court finds the existence of a pretermitted heir, the court Will award that heir, his or her intestate share of the estate.

For example, Mary wrote a Will leaving her estate to her three children. Mary later had a child out of wedlock and died shortly thereafter. Mary's Will did not mention the new baby. However, the court will find the baby a pretermitted heir and award the baby her intestate share of the estate, one-fourth.

30. WHAT IS A PRETERMITTED SPOUSE?
As with a pretermitted heir, a court will presume that a deceased spouse did not intend to disinherit a surviving spouse unless the intent to do so is specifically stated in the Will.

A pretermitted spouse is an surviving spouse who is not mentioned in the deceased spouse's Will. In all states, a surviving spouse will inherit from a deceased spouse's estate, under each state's laws of intestancy, if there had been no clause in the Will disinheriting the surviving spouse. When the Court finds the existence of a pretermitted spouse, it will award that spouse, his or her intestate share of the estate.

For example, Mary wrote a Will leaving her estate to her three children. Mary then remarried and died twenty years later. Mary's Will did not mention the husband. However, the court will find the new husband a pretermitted spouse and award to him his intestate share of the estate, usually a third.

31. WHAT SHOULD BE CONSIDERED IN MAKING A WILL?
A person first should consider the following factors before making a Will:
1. What specific bequests, gifts, are to be made?
2. How should the remainder of the estate be distributed?
3. Who should be the executor of the estate?
4. Should a bond be required on the executor?
5. What powers should be given the executor? How much should the court supervise the executor?
6. Should adopted or step-children inherit from the estate?
7. Should a testamentary trust be established?
8. Who should be nominated as guardian for minor children?
9. Should any debts be canceled that are owed by heirs or will they be deducted from the inheritances?
10. If assets are to be sold to pay debts, is there a priority as to how they will be sold? No Will should ever be created without first giving full consideration to the above. It simply makes no sense to leave such important matters to be decided by a judge who has no understanding of the decedent or the decedent wishes.

32. WILL A DIVORCE CUT OFF AN EX-SPOUSE'S INTEREST IN A WILL?

A few states, like California, have enacted laws that specifically prevent an ex-spouse from inheriting under a deceased ex-spouse's Will which had been drafted at the time of their marriage.

However, some states do not have such laws. In such states, an ex-spouse will be entitled to share in the estate because the decedent failed to rewrite the Will. The courts, in these states, take the view that decedent must have still wanted to make gifts to the ex-spouse because the Will was not changed. Based on that rationale, those courts will honor that perceived intention.

No one should ever assume that a divorce removes the rights of the ex-spouse to inherit under a Will. In cases of a divorce, a new Will or a Codicil should be drafted to specifically state that the ex-spouse is not inheriting under the Will.

In fact, a new Will should be written as soon as the divorce papers are filed. It's rare, but not uncommon, for a person to die during a divorce (in fact its been the basis of many mystery movies). In such an instance, the marriage is still in effect and surviving spouse receives property under the deceased spouse's old Will even though if the divorce had been granted the Will would have been invalidated.

33. WHAT RIGHTS DO STEPCHILDREN HAVE IN A STEPPARENT'S ESTATE?

Generally, step-children have no greater rights in a stepparent's estate than those of a total stranger. Unless the stepchildren were adopted, which then makes them the same as biological children under the law, step-children are viewed as strangers for inheritance purposes.

A stepchild may not be a pretermitted heir and has no right of inheritance under the law of intestancy. California has created a novel statutory provision that permits a person to claim a de facto adoption if certain elements are met. California requires that there be a parent-child relationship between the people and that an adoption was not possible because of some legal impediment. If these elements are met, the court will treat the person the same as an adopted child and award him or her an intestate share of the estate.

34. WHEN SHOULD A WILL BE CHANGED?

Unless changed, once a Will is drafted it is valid forever. As time goes on, a person's needs and circumstances change. A Will drafted years earlier may no longer fulfill the current needs and desires of the person. In such instances, a Will should be changed to reflect the true intent of the person.

The following changes in a person's life should immediately cause a review of the person's Will:

1. A change in marital status. Marriage makes the new spouse a pretermitted heir. A divorce, as stated above, might not cut the ex-spouse out of the Will.
2. Children are born or adopted. State laws allow unmentioned children to claim a portion of an estate as pretermitted heirs. However, these children might not receive under State Law what the decedent would have given them.
3. Stepchildren. In most states, stepchildren of a deceased have no rights to inherit under a stepparent's estate. Therefore, if a stepparent wishes to make dispositions to a step-child then that intent must be specifically stated in a Will.
4. The value of the estate changes so that the earlier gifts were too much, too little or there is now enough to give to others as well.
5. The intended heirs, executors, guardians or trustees have died.
6. Changes in estate or inheritance tax laws that make changing the Will advisable to save on taxes.
7. The necessity for a testamentary trusts for the surviving spouse or children no longer exists. Generally, a Will should be reviewed every few years for possible changes. Besides the changes above, tax laws change frequently and Wills should be reviewed to ascertain their effect on the estate.

35. WHAT IS AN ANCILLIARY PROBATE?

An ancilliary probate is a probate in a state other than one that was the decedent's permanent residence. Every state is responsible for probating the real and personal property located within it. This means that if a person owned property located in more than one state, then a probate may be required in each such state in addition to the state of the decedent's domicile. For example, George died with a home in Georgia and Alabama. In such a case, probates must be opened in both Georgia and Alabama for the houses in each state.

Additional problems may arise, if the states have differing requirements for a valid Will. For example if the domicile state requires two witnesses but the state with the ancilliary probate requires three witnesses, the Will may be invalid in the ancilliary probate state and the property located therein distributed by its law of intestancy.

36. WILL JOINTLY HELD PROPERTY BE SEIZED BY TAXING AUTHORITIES?

Some, but not all states, will freeze jointly held property such as bank accounts, real estate and brokerage accounts until the taxing entities for the state have had time to assess the value of the decedent's interest in the property. New Jersey and South Carolina, for instance, require ten day's written notice to the their taxing agencies before securities, deposits or assets of a decedent may be transferred, even to a joint tenant, outside of a probate.

In the states that freeze the assets pending a tax determination, a limited amount may nonetheless be transferred to a spouse or children without having to give the required notice. New Jersey permits up to $5,000 to be transferred to the surviving spouse without having to wait the required ten days.

The purpose of permitting limited transfer for use by the family is keep the spouse and family from destitution while the taxing authorities determine what amount of tax, if any, is owed. It is markedly unfair, in some situations, to seize the joint property of one person merely because the other joint tenant died. For that reason, the notice period is usually small.

37. WHAT IS A WILL CONTEST?

A Will Contest is a legal proceeding whereby some person, usually an heir or beneficiary of a Will, attacks or contests the validity of a Will or a distribution made under it.

A Will Contest results in a trial before the court to determine if the the Will was validly executed and if it should be enforced. The main contentions for contesting a Will are:
1. improper execution,

2. lack of competency,
3. lack of intent to make a Will,
4. pretermitted spouse,
5. pretermitted heir,
6. fraud, duress or under influence.

If the Will is successfully contested, the Probate Court may invalidate the entire Will or only the challenged portion of it. If the entire Will is invalidated, then the last valid Will is reinstated. If there is no such valid prior Will, then the estate will be distributed pursuant to the laws of intestacy.

38. CAN A NONRESIDENT BE THE EXECUTOR OF WILL?

Nearly all states permit nonresidents to serve as executors for probates in their states. However, some states have placed special restrictions on the out of state executors. In some states, out of state executors must post a bond even though the Will may have waived it. Other states, such as Wyoming require the out of state executor appoint a resident of the state as an agent to accept service of the court documents regarding the probate. Other states, limit the appointment of out of state executors to close relatives, brother, sister, parent of the deceased.

39. HOW MANY WITNESSES ARE NEEDED FOR A WILL?

Generally, only two witnesses are needed for a Will but a few states have rather eccentric requirements. Vermont for instance requires three witnesses. Louisiana follows the Napoleonic Code and requires three witnesses one of whom must be a notary public.

Remember that if a person has property out of state, an ancilliary probate may be required. In order to have the Will probated in another state, it must comply with that state's, as well as the decedent's home state's requirements for a valid Will. In the case of an ancilliary probate, if the Will does not comply with the ancilliary state's requirements, it will be declared invalid and t he estate distributed by the laws of intestacy.

40. HOW IS A WILL'S VALIDITY PROVEN?

All states require that proof be submitted that the decedent actually signed the Will. To do that, some states actually require some or all of the witnesses to come before the court and testify as to how the Will was signed. Other states, such as California, permit the witnesses to sign a declaration called a Proof of Subscribing Witnesses. In it, the witness swears under penalty of perjury that the witness actually saw the testator sign the Will.

A few states, like Louisiana, permit witnesses to sign the Will before a notary public. When this is done, the Will is said to be self-authenticating and the witnesses need not appear in court to validate their signatures.

When the witnesses are dead or unavailable and their signatures were not notarized, some states, California for instance, permit handwriting experts to testify that that the decedent signed the Will. This is a last resort and is difficult if the decedent had a long illness that affected his signature. For that reason, it is a good idea to use witnesses who are younger and in better health than the testator.

41. WHAT HAPPENS IF THE EXECUTOR NAMED IN A WILL DIES?

A Probate Court will not declare any Will invalid merely because the named executor dies or becomes unfit for any reason to perform the duties of an executor.

In such a situation, if the Will nominates a successor executor, the court will appoint that nominated person the successor executor providing he or she is qualified to act under the laws of the state where the probate is occurring.

In the event no successor executor is named or the named successor executor can not act for any reason, then the court will appoint an executor. The court appointed executor will have to post a bond unless it is the public administrator for the County.

In order to save the estate money, it is always a good idea for the Will to name at least one successor executor or executrix.

42. HOW ARE FUNERAL BILLS PAID?

Funeral bills are paid out of the estate. They are granted a priority over other bills. That is, they are among the first bills paid once the estate has been marshalled (assembled).

Many people today make their own funeral arrangements by paying for the service ahead of time. Many states, such as Ohio, Nevada, South Dakota and Washington require some, if not all, of the money paid under a pre-need plan to be placed in a trust fund. In the event the funeral home goes out of business, the money is returned to the client.

Sometimes, a person purchases a funeral policy to pay the funeral expenses. In such cases, the insurance company could pay insurance proceeds directly to the funeral home. Some states, such as Maryland and Tennessee require all payments on funeral policies to be made to the estate and forbid funeral homes being named the beneficiaries on such policies.

43. WHAT IS A CREDITOR CLAIM?

After a probate is opened, a notice of the probate proceeding is published in the newspaper of general circulation for the area where the decedent lived.

The purpose of this publication is to inform the creditors of the decedent that a death has occurred. The publication also informs the creditors that they have a fixed period of time ranging from four months to six months to file claims with the probate court for the amounts they claimed are owed. If any creditor that was given valid notice, either directly or by publication fails to file the claim within the statutory period of time, then the creditor is barred from recovery.

The cut off period enables the trustees to close down the estate as of a certain date. Otherwise, the probate would be open forever while old unpaid claims are being submitted.

Once filed, the executor must approve or reject a claim. If the claim is approved, it will be paid from the estate at the closing. If the claim is rejected, then the creditor has a fixed time to file a lawsuit to collect the claim or collection is permanently barred.

This creditor period is the main reason for the delay in closing a probate and distributing the estate. The advantage of the revocable trust is that the property is transferred immediately. The disadvantage is that creditor claims follow the estate. However it is going to be paid, it makes better sense to pay it immediately through a trust than wait months for the action to work its way through the courts.

44. WHAT HAPPENS IF THE ESTATE IS NOT LARGE ENOUGH TO PAY ALL OF THE CREDITORS?

If the estate is not large enough to pay all of the creditors, then the personal representative will first sell the secured property. The representative will apply the proceeds from the sale of the secured property to the secured creditors, those persons or entities holding loans secured by designated property. The proceeds from the sale of the secured property is applied to value of the secured creditors claims against the estate. If the proceeds are not enough to cover the claim, then the secured creditors will have an unsecured claim for the unpaid balance. Any amount received in the sale over the amount of the claim is paid to the estate.

After the secured creditors sell the secured property, all of the unsecured creditors then divide the remaining estate according to their percentage of claims against the estate. For example, Ed dies owing George $50,000 secured by a printing press. The executor of the estate sold the press for $30,000 and paid it to George. The remaining $20,000 became an unsecured debt of George against the estate. Ed's estate totaled $100,000 with $200,000 in unsecured claims. George's $20,000 unsecured claim is 10% of the total unsecured claims. Therefore George receives 10% of the unsecured estate which is $10,000.

45. WHAT IS A FAMILY ALLOWANCE?

Many states, like California, permit a surviving spouse or minor children to claim a fixed amount from their spouse or parent's estate free from all creditor claims.

This family allowance can be, in some states, in addition to anything bequeathed in the Will. In other states, if an election is made to take a family allowance, the heir can not take under the Will.

The family allowance can also be taken despite the terms of the Will. For example, the Will may specifically give the wife nothing but the wife may still be entitled to the family allowance under state law.

A family allowance was one for the means used by the states to replace dower and curtesy. In a small estate, the family allowance is the only way that the family may receive anything from the decedent's estate.

46. WHAT HAPPENS IF BOTH THE HUSBAND AND WIFE DIE AT THE SAME TIME?

A simultaneous death occurs when both the husband and wife die so closely in time together that it can not be ascertained with certainty who died first.

When there is a simultaneous death, each spouse's estate is distributed as though the other spouse had died first. In such a case, the husband's estate would pass to his heirs in the manner it would have passed had the wife actually died first. The wife's estate would pass to her heirs in the manner it would have passed had the husband actually died first. Jointly held property is divided equally among the two estates.

Every state except Alaska and Louisiana have adopted the Uniform Simultaneous Death Act which covers this situation. Many Wills avoid this problem altogether by simply containing clauses that requires the spouse or other heir to survive the testator by a fixed period of time in order to inherit, usually, sixty (60) days.

47. HOW LONG DOES IT TAKE TO SETTLE AN ESTATE?

The time to settle an estate varies from state to state and is dependent on whether there is litigation or any creditor claims to contend.

In California, it takes a minimum of six (6) months to close an estate. Four months is the statutory creditor claims period and the other two is the general period of public notice for opening an closing an estate.

Some states require that an executor actually close the estate within a fixed period of time or explain why not to the probate court. In Kansas, the mandatory time to close an estate is nine (9) months. In Wyoming, one year is time period to close an estate.

Where litigation is involved, years may pass before an estate can be closed. If a revocable trust is used, there is no estate to close because the trust estate passes immediately upon death to those next entitled to receive it under the terms of the trust.

48. IS THE PERSONAL REPRESENTATIVE RESPONSIBLE FOR PAYMENT OF TAXES?

The personal representative appointed by the court is responsible for the payment of all taxes owed by the estate from the assets in the estate.

If the personal representative distributes the estate before payment of all of the taxes due and owing, the representative may become personally liable for the taxes to the extend of the property transferred.

For example, if the representative distributes $50,000 to the heirs and the IRS then determines that an additional $60,000 is owed in taxes, the personal representative may be responsible for any portion of the $50,000 not recovered from the heirs.

49. WHAT CAN A PERSONAL REPRESENTATIVE DO TO LIMIT LIABILITY FOR TAXES?

Under the Internal Revenue Code, a personal representative can file a request with the IRS and sometimes the state taxing agency, for a final assessment of the taxes owed by the estate. Normally, the IRS has three years in which to assess additional taxes.

However, if the personal representative makes a request for a prompt assessment, the IRS has to complete the assessment within eighteen (18) months.

After the assessment is done, the personal representative can pay the tax, distribute the remaining estate to the heirs and be discharged without an liability for future taxes.

50. WHAT IS AN ACCOUNTING?

The personal representative is required to file an inventory with the court when the estate is opened. An inventory is a complete listing of every asset in the estate and its value.

While the estate is open, the representative is required to keep track of every penny received or spent by the estate. Before the estate can be closed, the representative is required to account for every penny that came in and left the estate. There must be a complete accounting for the estate.

All of the heirs can agree to waive an accounting. The accounting may be unnecessary because the heirs trust the executor or it may seem too costly given the difficulty or expense in performing it. Unless the accounting is waived, the estate will not be closed without one.

51. WHAT IS THE FINAL JUDGMENT OF DISTRIBUTION?

After the accounting has been performed and either accepted by the court or waived by the heirs, the court will order distribution of the estate. In its final judgment, the court will order which creditor claims are to be paid and how the final distribution of the heirs is to be made.

The final judgment acts as a deed for real property. Recording the final judgment is the same as having received a deed from the personal representative for the real property distributed under the final judgment.

52. WHAT HAPPENS ON AFTER-DISCOVERED PROPERTY?
An estate can always be reopened if property not covered by the terms of the final judgment is discovered.

Many final judgments have what is called an omnibus clause which states how such after-discovered property is to be distributed so as as to avoid the necessity of reopening the estate. Generally such an omnibus clause states, "The remainder of the estate a long with any undiscovered property shall be distributed as follows: ..."

When an omnibus clause is used in the final judgment of the probate court, there is usually no reason to reopen the probate because of after-discovered property.

Finding after-discovered property may result in additional estate or inheritance taxes. The taxes go with the property. So, if additional taxes would be owed because of the existence of this newly discovered property, the heirs receiving the property will be responsible for the taxes to the extent of the value of the assets received from the estate.

53. WHAT HAPPENS IF AN HEIR CAN'T BE FOUND?
If an heir is to receive property from an estate but can't be found, then the Probate Court will order the property of the heir to be delivered over to the County Treasurer, County Administrator or other designated agent.

The agent will hold the property for the missing heir until the heir or a person acting for the heir or his estate applies for release of the property. Payment to the designated agent relieves the personal representative of further responsibility to the heir.

When the property consists of real or personal property, other than cash, the court may order the property to be sold, converted to cash and kept in an interest bearing account.

If the money in the bank account is not claimed within a fixed statutory period of time, which varies for each state, the money is then transferred over to the state as escheated property.

54. WHAT IS STEPPED-UP BASIS?

The basis (value for tax purposes) of property received from a decedent regardless of whether it comes from a trust or a probate is its fair market value as of the date of death. For example if a person bought a home for $10,000 and upon death it was worth $40,000, the basis of the property when the heirs receive it will be $40,000. If the heirs sell it for $40,000, no capital gain taxes will be due.

Community property is considered owned by both spouses and is given special tax treatment. Under federal law, when one spouse dies, the basis of both halves of the community property will be increased to fair market value. This is a great tax advantage. For example, if a couple bought a home for $20,000 that had increased to $500,000 upon the husband's death. The basis for the husband's share in the community property is increased to fair market value $250,000. Under the special treatment for community property, the wife's share is also increased to fair market value $250,000.00. As such, the surviving wife can sell the house for $500,000 without having to pay any capital gain taxes.

If the spouses held the house as joint tenants, then only the husband's half would have been increased to fair market value. The wife's basis for her half would have remained at $10,000. If the wife later sold the house for $500,000, she would have had to pay capital gain tax of $240,000 ($500,000 -$260,000 total basis).

The stepped-up basis for community property is therefore a great tax advantage over simple jointly held property status between spouses.

12
ESTATE PLANNING

12. ESTATE PLANNING

We all will die. That is the one of the two sad truths of life for which all are in agreement. Whether we come back in reincarnated form or pass or to a higher plane of existence, we will nevertheless travel to a realm where no one ever returns.

We can not take it with us. That is the second truth of life for which all nod their heads in agreement. Of course, that is not to say that people have no tried to do so. The Pharoahs of Ancient Egypt, the Mayans in Central America and the Celtic tribes in Europe all attempted and failed to take their worldly good with them.

So given these truths, what then is left for us to do? Lacking a philosophical bent, this chapter offers only a practical and pragmatic answers for the living. The only answer that makes sense is that if a person can not take the estate with him, then it should be given to those, after death, whom the person cared. For most people that means simply giving the estate to family members and loved ones. If the estate is going to be given away, then it makes sense to give it to loved ones rather than to strangers or the government in the form of unnecessary and avoidable taxes.

The purpose of estate planning is to help a person build an estate as large as possible during life and upon death to pass as much of it as possible to the loved ones. This chapter attempts to educate the user of the various types of available estate planning.

1. WHAT IS AN ESTATE PLAN?

An estate plan is a general term for the adopted procedure by which a person intends to preserve the assets of his or her estate during life and then distribute them after death.

The main considerations in estate planning are the avoidance of probate, reduction of estate and inheritance taxes and the quick distribution of the estate to the designated heirs.

A complete estate plan will consider methods for the preservation of the estate during life by maximizing income while reducing to the extent possible, given the circumstances of the individual, the amount of income taxes that must be paid.

2. WHAT ARE THE COSTS OF PROBATING A WILL?

The costs for incurred in probating a Will are large. A probate is usually one of the most expensive expenditures made by a person. An old joke, which is wryly true, is that if the person weren't already dead, the cost to probate his estate would kill him.

Probate costs include courts fees, appraisal fees, attorney fees and executor fees. Court costs and appraisal fees are modest, usually around $200 for an average estate. The real cost is for the attorney and executor fees.

The maximum amount of attorney and executor fees are set by statute and approved by the court. They are based upon the size of the estate (value of the property to be probated) and increases as the estate increases.

In California, for example, attorney and executor fees are calculated as follows:
1. Four percent (4%) of the first $15,000 maximum $600.00
2. Three percent (3%) of the next $85,000 maximum $2,550.00
3. Two percent (2%) of the next $900,000 maximum $18,000.00
4. One percent (1%) of the next $15,000,000 and one half a percent (.5%) thereafter.

An estate of $100,000 if probated in California would have have to pay maximum attorney and executor fees of $6,300.00, $3,150 each to the executor and attorney. This is a maximum fee. The attorney and executor can agree to take less or no fee at all.

The avoidance of probate fees is a major inducement for implementing an estate plan. When a revocable trust is utilized, there are no probate fees because the estate passes immediately to the designated beneficiaries in the trust. No court proceeding is needed to transfer the property of a trust so no attorney is needed.

3. HOW CAN PROBATE BE AVOIDED?

There are several means available for a person to utilize in order to avoid having to probate his or her property. The probate avoidance vehicle are:
1. Summary probate proceedings, if available, in the decedent's state. A summary probate is a abbreviated procedure for small estates or when the entire estate goes to the surviving spouse. Many states have

adopted special procedures to by-pass the expense and long delay in probating such estates.
2. Giving the estate away while alive,
3. Placing the property into joint tenancy with the proposed heirs. Upon death, title for the property passes immediately without probate to the surviving joint tenants. Real property held in joint tenancy passes to the survivors without a probate by the recordation of a notice of the death of a joint tenant.
4. Placing the estate into a revocable trust which passes the estate to the designated beneficiaries immediately upon the decedent's death. This is the most popular form of estate planning because it is fast and bestows the maximum amount of control and property over the estate.

In order to determine the type of estate planning best suited to an individual, the person must fully understand the size of the estate, how the person wishes to distribute it and the amount of control the person wishes to give up in order to effectuate the estate plan.

4. WHAT ARE THE DISADVANTAGES OF USING JOINT TENANCIES FOR AVOIDING PROBATES?

There are three main disadvantages in doing a joint tenancy:
1. Putting the property into joint tenancy is an immediate gift of half or more of the property. This means that property placed into joint tenancy becomes attachable to satisfy the debts of the other joint tenants upon the creation of the joint tenancy. For example, if a house was put in joint tenancy with a child and, as a result of a lawsuit, a creditor of the child gets a judgment, the creditor could seize and sell the child's half interest in the house.
2. There may be gift taxes due on the gift if the value of the gift exceeds $10,000.00 or the unified credit had been used up by previous gifts. (There is no federal gift tax on gifts to a spouse if the spouse is an American citizen.)
3. There is no stepped-up basis for property placed in joint tenancy. The basis of the property remains the donee is the same as in the hands of the person who made the gift. Whereas property obtained through a probate or a revocable trust has its basis stepped-up to fair market value basis and can be immediately sold without having to pay a capital gain tax. The main disadvantage in creating a joint tenancy is that half or

more of the property is given up immediately. An example is when a parent puts a house in joint tenancy with a married son. If the son gets a divorce, the wife might, in some states, be awarded the son's interest in the house, something the parent never intended.

5. WHAT IS A DURABLE POWER OF ATTORNEY?

A general power of attorney is a written document that gives a person called the attorney in fact the authority to act on the principal's behalf. A general power of attorney lapses and become invalid when the principal becomes incompetent. At the time it is needed most, when the principal is no longer to act for himself, a general power of attorney lapses, becomes invalid and the right of the attorney in fact to act for the principal ceases.

To address this situation, most states have adopted the Uniform Durable Power of Attorney Act. Under the Act, a durable power of attorney will continue in full force and effect even though the principal subsequently became incompetent. A durable power of attorney must contain specific language stating the intent of the principal that the power of attorney will continue during the period of incompetency and incapacity.

A durable power of attorney has the effect of eliminating and replacing the necessity of a voluntary conservatorship. A durable power of attorney can also give the attorney in fact the power to make all or just specific health care decisions for the principal in the event that the principal becomes unable to do so. A sample durable power of attorney form follows this chapter for reference. Durable power of attorney forms, for a particular state, can usually be purchased at office supply or stationary stores.

6. WHAT IS A LIVING WILL?

A Living Will is not a Will for probate purposes. Rather, it is a document that serves as directive to a treating physician and the world at large that the person executing it does or does not want to be kept alive using extraordinary means. A Living Will is used to ascertain the intent of the person in the event that he or she is unable to make the health care decisions at the time it is necessary to do so. A sample Living Will Declaration follows this chapter.

Many states presume a person wants extraordinary means to be used to kept alive and will order it to be used unless the pers on had previously made a living will stating the opposite intent. Living Wills should be used in addition with Durable Powers of Attorney for Health Care in order to assure that a person's wishes are most likely fulfilled in this most dire of situations.

7. WHAT IS A REVOCABLE TRUST?

A revocable trust is usually the best means of estate planning. The creator of the trust, called the Trustor, places his or her entire estate into the revocable trust. The trustor usually is also the trustee, the person who manages the estate and the prime beneficiary.

Upon the trustor's death, the person named, in the trust document, as the successor trustee takes over immediately without court approval being needed. Then depending on the terms of the trust, the new trustee either dissolves the trust and distributes the assets immediately in the manner designated in the trust document or continues to operate the trust in the manner directed by the trust document.

Since there is no probate, there is no probate costs incurred. The savings for the estate when a revocable trust is used will usually be several times the cost of the creation of the trust.

Because the trust is revocable, the trustor can at any time alter, amend or revoke it. If the trust is revoked the trust assets immediately return to the trustor. A sample revocable trust follows this chapter. This sample trust is just for use as an example only for a person dying without a spouse and survived by children.

8. WHAT IS A POUR OVER WILL?

A Pour Over Will is a special Will used in conjunction with a revocable trust. It places all property into the trust that the decedent forgot or failed to do while alive. Unfortunately, property not placed into the trust prior to the trustor's death may require a probate if the size of the assets are large enough that the summary procedures can not be used.

In a real case, the trustor forgot to place a piece of property in Hawaii into a California Trust which the trustor had created. The executor of the Pour Over Will was required to open a Hawaiian probate in order to get permission to put the property into the trust. Having to probate the non-trust property needlessly cost eleven thousand of dollars when the trustor could have done it during his life for just the cost of recording a deed into the trust, usually about $10.00.

Another example of the need for a Pour Over Will would be if a person hits a lottery for fifty million dollars and drops dead in the excitement. The Pour Over Will will place the money into the trust after it has been probated. Once placed in the trust, the money will be managed in accordance with the trust terms.

9. WHAT IS A LIFE INSURANCE TRUST?

A typical vehicle used in estate planning is the creation of an insurance trust. The trustor creates an irrevocable trust with someone else as the trustee and takes insurance policies out on his or her life. The ownership of insurance policies on the trustor's life is given to the trust and the trust is made the beneficiary of the insurance policies.

When the trustor dies, the insurance proceeds will be paid into the trust but the value of the insurance proceeds will not be included into the trustor's estate for estate tax purposes if the trustor lived more than three years after placing the policies into the trust.

Creating an insurance trust could save many thousands of the dollars in estate taxes by keeping the insurance proceeds out of the decedent's estate for tax purposes. For example, if the decedent had a $200,000 estate and a one million dollar insurance policy then the estate would be worth $1,200,000 upon the decedent's death. Since the federal government taxes any estate over $600,000, the remaining $600,000 in the estate will be taxable. If an insurance trust had been used, the one million dollars in insurance proceeds would not be included in the decedent's estate and thus not be taxable.

10. WHAT IS A MARITAL DEDUCTION?

Under federal law there is no federal gift or estate taxes on property transferred between spouses. This is an unlimited credit that has only has only two exceptions:
1. It must be an actual gift. If the gift is in trust then all of the income must go to the spouse.
2. The spouse receiving the gift must be an American citizen. Gifts to a non-citizen spouse are not eligible for for the unlimited deduction but

are are eligible for a $100,000 annual exclusion under Section 2523 of the Internal Revenue Code. Likewise property passing from an American spouse to an alien spouse, after death, does not qualify for an unlimited marital deduction either. Special tax rules apply for such transfers and a tax consultant should be consulted if the estate of the American spouse exceeds six hundred thousand dollars ($600,000.)

Therefore, a person can generally pass his or her entire estate to a surviving spouse without incurring any federal estate taxes. This may not ultimately be the best estate planning because if the property given to the surviving spouse boosts the surviving spouse's estate over $600,000 then upon the surviving spouse's estate will have to pay estate taxes. Any gift to a surviving spouse that would boost his or her estate over the $600,000 in value should be made after first using up the decedent's unified credit discussed below.

11. WHAT IS THE UNIFIED CREDIT?

Every person is permitted to transfer assets totaling $600,000 by either gift or death without incurring a gift or estate tax under federal law. For example, a person can give $275,000 in gifts while living and pass an estate of $325,000 after death without the estate having to pay any federal gift or estate taxes.

About half of the states impose their own estate and inheritance taxes. These taxes should also be a consideration in estate planning. The Internal Revenue Code permits a slight credit for state death taxes to be applied against the federal estate.

The significance of the $600,000 unified credit is that it permits a husband and wife to give to their children a total combined estate of $1,200,000 before incurring any estate taxes. A person giving his or her entire estate to a surviving spouse, is not taking advantage of the unified credit. Not using the unified credit is ill-advised when the surviving spouse's estate exceeds $600, 000.

12. WHAT IS THE ANNUAL EXCLUSION?

Under federal tax law, every individual may make an annual gift of $10,000.00 per year per person without incurring a gift tax or having the gift applied towards the $600,000.00 unified credit. A parent having four children could give $10,000.00 each for a total of $40,000 free of gift taxes. The advantage of making these gifts is that they provide a means to help reduce the size of the estate to below $600,000 and thus reduce if not eliminate federal estate taxes.

An alien spouse does not qualify for the unlimited marital deduction. In place of the unlimited marital deduction, an alien spouse is permitted to receive, as gift for the other spouse, one hundred thousand dollars ($100,000) per year tax-free.

13. ARE REVOCABLE TRUSTS VALID ELSEWHERE?
All fifty states and the federal government accept as valid a revocable trust. If the trust was validly created in the original state, then all the other states will honor and enforce it.

Provisions can also be placed into a trust document stating that the terms of the trust are to be administered by the laws of a certain designated state. If so, all states will apply the laws of the designated state in administrating the trust. Therefore even if the trustor moves to another state, the trust will still remain valid and in effect.

14. WHAT IS A QTIP TRUST?
A QTIP Trust is a special trust whereby the trustor's spouse is given all of the income from the trust with the principal being distributed to others, usually the children or grandchildren, upon the surviving spouse's death. QTIP stands for Qualified Terminal Interest Property and is a fancy name for property given to spouse in a certain type of trust.

A QTIP Trust gives the option to the surviving spouse to have the trust property treated as a gift to the surviving spouse for estate tax purposes. If the election is made, then the value of the trust will be treated as a spousal gift and exempt from tax under the unlimited marital deduction. On the surviving spouse's death, the value of the trust assets will be included in the surviving spouse's estate for determination of the surviving spouse's estate tax.

Depending on the size of the surviving spouse's estate it may or may not be good financial planning to make the QTIP election and have the value of the trust included in the surviving spouse's estate. For example if the surviving spouse's estate was $100,000 and the QTIP Trust was $1,000,000 and the unified credit of the deceased spouse had previously been used, making the election would save the trust from paying federal estate taxes until the surviving spouse dies. In the meanwhile, the surviving spouse could draw a higher interest from the investment of the pre-taxed $1,000,000. The disadvantage is that if the surviving spouse's estate grows greatly after making the election, more tax may ultimately be paid upon the death of the surviving spouse, than would have been paid if no election had been made.

15. WHAT IS AN A-B TRUST?

The A-B Trust is the common name give to the general type of revocable trust used by a married person with children and the trustor's estate exceeds $600,000.00. It is also called a marital trust or a by-pass trust.

The trust exists for the benefit of the trustor during his life. At the trustor's death, the trust is divided into two parts, the first $600,000 or the remaining unused unified credit whichever is smaller is placed into the B trust and the rest in placed in the A trust.

The sole beneficiary of the A trust is surviving spouse. The surviving spouse has ownership of the A trust and usually has the power to terminate it and receive the assets in her own name. Since assets in the A trust go to the wife, there is unlimited marital deduction, if the spouse is a U.S. citizen and therefore is not subject to federal estate taxes. Upon the surviving spouse's death all of the property in Trust A will be included in the surviving spouse's estate for calculation of estate taxes. For example, upon the husband's death, his two million dollar estate was divided $600,000 to Trust B and $1,400,000.00 to Trust A. Upon the wife's death, Trust A had grown to $1,700,000. In addition, the wife had $500,000 of her own estate. So, for tax purposes, the wife's taxable estate will be $2,200,000.00.

The beneficiaries of the B trust are the children. Income may be applied for the surviving spouse but the trust does not qualify for a marital deduction. It does qualify for a deduction to the extent of the trustor's unused unified credit. Thus there is no federal estate tax for this trust either. In the above example, if the assets in Trust B increased to $1,000,000 at the time of the wife's death, no estate taxes will be due because the property placed into the Trust was originally tax-free. If $800,000 was originally placed into Trust B, the excess $200,000 would be taxable. After the taxes are paid, no additional estate taxes will be charged against it upon the death of the wife.

16. WHAT PROPERTY CAN BE PLACED INTO A REVOCABLE TRUST?

All of the property of the trustor can and should be placed into the trust. Anything left out of the trust will have to be probated unless it is joint tenancy property, insurance policies with designated beneficiaries other than the decedent's estate or otherwise qualifies for summary probate proceedings.

Any property that has a title must have the title specifically changed over into the name of the trust. Merely stating in the trust agreement that such titled property is to be placed into the trust is insufficient to legally put the property into the trust.

A common example is when the trustor owns a home. Since a home has a title document, the title must be changed to make the owner trust. A quitclaim deed by the trustor to himself for herself as trustee of the trustee must be executed and recorded. This is simple to do and usually is done when the trust is created.

17. HOW IS A TRUST CREATED?

A trust is created very easily. The trust document is drafted usually by an attorney, and directs how the trust estate will be administered and distributed. The trustee acts in accordance with the terms of the trust.

The trustor and trustee must both sign the trust document. If the trustor is also the trustee he or she signs the trust agreement twice in both capacities.

The final requirement is that that trust be funded. Funding the trust requires that the trustor place into the trust all of the property the trustor wishes to be in the trust.

Personal property that does not have a title such as a television or furniture is transferred automatically by a statement in the trust document stating the intent of the trustor to put into the trust all personal wherever located. Property that has a title, such as a house, must have the title specifically changed to make the trust the owner. Merely stating an intent to place the house or other property that has a title into the the trust is insufficient. The only way to put property that has a title into a trust is to actually change the title on the property so that the trust is listed on the title documents as the owner.

18. WHAT ARE THE INCOME TAX EFFECTS FOR THE TRUST?

A revocable trust is considered for tax purposes a grantor trust. A grantor trust, under the Internal Revenue Code is a type of trust created for the benefit of the person creating it. In such a trust, all of the income from the trust is attributed to the grantor for tax purposes.

Since all of the income is attributed to the grantor, as long as he or she is alive, the grantor remains liable for the income taxes. A revocable trust does not save the grantor any money on income taxes because it is not designed to do that. A revocable trust exists to avoid probate and save estate taxes not income taxes.

19. WHAT IS A GENERATION SKIPPING TRUST?

A generation skipping trust is a trust that, as the name implies, skips one or more generations. A trust by a grandparent for grandchildren that by-passes the parents is a generation skipping trust. The main exception is when there are no parents surviving the grandchildren, then it is treated as a direct trust.

A generation skipping trust is complicated tax-wise. It is easy to create but because of the inherent tax consequences, a generation skipping trust should not be created without first consulting a tax advisor. Generally, one million dollars can be placed in a generation skipping trust without incurring an estate or gift tax (provided the uniform credit had not been used previously).

20. HOW IS A GENERATION SKIPPING TRUST TREATED?

A million dollars may be transferred in a generation skipping trust tax free. Any amount placed in the trust over one million dollars is taxed at a rate of 50% when ever a distribution is made. A distribution is deemed to have been made when the parents of the grandchildren die or the grandchildren receive money from the trust. The purpose of this law is to avoid amassing huge estates by not paying taxes. These trusts only affect very wealthy people.

The tax consequences of a generation skipping trust are so great no one should consider funding one with over $600,000 without speaking with a tax advisor.

21. WHAT IS THE ESTATE TAX RATE?

The federal estate tax is graduated and increases as the size of the estate increases over the unified credit. For example, a taxable estate of $100,000 has a tax of $23,800.00. A taxable estate of $250,000 has a tax of $70,000. A taxable estate of $500,000 has a tax of $155,800.00. A taxable gift of $2,500,000.00 has a tax of $1,025,800.00.

22. WHAT ARE GIFT TAXES?

The federal gift tax is graduated and increases as the size of the gift increases over the unified credit. For example, a taxable gift of $100,000 has a tax of $23,800.00. A taxable gift of $250,000 is $70,800. A taxable gift of $500,000 has a tax of $155,800.00. A taxable gift of $2,500,000 has a tax of $1,025,800.00.

23. DOES A TAX RETURN HAVE TO FILED FOR A GIFT?

A gift tax return is required to inform the IRS of any gifts in excess of the annual exclusion ($10,000.00) per person. In other words if a gift of $11,000.00 is made to a son, a gift tax return must be filed to show that a taxable gift of $1,000.00 was made. This will either be deducted from the unified credit of $600,000 or the tax will be paid by the donor.

24. CAN A TRUST BE IRREVOCABLE?

A trust can be made irrevocable and sometimes it makes good financial estate planning to do so. In order for assets in a trust not to be included in trustor's estate, the trustor must not have control over the trust or the reasonable expectation that the t rust will revert back to the trustor.

If the trust is revocable, then the trustor has a great deal of control over the trust. For that reason, the fair market value of the assets of the trusts will be included in the trustor's estate upon death for estate tax calculations.

If the trust is made irrevocable and the trustor has no control over the trust, then upon his or her death the assets in the trust including appreciation all appreciation in value will not be included in the trustor's estate. This could pass a great deal of appreciation to the trustor's heirs without having it taxed.

It is because a life insurance trust is irrevocable that the proceeds of the insurance on the decedent are not included in his or her estate.

Gifts made within three years of a person's death will normally be included into the person's estate for tax purposes even if gift taxes had been paid on the gift (credit will be given for the gift taxes that had previously been paid.)

25. CAN A CONSERVATOR CREATE A REVOCABLE TRUST FOR THE CONSERVATEE?

Some states, like California, have statutes that permit a conservator to make a revocable trust for the conservatee. Such states usually require that the distribution of the trust be the same as the terms of the Last Will and Testament previously drafted by the conservatee.

The purpose behind the revocable trust must be to avoid probate and not to change the distribution of assets that the conservatee had decided upon when he or she were competent. The situation may be different if the conservatee did not have a Will. In such a case, the trust must be in accordance with the state's laws of intestancy. The estate must be distributed in the same manner that it would have been distributed if a probate had occurred.

26 WHEN MUST A FEDERAL ESTATE TAX RETURN BE FILED?

The federal estate tax return Form 706 is required to be filed whenever the decedent had an estate greater than $600.000. The requirement to file the estate tax return does not depend on whether there will be any taxes due or if a probate is necessary. As long as the estate is greater than $600,000, the tax return has to be filed.

For example, a tax return would still have to be filed even if the entire estate was going to the surviving spouse under a trust and was entirely exempt from estate tax as a result of the unlimited marital credit.

Likewise, a federal estate tax return would have to be filed even if the entire estate was being given to charities exempt from tax under the Internal Revenue Code.

27. WHEN DOES THE TRUST TERMINATE?

A trust must terminate within twenty one years after the death of someone alive and mentioned in the trust when it was created. In other words, the trust must be totally distributed within twenty one years of the death of the last person alive when the trust was created. This is known as the Law of Perpetuities.

If it appears that the trust would continue after the death of the person mentioned in the trust document, the trust is invalid. Clauses are usually inserted in the trust document to guarantee that the trust will not violate the Law of Perpetuities.

Except for the Law of Perpetuities, a trust terminates whenever the trustor stated it would terminate under the terms of the trust agreement. Usually, it terminates on the death of the surviving spouse or the death of the trustor's last child.

28. WHAT IS A CHARITABLE GIFT FOR INCOME TAX PURPOSES?

Under the federal tax code, a person, while living, can make gift to a qualified charity and receive an income tax deduction for the gift. Gifts made by a decedent's estate do not qualify for a charitable income tax deduction.

The maximum deduction is 50% of the taxpayer's adjusted income for the year with the balance of the gift being carried over for the next five years.

Where the gift is appreciated property instead of cash, the amount of the deductible is reduced to 30% rather than the 50% unless special elections are made. Because of the complexity of the tax law in this area, any large gifts to a charity should only be made after consulting a tax professional.

29. HOW MUCH IS THE CHARITABLE DEDUCTION FOR GIFTS MADE AFTER DEATH?

Charitable gifts made by a decedent after death, regardless of whether they were made through a will or trust, are allowed full deductions of fair market value from the decedent's estate for federal estate tax purposes. As a result, federal estate taxes are reduced when charitable gifts are made as opposed to gifts to ordinary persons or entities.

For example, if a decedent had an estate worth $1,000,000 and gave $400,000 to a charity then the decedent's estate would deduct that $400,000 gift leaving an estate of $600,000. The $600,000 would be equal to the decedent's unified credit so there would be no federal estate tax owed.

30. WHAT IS A CHARITABLE REMAINDER TRUST?

A charitable remainder trust is an inter vivos (living) trust, a trust made during the lifetime of the trustor. Property is placed into a irrevocable trust with a charity as a beneficiary. The trustee, who is usually the charity, is instructed to pay fixed percentage of the trust assets to the trustor for the life of the trustor.

The trustor is given a tax deduction for the value of the gift to the charity. The trustor pays ordinary income tax on the payments received from the trust.

The gift to the charity is tax free. Since the charity is tax exempt, it can sell the appreciated property without having to pay capital gains. The charity can reinvest the proceeds of the sale and pay the trustor from the interest on the investment. Because the charity can invest the whole amount without paying capital gains, it can generate more interest income from the sale than the person who transferred it to the trust. For this reason, it is better to place highly appreciated property that is not earning a gr eat deal of income, such as idle land, into the trust. The return that the trustor gets, from the trust, is higher than if the assets had been sold and reinvested by the trustor because capital gain taxes would have had to be paid on the trustor's sale of the highly appreciated property.

This is an excellent vehicle for estate planning for well to do people. Life insurance policies can be bought with the trust payments that will replace the value of the property transferred to the trust.

31. WHAT ARE TAX FREE MUNICIPAL BONDS?

Most states issue bonds at relatively low rates, around six percent (6%) to help pay for their government services, hence the name municipal bonds.

Most such bonds are both federally and state tax exempt. Because they are tax exempt, they can be an excellent investment for a person that is paying taxes. For example a tax free bond at 6% bought by a person in a 33% total tax bracket would be equivalent to a 9% taxable bond. Given the fact that most municipal bonds are backed by the full face and credit of a government entity and rated for risk they may be more safe than private bonds. However the buyer should consult with a broker before buying such bonds.

Municipal bonds may be bought directly from the government in a bond fund operated by a brokerage house.

32. WHAT IS A ZERO COUPON BOND?

A zero coupon bond is a bond issued by the Treasury as a Strip Bond, a Corporation or a Municipal at a deep discount and can only be redeemed at a specified date in the future for a specified amount. For example, a $60,000 corporate zero coupon bond might mature in fifteen years. It would be sold for $17,000.00

The purchaser of the bond pays tax each year on the accrued but unpaid interest in the bond unless the bond is a tax free zero coupon municipal bond.

33. WILL PUTTING REAL PROPERTY INTO A REVOCABLE TRUST TRIGGER A REASSESSMENT OF PROPERTY TAXES?

Placing a piece of real property into a trust should not trigger a reassessment of property taxes because the transfer is not really a sale or conveyance of the property.

The property is put into a revocable trust which the owner can terminate at any time and receive back. California law specifically states that merely placing real property into a revocable trust for estate planning purposes does not trigger reassessment as long as the grantor is alive.

This is just common sense. Reassessment occurs when there is a change of ownership. Placing the real property into a revocable trust is not really a change in ownership because the trustor still controls it and can, at any time, have the property returned to him.

34. CAN CREDITOR ATTACH A TRUST FOR PAYMENT OF THE TRUSTOR'S DEBTS?

Most states will allow creditors to attach any revocable trust for the payment of debts or other obligations owed by the trustor.

The rationale for the allowing the attachment is that the trustor has effective ownership of the trust assets by the fact that he can, at any time, revoke the trust and receive the property in his own name. A court has the power to order the trustor to terminate the trust and receive the assets back so that the trustor's creditors can be paid.

35. CAN CREDITORS OF A BENEFICIARY ATTACH ASSETS OF THE TRUST?

Most trusts have clauses in them that state that the interest of the trust beneficiaries can not be attached to pay the debts or obligations of any beneficiary. This provision is called a spendthrift clause.

Courts will enforce spendthrift provisions and deny any attachments, except in a revocable trust where the trustor is also the beneficiary whose trust interest is being attached.

If there is no spendthrift clause, then the trust can be attached to pay a beneficiary's debts. In addition, most states permit a beneficiary's share of a trust to be attached to pay spousal or child support obligations even if there is a spendthrift clause in the trust.

California has recently passed legislation stating that a spendthrift clause will not shield a trust from attachment for payment of a tort judgment against a beneficiary.

36. CAN A TRUST REPLACE A STATE'S DOWER OR CURTESY LAWS?

If the provisions of a trust are in conflict with a state's law regarding how much of a decedent's estate goes to the surviving spouse, then the surviving spouse has an election of whether to take his or her share of the trust or to insist on receiving his or her statutory share of the estate.

If the spouse elects to take the statutory share, the trust will pay over enough assets as necessary to do so and then distribute the remainder of the trust in accordance with the terms of the trust.

To avoid this problem, in such states that have statutory provisions for providing for a surviving spouse, the spouse should disclaim his or her statutory rights and agree to take only the disposition given under the trust as of the date executed.

If the trust does not give the surviving spouse, at least his or her statutory share, then the trustor should consult with an attorney for advise on the legal consequences before proceeding.

37. IS THERE A GIFT TAX FOR SETTING UP A TRUST?

If the trust is revocable, there is no gift tax because the trustor can always revoke it. All income is still taxed to the trustor.

If the trust is irrevocable but the trustor is the beneficiary, then there is no gift tax because the trust is still for the trustor's benefit. Such a trust is called a grantor's trust and all trust income is taxed to the trustor.

If the trust is for the spouse, there is no gift tax because of the unlimited marital deduction. If the trust is for someone other than the trustor or the trustor's spouse, the general rule is that a gift tax is owed. The gift tax must either be paid or deduction taken from the unified credit or annual exclusion.

38. IS IT DIFFICULT TO SELL PROPERTY IN A TRUST?

Property in a trust is sold like any other property that is not in the trust. All that is needed to sell real property from a trust is a deed executed by the trustee. The trustee merely signs the deed as the representative for the trust and upon recordation title is passed. For example, the deed from the trustee will read: "John Doe , Trustee of the John Doe Revocable Trust hereby deeds, conveys, sells, and transfers to John Smith all right, title and interest in the following property:"

39. WHEN DOES THE TRUST HAVE TO FILE AN INCOME TAX RETURN?

As long as the grantor of the revocable trust is the trustee and treated as the owner of the trust, no tax return for the trust should be filed. The income and deductions for the trust should be listed on the grantor's personal tax return.

A Form 1041 should be filed by the trust when the grantor is not considered the owner. This return should then list to whom the any distributions of income was made and pay the trust income tax on any income not distributed.

When the grantor is no longer the trustee, a trust tax return should be filed.

40. WHAT IS THE 55 YEAR OLD EXCLUSION FOR SALE OF A HOUSE?

An excellent asset for estate planning is a home that has has appreciated greatly over the years. The Internal Revenue Code permits a one-time exclusion of gain up to $125,000.00 from the sale of a home, lived in three years, by a person over 55 years of age.

This gain can, if large, help provide for the retirement of the owner or help start a new business. This is one of the few tax benefits that remain in the Internal Revenue Code that permits a sizable amount of capital gain to be realized without incurring capital gain taxes.

41. CAN A TRUST'S ADMINISTRATION BE REVIEWED BY A COURT?

A common fear that many people have is that the trust will be mismanaged and no one will be able to stop it. There is little to worry on that score. All states permit concerned persons to petition the court for review of the administration of a trust.

A trustee is a fiduciary and owes both the trust and the beneficiaries a fiduciary duty to act reasonably and responsibly. If the court finds that a trustee has breach his or her duty of care, it will remove the trustee and surcharge (find the trustee liable) for all of the damages caused by the trustee's misconduct.

Even if the trust document states otherwise, probate courts will always have the power to review the actions of a trustee. The court will never permit a trustee to misuse the faith and power of his position and hide behind the trust document to avoid judicial scrutiny. Anyone, not just the beneficiaries, can take their suspicions of abuse to the court who will investigate. In Bakersfield, California, an attorney conspired with a trustee to raid an elderly woman's trust. Concerned neighbor's expressed their concern to the court which ordered an investigation. Ultimately, the attorney was sentenced to seven years in prison. The defense that everything was done in accordance with the terms of the trust was not persuasive.

42. CAN A TRUSTEE RESIGN?

A trustee can always resign. In such a case, the trustee is replaced just as though the trustee had died. Most trust agreements contain a list of proposed successor trustees to replace dying or resigning trustees. If the trust does not provide for a successor trustee and the trustor is dead or did not retain the right to amend or revoke the trust, then the probate court will appoint a trustee. No trust will ever fail just because the trustee died or resigned.

Before a trustee can resign, the trustee, unless the trustor is the trustee, will be required to provide a full accounting of the trust business during the time that trustee managed it. All of the beneficiaries may waive the together waive the accounting.

43. IS THERE A REQUIRED BOND FOR A TRUSTEE?
Normally, the trustor waives any bond for any trustee or successor trustee named in the trust document. After all, such a bond would be paid for by the trust and thus diminish the trust estate. If the trustor did not have faith in the named trustees, then they should not have been named.

In the event of a court appointed trustee, the court will require a bond unless all of the beneficiaries agree to waive it.

44. HOW MUCH IS THE STANDARD ESTATE PLAN?
The standard estate which includes the revocable will, durable power of attorney, living will, and pour over will is usually between $500.00 and $1,100.00 depending on the type of trust used. There are different types of the trusts depending on the type of trust needed to accomplish the trustor's intent. Different trusts are used depending on whether the grantor is single or married with or without children and if the trust is a joint trust between the spouses. Special trust such as life insurance trust, generation skipping trusts or charitable trusts can also be part of an estate plan and obviously will increase its cost.

45. CAN BOTH SPOUSES CREATE A REVOCABLE TRUST TOGETHER?
A common estate plan is for both spouses create one joint revocable trust. In the joint trust, both spouses place all of their property into the trust. The spouses' property is listed on schedules marked his, her and theirs. On the death of the first spouse, the trust is divided into separate trusts for the surviving spouse and their children or heirs, if any.

This joint trust is usually the most economical estate plan because it plans for both estates. The cost for doing the joint estate plan is almost always less than what it would cost to do a separate estate plan for each spouse.

The trust is totally revocable during the joint lifetimes of the spouse. Either spouse may terminate it at any time. Upon the death of the first spouse, the trust usually becomes irrevocable as to the property of the deceased spouse but the surviving spouse usually retains full power to revoke the trust as to the property that he or she contributed into it. This type of trust gives the spouse maximum control over their assets and is very flexible to accommodate future changes in the surviving spouse's life following the death of the first spouse. Following this chapter, for reference purposes only, is a joint revocable trust of a married couple.

46. HOW IS A TRUST REVOKED?

If a trust is revocable, all that is needed for an effective revocation is for the trustor to notify the trustee in writing that the trust is terminated as of a certain date and to demand the trust assets be paid over to the trustor.

When the trustor is the trustee, he or she simply affixes a letter to the trust document revoking the trust and executes new deeds from the trust back to the trustor as an individual.

Revocation is simple and quick that is one of the prime advantages of the trust over any other form of estate planning in that the control over the assets of the trust are never lost. Until the trustor actually dies, he or she retains the ability to immediately revoke and terminate the trust merely by stating that the trust is revoked.

47. CAN ACCOUNTINGS BE ORDERED FOR THE TRUST?

Most trusts require annual accountings to be made unless the grantor is the trustee or all the beneficiaries waive them. In addition, anyone concerned person, not just a beneficiary, who feels that the trust is being mismanaged, can seek a court order directing the trustee to perform an accounting. The court can order an accounting even if the trust agreement waives them.

A major concern that many people have over a trust is that after their death the trustee may take and otherwise mismanage the trust assets and the beneficiaries will be helpless. Such is never the case. The probate court always has jurisdiction to oversee every trust, whether or not such jurisdiction is spelled out in the trust document. No court will ever let a Trustee intentionally mismanage or steal trust assets. Anyone, not just beneficiaries, can raise their concerns to the court which will order a hearing to investigate the matter.

48. HOW IS THE TRUSTEE REPLACED IF THE TRUSTOR BECOMES INCOMPETENT?

Most trusts have language that a successor trustee takes over when the trustee becomes unable to perform the duties of the trustee. This may cause problems when the trustee is the trustor and does not believe himself or herself to be incompetent.

To alleviate the problem, many agreements permit a trustee to be replaced when two competent doctors determine the trustee to be incompetent. Likewise, if a court adjudges a person incompetent the successor-trustee will take over immediately.

49. CAN COMMUNITY PROPERTY BE CHANGED INTO SEPARATE PROPERTY?

Community property is property acquired by a husband and wife during a marriage in a manner other than by gift, devise or bequest. Community property is considered to be jointly owned equally by each spouse. Each spouse can pass their interest in the community property by deed or Will.

In a community property state, the spouses may enter into property settlement agreements whereby the community property is divided among them as separate property. There may be reasons for doing this other than a divorce such as one spouse wishing to borrow against his or her share of the property while the other spouse wish to do so.

California freely allows spouses to change separate property into community property and vice versa, this is called transmutation of the property. The ability to change the status of property is beneficial for acquiring the stepped up basis in the surviving spouse's share of community property on the death of the first spouse. It permits the changing of joint tenancy property to community property and thus gives the surviving spouse the tax advantage of a stepped up basis in the property.

Community property, in the absence of a Will, usually, as in California, will pass to the surviving spouse without a probate. Unfortunately, title companies will not insure community property passing to a surviving spouse unless it has gone through a probate or a trust. To address this matter, California created a spousal property petition procedure wherein a spouse would petition the probate court for confirmation of the property being distributed under a Will or under its intestacy laws. This is a simpler, faster and cheaper summary probate proceeding, adopted by California, to pass property easily to a surviving spouse.

50. SHOULD BANK ACCOUNTS BE IN A TRUST OR IN JOINT TENANCY?

A person may have his or her bank accounts placed in joint tenancy with the spouse of children. The problems with this are, as stated above, the same as with all joint tenancy property. The opening of joint bank accounts is a legal gift of one half of all money placed into the account. The account may thus be attached to pay the other joint tenant's debts.

If a revocable trust is used, all that is needed to avoid probate is just to retitle the account so that the trust is the new holder. The trustor controls the trust which controls the bank account. The bank will want to see the trust document to make sure that the trust actually exists and to identify the successor trustee but this happens at the time. The use of a trust as the owner of the bank account assures that it will not be attached to pay any debts but the trustor's.

51. MUST A TRUST BE RECORDED?

A revocable trust does not ever need to be recorded. Unlike a Will, it is a private document. The only documents that need recordation are the deeds transferring real property into the trust.

In some states, a revocable trust is required to be registered with the probate court. To register, a short statement is filed listing the trustee and giving some basic information. Registration gives the court jurisdiction to oversee the trust. There are no penalties, however, for failure to register.

The states requiring registration are Alaska, Colorado after the death of the grantor but no registration is required if there is an immediate distribution to the beneficiaries, Florida but it isn't mandatory, Hawaii, Idaho, Maine, Michigan, Nebraska but it isn't mandatory, New Mexico and North Dakota.

(SAMPLE POUR OVER WILL FOR WIFE PUTTING INTO HER REVOCABLE TRUST ANY PROPERTY NOT IN IT.)

LAST WILL AND TESTAMENT

OF
AGNES MILICENT HOWARD

I, _____AGNES MILICENT HOWARD_____ a resident of MENDOCINO County, __CALIFORNIA__ declare this to be my LAST WILL AND TESTAMENT.

Paragraph One: I revoke all Wills and Codicils that I have previously made.

Paragraph Two: I am married to __JASON HOWARD__ and all references in this Will to my husband are to him. I have the following children, __FELICITY HOWARD, ALLEN HOWARD and ALICE HOWARD_____

The terms 'my child" and "my children" as used in this Will shall include any other children born to or adopted by me.

Paragraph Three: I confirm to my husband his interest in our community and marital property.

Paragraph Four: I give my entire estate, including all of my real and personal property to the Trustee then in office under the Trust designated as the ____HOWARD____ REVOCABLE TRUST of which _AGNES MILICENT HOWARD AND JASON HOWARD_ are grantors and _AGNES MILICENT HOWARD and JASON HOWARD_ was designated as Trustee. I direct that my entire estate shall be added to, administered, and distributed as part of that trust, according to the terms of the trust and any amendment made to it before my death. To the extent permitted by law it is not my intention to create a separate trust by this will or to subject the trust or the property added to it to the jurisdiction of the probate court.

Paragraph Five: If the disposition in Paragraph Four is inoperative or is invalid for any reason, or if the trust referred to in Paragraph Four fails or is revoked, I incorporate here by reference the terms of the trust, as originally executed without giving effect to any amendments made subsequently, and I bequeath and devise my entire estate to the Trustee named in the Trust as Trustee to be held, administered and distributed as provided in this instrument.

Paragraph Six: Except as provided in this Will, I have intentionally omitted to provide herein for any of my heirs living at the date of my death.

Paragraph Seven: If any beneficiary under this Will in any manner, directly or indirectly, contests or attacks this Will or any of its provisions, any share or interest in my estate given to that contesting beneficiary under this Will is revoked and shall be disposed of in the same manner provided herein as if that contesting beneficiary had predeceased me without issue.

Paragraph Eight: I nominate ___JASON HOWARD___ as Executor of my estate to serve without bond. If for any reason, ___JASON HOWARD___ shall fail to qualify or cease to act as my Executor, then I nominate ___FELICITY HOWARD___ as Alternate Executor of my estate to serve without bond. The term Executor as used in this Will shall include any personal representative of my estate.

Paragraph Nine: I direct that all inheritance, estate, or other death taxes that may by reason of my death be attributable to my probate estate or any portion of it, including any property received by any person as a family allowance or homestead, shall be paid by my Executor out of the residue of my estate disposed of by this Will, without adjustment among the residuary beneficiaries, and shall not be charged against or collected from any beneficiary of my probate estate.

Paragraph Ten: I grant my Executor the following powers under the terms of this Will:

1. To retain any such property without regard to the proportion such property or similar held may bear to the entire amount held and whether or not the same is of the class in which fiduciaries are authorized by law or any rule of court to invest funds;

2. To sell any such property upon such terms and conditions as may be deemed proper at either public or private sale, either for credit for such period of time as may be deemed proper or for cash and with or without security; and the purchaser of such property shall have no obligation to see to the use or application of the proceeds of sale; to exchange, lease, sublease, mortgage, pledge or otherwise encumber any such property upon such terms and conditions as may be deemed advisable; to grant options for any of the foregoing and to make any lease or sublease, including any oil, gas or mineral lease, for such period of time and to include therein any covenants or options for renewal as may be deemed proper without regard to the duration of any

trust subject only to such confirmation of court as may be required by law.

3. To invest and reinvest in and to acquire by exchange property of any character, foreign or domestic, or interests or participations therein, including by way of illustration but not of limitation, real property, mortgages, bonds, notes, debentures, certificates of deposit, capital, common and preferred stocks, and shares or interests in investment trusts, mutual funds or common trust funds, without regard to the proportion any such property or similar property held may bear to the entire amount held and whether or not the same is of the class in which fiduciaries are authorized by law or any rule of court to invest funds;

4. To hold any personal property in any state; to register and hold any property of any kind, whether real or personal, at any time held hereunder in the name of a nominee or nominees; and too take and keep any stocks, bonds or other securities unregistered or in such condition as to pass by delivery;

5. To employ in the exercise of absolute discretion investment counsel, accountants, depositaries, custodians, brokers, attorneys and agents, irrespective of whether any person so employed shall be a fiduciary hereunder or a firm or corporation in which a fiduciary hereunder shall have an interest and to pay them the usual compensation for their services out of the principal or income of the property held hereunder in addition to and without diminution of or charging the same against the commissions or compensation of any fiduciary hereunder; and any

fiduciary who shall be a partner in any such firm shall nevertheless be entitled to receive his share as partner of the compensation paid to such firm.

      6. To continue the operation of any business belonging to my estate for such time and in such manner as my Executor may deem advisable and for the best interests of my estate, or to sell and liquidate the business at such time and on such terms as my Executor may deem advisable and for the best interests of my estate. Any such operation, sale, liquidation by my Executors, in good faith, shall be at the risk of my estate and without liability on the part of my Executor for the resulting losses.

      Paragraph Eleven: This Last Will and Testament shall be construed, regulated, and governed in all respects not only as to administration but also as to its validity and effect by the laws of the State of ____CALIFORNIA____.

      Paragraph Twelve: As used in this Will, the term "issue" shall refer to lineal descendants of all degrees, and the terms "child", "children", and "issue' shall include adopted persons.

      Paragraph Thirteen: This Last Will and Testament has been executed in duplicate. Upon my death, either duplicate original will may be offered for probate. If upon my death, the Will in my possession can not be found, it is not to be presumed that I destroyed or revoked the Will.

      I subscribe my name to this Will on this date January 15, 2002 at ____Ukiah, California____.

                                      AGNES MILICENT HOWARD

On the date last written above, __AGNES MILICENT HOWARD__ declared to us the undersigned that the foregoing instrument consisting of six (6) pages including the page signed by us as witnesses, was her LAST WILL AND TESTAMENT and requested us to act as witnesses to it. She thereupon signed the Will in our presence, all of us being present at the time. We now, at her request, in her presence and in the presence of each other, subscribe our names as witnesses.

_____

residing at _____

_____

residing at _____

_____

residing at _____

LIVING WILL DECLARATION

To My Family, Doctors and All Those concerned with my care:

I, _____, being of sound mind, make this statement as a directive to be followed if I become unable to participate in decisions regarding my medical care.

If I should be in an incurable or irreversible mental or physical condition with no reasonable expectation of recovery, I direct my attending physician to withhold or withdraw treatment that merely prolongs my dying. I further direct that treatment be limited to measures to keep me comfortable and relieve pain.

In the event that at the time this declaration is being considered, I am pregnant then I specifically state that I
   1. want the treatment withheld even though it may result in an abortion. _____
   2. do not want such treatment withheld if it will result in an abortion. _____
(Cross out inapplicable language and sign on the appropriate line.

These directions express my legal right to refuse treatment. Therefore I expect my family, doctors and everyone concerned with my care to regard themselves as legally and morally bound to act in accord with my wishes, and in so doing to be free of any legal liability for having followed my directives.

I especially do not want: _____
_____
_____

Other instructions or comments: _____
_____
_____

Proxy Designation Clause: Should I become unable to communicate my instructions as stated above, I designate the following person to act in my behalf:

Name: _____

Address: _____

Phone: _____

If the person I have named above is unable to act in my behalf, authorize the following person to do so:

- 1 -

Name: _____

Address: _____

Phone: _____

Signed _____ Date _____

Witness _____

Witness _____

STATE OF

COUNTY OF

On _____, before _____
personally appeared personally known to me or proved to me on the
basis of satisfactory evidence to be the person whose name is
subscribed to the within instrument and acknowledged to me that
he/she executed the same in **his/her** authorized capacity and that by
his/her signature(s) on the instrument the person or the entity
upon behalf of which the person acted, executed the within
instrument.

WITNESS MY HAND AND OFFICIAL SEAL.

_____

DURABLE POWER OF ATTORNEY

KNOW ALL PEOPLE BY THESE PRESENTS, that I, _____ _____ residing at _____ _____ phone number _____ do declare this to be a **DURABLE POWER OF ATTORNEY.**

THIS POWER OF ATTORNEY SHALL NOT BE AFFECTED BY SUBSEQUENT INCAPACITY OF THE PRINCIPAL.

I hereby revoke all prior powers of attorney regardless of the type or to whom they may have been given.

I hereby nominate, constitute and appoint _____ _____ whose address and telephone number are: _____ _____ as my true and lawful attorney in fact, for me and in my name, place and stead, and for my use and benefit, to exercise the following powers:

(1) **TO MAKE HEALTH CARE DECISIONS ON MY BEHALF.** Health care decisions means decisions on my care, treatment, or procedures to be utilized in order to maintain, diagnose or treat my physical condition. This **DURABLE POWER OF ATTORNEY**, as it relates to health care decisions, does not carry with it the power to authorize any of the following acts:

        (A) Any commitment or placement in a mental health facility;

        (B) Any convulsive treatment; or

        (C) Any psychosurgery.

Furthermore, I hereby expressly authorize any physician,

hospital, and any other person or organization, to release and disclose to my agent any information any of them may have concerning any treatment, diagnosis, recommendation, or other facts, which they may have concerning my physical condition and any health care, counsel, treatment, or assistance provided to me either before or after the execution of this power of attorney, any privilege hereby being expressly waived as to such disclosures. This waiver shall extend to communications to my agent only and shall not be deemed a general waiver of the privilege. My agent may, however, authorize release of such information to such third persons as my agent deems to be reasonable or necessary in the exercise of the powers granted in this instrument.

(2) Subject to any limitations in this document, my agent has the power and authority to do all of the following:

(A) Authorize an autopsy;

(B) Make a disposition of a part or parts of my body under the Uniform Anatomical Gift Act; and

(C) Direct disposition of my remains State law.

(3) Subject to any limitations in this document, I hereby grant to my agents full power and authority to act for me in my name, in any way which I myself could act, with respect to the following matters as each of them to the extent that I am permitted to act through an agent.

(A) Real estate transactions;

<u>**DURABLE POWER OF ATTORNEY**</u>

(B) Tangible personal property transactions;

(C) Bond, share and commodity transactions;

(D) Financial institution transactions;

(E) Business operating transactions;

(F) Insurance transactions;

(G) Retirement plan transactions;

(H) Estate transactions;

(I) Claims and litigation;

(J) Tax matters;

(K) Personal relationships and affairs;

(L) Benefits from military service;

(M) Records, reports and statements;

(N) Full and unqualified authority to my agents to delegate any and all of the foregoing powers to any person or persons whom my agents shall delegate.

(4) To ask, demand, sue for, recover, collect, and receive such sums of money, debts, dues accounts, legacies, bequests, interest, dividends, annuities, and demands whatsoever as are now or shall hereafter become due, owing payable or belonging to me and have, use, and take all lawful ways and means in my name or otherwise, and to compromise and agree for the acquittance or other sufficient discharge of the same;

(5) For me in my name, to make, seal, and deliver, to bargain, contract, agree for, purchase, receive, and take lands, tenements, hereditaments and accept the possession of all lands,

DURABLE POWER OF ATTORNEY

and deeds of assurances, in the law therefor, and to lease, let demise, bargain, sell, remise, release, convey, mortgage, and hypothecate lands, tenements and hereditaments upon such covenants as they shall think fit;

(6) To sign, endorse, execute, acknowledge, deliver, receive, and possess such applications, contracts, agreements, options, covenants, deeds, conveyances, trust deeds, security agreements, bills of sale, leases, mortgages, assignments, insurance policies, bills of lading, warehouse receipts, documents of title, bills, bonds, debentures, checks, drafts bills of exchange, notes, stock certificates, proxies, warrants, commercial paper, receipts, withdrawal receipts and deposit instruments relating to accounts or deposits in or certificates of deposits of, banks, savings and loans or other such institutions or associations, proof of loss, evidences of debts, releases and satisfaction of mortgages, judgments, liens, security agreements, and other debts and obligations, and such other instruments in writing of whatever kind and nature as may be necessary or proper in the exercise of the rights and powers herein granted.

(7) Also to bargain and agree for, buy, sell mortgage, hypothecate, and in any and every way and manner deal in and with goods, wares and merchandise, choses in action, and to make, do and transact all business of whatever nature and kind;

(8) Also for me and in my name, and as my act and deed, to sign, seal execute, deliver, and acknowledge such deeds, leases,

DURABLE POWER OF ATTORNEY

mortgages, hypothecations, bottomries, charter parties, bills of lading, bills, notes, receipts, evidences of debt, releases and satisfaction of mortgages, judgments and other debts, and other such instruments in writing of whatever kind and nature as my be necessary and proper;

(9) To have access at any time or times to any safe deposit box rented by me, wheresoever located and to remove all or any part of the contents thereof, and to surrender or relinquish said safety deposit box, and any institution in which such safe deposit box is located shall not incur any liability to me or to my estate as a result of permitting my agent to exercise this power.

(10) I hereby expressly authorize any attorney of mine, past or present, to release and disclose to my agent any information any of them may have concerning my legal affairs or other facts, which they may have concerning my personal affairs and any legal service, counsel or assistance provided to me either before or after the execution of this power of attorney, any privilege hereby being expressly waived as to such disclosures. This waiver shall extend to communications to my agent only and shall not be deemed to authorize a release of information to third parties and shall not be deemed a general waiver of the privilege. My agent may, however, authorize release of such information to such third persons as my agent deems to be reasonable or necessary in the exercise of the powers granted in this instrument.

(11) Giving and granting unto said attorney in fact full power

DURABLE POWER OF ATTORNEY

and authority to do and perform every act necessary, requisite or proper to be done in and about my property as fully as I might or could do if personally present, with full power of substitution and revocation, hereby ratifying and confirming that my said attorney shall lawfully do or cause to be done by virtue hereof.

THE ATTORNEY IN FACT UNDER THIS DURABLE POWER OF ATTORNEY IS SPECIFICALLY NOT GIVEN AND DOES NOT HAVE THE AUTHORITY OR POWER TO REVOKE, AMEND OR ALTER ANY REVOCABLE OR IRREVOCABLE TRUST THAT I HAVE CREATED OR MAY CREATE IN THE FUTURE.

If _____ is not available or becomes ineligible or unable for any reason to act as my agent and to make decisions for me, or if I revoke appointment or authority to act as my agent, then I designate and appoint _____ _____ address _____ _____ phone number _____ as my alternative, true and lawful attorney in fact with all of the powers enumerated above INCLUDING THE POWER TO MAKE HEALTH CARE DECISIONS ON MY BEHALF.

IN WITNESS WHEREOF, I have hereunto signed my name on this _____ day of _____, at _____.

I am aware that I have the following rights regarding this DURABLE POWER OF ATTORNEY.

1. THIS DOCUMENT GIVES TO THE PERSON WHO I DESIGNATE AS MY DURABLE POWER OF ATTORNEY

ATTORNEY IN FACT THE POWER TO MAKE HEALTH CARE DECISIONS FOR ME SUBJECT TO THE LIMITATIONS AND STATEMENT OF MY DESIRES THAT I HAVE INCLUDED IN THIS DOCUMENT. The power to make health care decisions for me may exclude consent, refusal of consent, or withdrawal of consent to any treatment, service or procedure to maintain, diagnose or treat physical or mental condition. I may state in this document any type of treatment or placements that I do not desire.

(2) The person who I designated in this document has a duty to act consistent with my desires as stated in this document or otherwise made known or, if my desires are unknown, to act in my best interests.

(3) Except as I have otherwise specified in this document, the power of the person who I have designated to make health care decisions for me may include the power to consent to my doctor not to give treatment or to stop treatment which could keep me alive.

(4) UNLESS I SPECIFY A SHORTER PERIOD IN THIS DOCUMENT, THIS POWER WILL EXIST FOR SEVEN (7) YEARS FROM THE DATE I EXECUTED THIS DOCUMENT AND, IF I AM UNABLE TO MAKE HEALTH CARE DECISIONS FOR MYSELF AT THE TIME THE SEVEN (7) YEAR PERIOD ENDS, THIS POWER WILL CONTINUE TO EXIST UNTIL THE TIME I BECOME ABLE TO MAKE HEALTH CARE DECISIONS FOR MYSELF.

(5) Notwithstanding this document, I have the right to make medical and other health care decisions for myself so long as I can give informed medical consent with respect to the particular

DURABLE POWER OF ATTORNEY

decision. In addition, no treatment may be given to me over my objection, and health care to keep me alive may not be stopped if I object.

(6) I HAVE THE RIGHT TO REVOKE THE APPOINTMENT OF THE PERSON DESIGNATED IN THIS DOCUMENT BY NOTIFYING THAT PERSON OF THE REVOCATION IN WRITING.

(7) I HAVE THE RIGHT TO REVOKE THE AUTHORITY GRANTED TO THE PERSON DESIGNATED IN THIS DOCUMENT TO MAKE HEALTH CARE DECISIONS FOR ME BY NOTIFYING THE TREATING PHYSICIAN, HOSPITAL, OR OTHER HEALTH CARE PROVIDER ORALLY OR IN WRITING.

(8) The person designated in this document to make health care decisions for me has the right to examine my medical records and to consent to their disclosures unless I limit this right in this document.

DATED: _____

_____

ATTESTATION

I declare under penalty of perjury under the laws of the State of _____ that _____ the person who signed this document is personally known to me or proven to me on the basis of convincing evidence to be the Principal, that the Principal signed or acknowledged to this

DURABLE POWER OF ATTORNEY

DURABLE POWER OF ATTORNEY in my presence, that the Principal appears to be of sound mind and under no duress, fraud, or undue influence; that I am not the person appointed as attorney in fact by this document; and, that I am not a health care provider, the operator of a community care facility, or an employee of an operator of a community care facility, the operator of a residential care facility for the elderly, nor an employee of an operator of a residential care facility for the elderly.

    I further declare under penalty of perjury under the laws of the State of _____ that I am not related to the Principal by blood, marriage, or adoption, and, to the best of my knowledge, I am not entitled to any part of the estate of the Principal upon the death of the Principal under a Will now existing or by operation of law.

DATED: _____

DURABLE POWER OF ATTORNEY

-9-

CERTIFICATE OF ACKNOWLEDGMENT OF NOTARY PUBLIC

STATE OF _____

COUNTY OF _____

On this day of _____ before me, the undersigned, personally appeared _____ personally known to me or proved to me on the basis of satisfactory evidence to be the person whose name is subscribed to this instrument, and acknowledged that she executed it. I declare under penalty of perjury that the person whose name is subscribed to this instrument appears to be in sound mind and under no duress, fraud or undue influence.

_____

DURABLE POWER OF ATTORNEY

REVOCABLE TRUST

TRUST SUMMARY-THIS PAGE IS NOT PART OF THE TRUST

THIS TRUST IS SPECIFICALLY DESIGNED FOR AN ESTATE OF LESS THAN $600,000.00. IF THE COMBINED ESTATE SHOULD LATER EXCEED $600,000, THEN THE TRUST SHOULD BE REVIEWED FOR POSSIBLE CHANGES TO AVOID OR REDUCE FEDERAL ESTATE TAXES.

NAME OF THE TRUST: _____

DATE ESTABLISHED: _____

NAME OF GRANTOR: _____

NAME OF TRUSTEE: _____

SUCCESSOR TRUSTEE: _____

FEDERAL I.D. NUMBER: NOT NEEDED UNLESS THE TRUSTEE IS SOMEONE OTHER THAN THE GRANTOR

KEEP SEPARATE RECORDS FOR THIS TRUST. ALL INCOME OR LOSSES OF THE TRUST ARE REPORTED ON THE GRANTOR'S SEPARATE TAX RETURN. SO LONG AS THE GRANTOR IS THE ONLY TRUSTEE, YOU DO NOT HAVE TO FILE AN INCOME TAX RETURN FOR THE TRUST.

DO NOT WRITE ON THIS AGREEMENT, CHANGE IT, OR REVOKE IT WITHOUT YOUR ATTORNEY'S ADVICE.

FOR TRUST BUSINESS, ALWAYS SIGN:

TITLE OF ALL ASSETS IN THIS TRUST SHOULD BE TAKEN AS FOLLOWS:

LAW OFFICE OF MICHAEL LYNN GABRIEL
643 B SOUTH MAIN STREET
UKIAH, CA. 95482
(707) 468-0268

REVOCABLE TRUST

This Agreement is made this _____ day of _____ between _____ (hereinafter called the "Grantor"), and _____ (hereinafter called the "Trustee");

The Grantor hereby assigns, transfers, conveys and sets over unto the Trustee all his right, title and interest in and to the property set forth and described in Schedule A annexed hereto. The Trustee does hereby acknowledge the receipt of said property.

The Trustee further agrees to have, hold, administer and manage said property together with any additions thereto (hereinafter referred to as the "**TRUST FUND**") upon the following express terms and conditions of this Trust Agreement:

BENEFICIARIES' INTERESTS

FIRST: It shall be the Trustee's duty and responsibility to take, receive, hold, administer, manage, invest and reinvest the Trust Fund. The Trustee shall also collect the rents, interest, dividends, and other income therefrom and, after deducting all proper charges and expenses, shall pay directly to the Grantor, or apply to or for the use of the Grantor, all of the net income derived from the Trust Fund. In addition, the Trustee shall pay all or so much of the principal thereof as the Trustee shall in its sole and uncontrolled discretion shall determine, irrespective of any other source of income, support, maintenance or benefit of the Grantor. Following the death of the Grantor, the Trustee shall (subject to the provisions of the SEVENTH ARTICLE hereof) convey, transfer, pay over, and deliver the entire principal of the Trust Fund as then constituted to the Grantor's Children, _____

_____

then living per stirpes. The Trustee shall divide the Trust Fund into a many parts or shares as there are children and descendants of deceased children surviving the Grantor, the shares of the children surviving to be equal and the shares of the descendants of each deceased child to be in the aggregate the amount that would have been set aside for the benefit of such deceased child had he or she survived and to equal among themselves, per stirpes and not per capita.

ADDITIONS TO THE TRUST

SECOND: Property may be added and transferred to the Trust at any time and from any source with the Trustee's consent. Such added property shall thereupon become a part of the TRUST FUND and shall thereafter be held upon the same terms and conditions as the property originally transferred.

REVOCABILITY

THIRD: During the lifetime of the Grantor, this Trust may be

REVOCABLE TRUST

be revoked in whole or in part by the Grantor by delivering written notice to the Trustee. In the event of such revocation, the entire Trust Fund or the revoked portion thereof shall revert to the Grantor as the Grantor's sole and separate property. In addition, the Grantor reserves the right by a written instrument signed and acknowledged by the Grantor and delivered to the Trustee, in whole or in part, to modify, alter, and amend this trust agreement on any matter. The Grantor may, at any time, withdraw any or all of the property held in the Trust. Such withdrawn property shall thereafter be free of the terms or provisions of this Trust.

GOVERNING LAW

FOURTH: This Trust has been created and accepted by the Grantor and the Trustee in the State of _____, and the validity, construction and all rights under this Trust Agreement shall be governed by the laws of the State of _____. If any provision of this Trust Agreement shall be invalid or uneforceable, the remaining provisions shall continue to be fully effective.

Titles and headings contained in this Trust Agreement shall not be deemed to govern, limit, modify or in any manner affect the scope, meaning or intent of the provisions hereof.

PAYMENTS TO MINORS

FIFTH: If any property held shall be distributable or payable to a minor, the Trustee in its sole discretion may:

(A). Transfer and pay over all or any such property to

a Guardian of the property of such minor wherever appointed without requiring ancillary guardianship or to a parent or person having care and custody of such minor without requiring such parent or person to qualify as guardian in any jurisdiction or a custodian for such minor under the Uniform Gifts to Minors Act of any State. The Trustee shall have no obligation to see to the use or application thereof or to make inquiry with respect to any other property available for the use of such minor, and the receipt therefor of such guardian, parent, person or custodian shall completely discharge the Trustee as to such transfer or payment; or

(B) Set aside all or any part of such property, title to which shall have vested absolutely in such minor, in a separate fund and hold the same until the minor shall become of age or sooner die. During such period, the Trustee may at any time or from time to time in the Trustee's sole discretion pay over all or any portion of such fund as provided in paragraph (A) hereof, or invest and reinvest the same and pay or apply to or for the use of such minor, all or so much of the principal thereof and the net income therefrom (including accumulated income), and accumulate any income not so paid or applied, as the Trustee may its sole discretion determine, irrespective of any other property available for the use of such minor.

The Trustee holding such a fund shall not be required to give bond or security or to render periodic accounts and shall be entitled to compensation as if the fund were a separate Trust.

<u>TRUSTEE POWERS</u>
<u>REVOCABLE TRUST</u>

<u>PAGE 4</u>

SIXTH: In the administration of this Trust, the Trustee shall have the following powers, all of which shall be exercised in a fiduciary capacity:

1. To retain any such property without regard to the proportion such property or similar property held may bear to the entire amount held and whether or not the same is of the class in which fiduciaries are authorized by law or any rule of court to invest funds.

2. To sell any such property upon such terms and conditions as may be deemed proper at either public or private sale, either for credit for such period of time as may be deemed proper or for cash and with or without security; and the purchaser of such property shall have no obligation to see to the use or application of the proceeds of sale; to exchange, lease, sublease, mortgage, pledge or otherwise encumber any such property upon such terms and conditions as may be deemed advisable; to grant options for any of the foregoing and to make any lease or sublease, including any oil, gas or mineral lease, for such period of time and to include therein any covenants or options for renewal as may be deemed proper without regard to the duration of any Trust and without approval of any court.

3. To invest and reinvest in and to acquire by exchange property of any character, foreign or domestic, or interests or participations therein, including by way of illustrations but not limitation, real property, mortgages, bonds, notes debentures,

certificates of deposit, capital, common and referred stocks, and shares or interests in investment trusts, mutual funds or common trust funds, without regard to the proportion any such property or similar property held may bear to the entire amount held and whether or not the same is of the class in which fiduciaries are authorized by law or any rule of court to invest funds.

4. To hold any personal property in any state; to register and hold property of any kind, whether real or personal, at any time held hereunder in the name of a nominee or nominees, and to take and keep stocks, bonds, or other securities unregistered or in such condition as to pass by delivery.

5. To employ in the exercise of absolute discretion, investment counsel, accountants, depositaries, custodians, brokers, attorneys and agents, irrespective of whether any person so employed shall be a fiduciary hereunder or a firm or corporation in which a fiduciary hereunder shall have an interest and to pay then the usual compensation for their services out of the principal or income of the property held hereunder in addition to and without diminution of or charging the same against the commissions or compensation of any fiduciary hereunder; and any fiduciary who shall be a partner in any such firm shall nevertheless be entitled to receive his share as partner of the compensation paid to such firm.

6. To retain any property or interest in property in the form received.

REVOCABLE TRUST
PAGE 6

7. To invest funds in stocks, bonds, notes, debentures or other securities, or property, real or personal (including any common r commingled fund), notwithstanding such securities or property may not be eligible investments for fiduciaries under statutory or general law, either as to the nature of the security or in relation to the other investments. It is the Grantor's intention that the Trustee shall have the power to make such investments as it may, in its unrestricted judgment, deems best.

8. To register any stock, bond, or other property in the name of a nominee, without the addition of words indicating that such security is held in a fiduciary capacity; but accurate records shall be maintained showing that such security is a trust asset and that the Trustee shall be responsible for the acts of the nominee.

9. To retain and carry on any business which may be accepted as a part of the trust fund, to acquire additional interest in any such business, to agree to the liquidation in kind of any corporation in which this Trust may have any interest and yo carry on the business thereof, to join with other owners in adopting any form of management for any business or property, in which this Trust may have an interest, to become and remain a partner, general or limited, in regard to any such business or property, incorporate any such business or property and to hold the stock or other securities as an investment, and to employ agents and confer on them authority to manage and operate such business, property or corporation, without liability for the acts of any such

REVOCABLE TRUST
PAGE 7

agent for any loss, liability or indebtedness of such business if the management is selected or retained with reasonable care.

10. To determine any questions which may arise as to what constitutes income and what constitutes principal, and such determination shall be conclusive as to all persons interested in the Trust (but, subject to such power and in except some unusual instance where it may be exercised to the contrary, shares of stock received by way of a stock dividend shall be deemed principal and not income).

11. To employ such agents and counsel and other persons as may be necessary, in the opinion of the Trustee, and to determine and pay them such compensation as may be deemed appropriate ny the Trustee.

12. To sell any property to or purchase any property from any other trust or share thereof created by a Grantor during the Grantor's life, or the Grantor's estate or of the estate of a Grantor's spouse or form any trust created by a Grantor's spouse by Will or during the Grantor's life, at the fair market value thereof as determined by the Trustee, even though the same person or corporation may be acting as Trustee of any such other Trusts, as Executor of the estate of the Grantor's spouse, or as the Grantor's Executor or Trustee of any Trust established by the Grantor.

13. To commingle, for the purposes of management and investment, the funds of this Trust with funds of any other Trust or Trusts created by a Grantor.

REVOCABLE TRUST
PAGE 8

14. To make loans, either secured or unsecured, in such amounts, upon such terms, at such rates of interest, to such persons other than a Grantor and to such firms or corporations other than those controlled by a Grantor, as the Trustee may deem advisable, including but not limited to the beneficiary of this Trust. It is the Grantors' intention that this provision be used to assist the beneficiary when the beneficiary is in need of funds without having to make a final distribution of principal to the beneficiary.

15. To exercise any and all powers not included herein which are authorized by the laws of the State of _____ which by reference is specifically incorporated herein as though fully set forth in its entirety.

16. In its fiduciary capacity, to exercise all powers in the management of the Trust Fund which any individual could exercise in his or her own right, upon such terms and conditions as it may deem best, and to execute and deliver any and all instruments and to do all acts which may be deemed necessary or proper to carry on the purposes of this Agreement.

17. To prosecute and defend actions, claims or proceedings for the protection of trust property and of the Trustee in the performance of the Trustee's duties.

18. To pay any sum distributable to a beneficiary, without regard to whether the beneficiary is under a legal disability, by paying the sum to the beneficiary or by paying the sum to another

person for the use or benefit of the beneficiary. No distribution under this instrument to or for the benefit of a minor beneficiary shall discharge the legal obligation of the beneficiary's parent's to support him or her in accordance with the laws of the state of the parent's domicile from time to time, unless a court of competent jurisdiction determines that this distinction is necessary for the minor's support, health, or education.

PAYMENTS TO ESTATE

SEVENTH: Upon the death of the Grantor, and on the written demand of the duly appointed and qualified Executor or Administrator of the Grantor's Estate, the Trustee shall pay to such Executor or Administrator out of the principal of the Trust Fund such amount or amounts as may be required to pay all estate, transfer, succession, inheritance, legacy, or other similar taxes payable by reason of the Grantor's death under the provisions of any tax law (including interest and penalties thereon) whether or not such taxes are attributable to the inclusion of the Trust Fund in the Grantor's gross estate for the purposes of such taxes.

The Trustee shall be under no duty or obligation to take part in determining the amount of such taxes (and interest and penalties thereon) and may rely upon the written certification of the Executor or Administrator of the Estate of the Grantor as to the amounts to be paid on demand as herein directed.

SUCCESSOR TRUSTEE

EIGHTH: On the death, resignation, or incapacity of the

Grantor _____ , then_____ shall serve as Successor Trustee. In the event _____ _____ , shall fail, for any reason to serve as Trustee, then _____ shall serve as Successor Trustee. In the event that _____ shall fail, for any reason to serve as Trustee, then the Superior Court of the State of _____ shall appoint the Successor Trustee.

Physical and mental incapacity shall be conclusively established if a doctor, authorized to practice medicine in the State of California, issues a written certificate to that effect. In the absence of such a certificate, the Successor Trustee or the beneficiaries may petition the court having jurisdiction over the the Trust to remove the Trustee and replace him or her with the Successor Trustee. The Successor Trustee or the beneficiary who so petitions the court shall incur no liability to any beneficiary of the Trust or to the substituted trustee as a result of this petition, provided the petition is filed in good faith and in a reasonable belief that the Trustee is physically or mentally incapacitated or otherwise cannot act.

The Grantor shall have the right at any time and periodically to appoint or to remove any Trustee and thereafter appoint a Successor trustee even though a Successor Trustee may be named in this Agreement. In such an event, the Successor Trustee named in this Agreement will follow the Successor Trustee appointed by the

REVOCABLE TRUST
PAGE 11

Grantors. The removal or appointment of a Successor trustee shall be made in writing, shall be attached to this Agreement at the time made, and shall take effect at then time states in the instrument. All Successor Trustees shall have the same duties and powers as are conferred upon the Trustee.

BOND

NINTH: No bond shall be required of any Trustee named in this Trust Agreement.

ACCOUNTING

TENTH: No Trustee shall be required to file any inventory or appraisal or any annual or other returns or reports to any court or to give bond, but shall render a report at least annually and within 120 days after the end of the tax year of this Trust to the beneficiary or to the beneficiary's guardian, if the beneficiary is a minor or is legally incompetent, showing the assets and liabilities of the Trust Fund, the income therefrom and the disposition thereof. The records of the Trustee with respect to the Trust Fund shall be open at all reasonable times to the inspection of the Grantor, the beneficiary or the beneficiary's guardian.

NO-CONTEST CLAUSE

ELEVENTH: Except as otherwise provided in this instrument, the Grantor has intentionally and with full knowledge omitted to provide for the Grantor's heirs. If any beneficiary under this Trust, singly or in conjunction with any other person or persons, contests in any court the validity of this Trust or of the

Grantor's Last Will or seeks to obtain adjudication in any proceeding in any court that this Trust or any of its provisions or that such Will or any of its provisions is void, or seeks to otherwise to void, nullify, or set aside this Trust or any of its provisions, then that person's right to take any interest given to him or her by this Trust shall be determined as it would have been determined if the person had predeceased the execution of this Trust without surviving issue. The provisions of this paragraph shall not apply to any disclaimer by any person of any benefit under this Trust or under any Will. The Trustee is hereby authorized to defend, at the expense of the Trust Estate, and contest, or other attack of any nature on this Trust or its provisions.

PERPETUITIES SAVINGS CLAUSE

TWELFTH: Any Trust created under this instrument shall, unless terminated earlier, terminate twenty-one (21) years after the death of the last survivor of all of the Grantor's issue living on the date of the Grantor's death. The Trust Estate shall then be distributed by the right of representation to those persons who are then entitled or authorized at the Trustee's discretion, to receive income distributions from the Trust.

CLAIMS OF CREDITORS

THIRTEENTH: The Trustee shall not be personally liable to any creditor or to any other person for making distributions from any Trust under the terms of this instrument if the Trustee has no

REVOCABLE TRUST
PAGE 13

notice of the claim of such creditor.

SEVERABILITY CLAUSE

FOURTEENTH: If any provision of this Trust instrument is unenforceable, the remaining provisions shall nevertheless be carried into effect.

NAME OF THE TRUST

FIFTEENTH: This Trust and the Trust contained herein may be referred to collectively as the _____ REVOCABLE TRUST or by the identifying name of the named beneficiary of any Trust hereunder from time to time or by such other designation as the Trustee may from time to time deem appropriate.

Property shall be deemed transferred to the Trustee and subject to the terms of this instrument if it has been registered in or assigned to the Trustee as Trustee of the _____ REVOCABLE TRUST , or to the Trustee as Trustee under a Declaration of Trust followed by the same date of this instrument, or to the Trustee U/D/T dtd (UNDER DECLARATION OF TRUST dated) followed by the date of this instrument, or in any other manner indicating its transfer to the Trustee as Trustee hereunder or under this Declaration of Trust.

ACCEPTANCE BY TRUSTEE

SIXTEENTH: The Trustee by joining in the execution of this Agreement hereby signifies their acceptance of this Trust.

BROAD SPENDTHRIFT CLAUSE

SEVENTEENTH: To the extent permitted by law, no interest of any beneficiary in the income or principal of any Trust hereby created shall be subject to pledge, assignment, sale, or transfer in any manner, nor shall any beneficiary have power in any manner to anticipate, charge, or encumber his or her interest, nor shall any interest of any beneficiary ne liable or subject in any manner while in the possession of the Trustee for the debts, contracts, liabilities, engagements, or torts of such beneficiary.

TRUSTEE COMPENSATION

EIGHTEENTH: For services as Trustee, all Trustees shall receive reasonable compensation for such services, provided, however, that any Trustee who contributes to the principal of any share of a Trust created under this Agreement shall not receive any fee for his or her services. A Corporate Trustee shall receive a fee based upon those set forth in the Trustee's regularly published fee schedule for similar services or such other fee as may be agreed upon the Trustee's appointment.

IN WITNESS WHEREOF, the parties have executed this instrument as of the date and year first written above.

GRANTOR

_____

TRUSTEE

_____

REVOCABLE TRUST
PAGE 15

REVOCABLE TRUST

DATED:

SCHEDULE A

All real and personal property wheresoever located including but not limited to the following:

1.

Grantor will change the title to all property to reflect the transfer into the Trust Estate.

REVOCABLE TRUST

DATED:

SCHEDULE A

All real and personal property wheresoever located including but not limited to the following:

1.

Grantor will change the title to all property to reflect the transfer into the Trust Estate.

CERTIFICATE OF ACKNOWLEDGMENT OF NOTARY PUBLIC

STATE OF CALIFORNIA

COUNTY OF MENDOCINO

On this day of_____ in the year 1992, before me appeared _____ personally known to me (or proved to me on the basis of satisfactory evidence) to be the person whose name is subscribed to this instrument, and acknowledge that executed it. I declare under penalty of perjury that the name of the person whose name is subscribed to this instrument appears to be of sound mind and under no duress, fraud, or undue influence.

_____

REVOCABLE TRUST
PAGE 17

REVOCABLE TRUST

TRUST SUMMARY-THIS PAGE IS NOT PART OF THE TRUST

THIS TRUST IS SPECIFICALLY DESIGNED FOR AN ESTATE OF LESS THAN $600,000.00. IF THE COMBINED ESTATE SHOULD LATER EXCEED $600,000, THEN THE TRUST SHOULD BE REVIEWED FOR POSSIBLE CHANGES TO AVOID OR REDUCE FEDERAL ESTATE TAXES.

NAME OF TRUST: _____

DATE ESTABLISHED: _____

NAME OF GRANTORS: _____

NAME OF TRUSTEES: _____

SUCCESSOR TRUSTEE: _____

FEDERAL I.D. NUMBER: NOT NEEDED AS LONG AS A GRANTOR IS A TRUSTEE

KEEP SEPARATE RECORDS FOR THIS TRUST. ALL INCOME OR LOSSES OF THE TRUST ARE REPORTED ON THE GRANTORS' SEPARATE TAX RETURN. SO LONG AS THE GRANTORS ARE THE ONLY TRUSTEES, THERE IS NO NEED TO FILE AN INCOME TAX RETURN FOR THE TRUST.

> DO NOT WRITE ON THIS AGREEMENT,
> CHANGE IT, OR REVOKE IT
> WITHOUT YOUR ATTORNEY'S ADVICE.

FOR TRUST BUSINESS, ALWAYS SIGN AS TRUSTEE OF THIS REVOCABLE TRUST

TITLE OF ALL ASSETS IN THIS TRUST SHOULD BE TAKEN AS TRUSTEE OF THIS REVOCABLE TRUST

REVOCABLE TRUST

On this _____ day of _____, _____
_____
(hereinafter referred to the "Grantors") have transferred, delivered, and paid over to themselves,_____
_____ (hereinafter together referred to as the "Trustee") the property described in Schedule A, which is annexed hereto.

STATEMENT OF INTENT

FIRST: The property described in Schedule A and all property subsequently transferred to this Trust at any time is hereby referred to as the "Trust Estate" and shall be held, administered, and distributed as provided below. It is the Grantors' intention that all community property transferred to these Trusts and the proceeds thereof, (called the **"COMMUNITY ESTATE"**) shall continue to retain its character as community property during the joint lives of the Grantors, subject, however, to all the terms and conditions of this instrument.

It is also the Grantors' intention that all quasicommunity property and separate property of either spouse and the proceeds thereof (called the **"SEPARATE ESTATE"** on Schedule A) shall continue to retain its character during the joint lifetimes of the Grantor, subject to all the terms and conditions of this Trust Agreement.

ADDITIONS TO TRUST

SECOND: Property may be added to the Trust at any time and from any source with the Trustee's consent. Such added property shall thereupon become a part of the Trust Estate and shall thereafter be held upon the same terms and conditions as the property originally transferred into this Trust.

DISPOSITIVE PROVISIONS

THIRD: (A) While both Grantors are alive, the Trustee shall pay to _____ as managers of the community property owned by _____ _____ or apply for their benefit, the entire net income of the community estate semi-annually, or more frequent installments. At the written request of _____ _____ as managers of the community property, the Trustee shall pay to him or her as much of the community property in the Trust Estate as the designated manager of the community property shall request.

(B) While both of the Grantors are alive, the Trustee shall also pay to each Grantor, or shall apply for his or her benefit, the entire net income of that Grantor's separate estate, semi-annually or in more frequent installments. On the written request of the Grantor who transferred the separate estate to the

REVOCABLE TRUST

PAGE 3

Trust, the Trustee shall pay to him or her so much of the principal of the separate estate Trust as such Grantor shall request.

(C) Following the death of the first Grantor, (hereinafter referred to as the **DECEDENT GRANTOR**) the Trustee shall pay to the **SURVIVING GRANTOR** or apply for his or her benefit the entire net income of the Trust semi-annually or in more frequent installments. If the Trustee deems that the net income of the Trust to be insufficient, the Trustee shall also pay or apply for the benefit of the **SURVIVING GRANTOR** from time to time so much of the principal from the Trust as the Trustee, in the Trustee's discretion, deems necessary for the **SURVIVING GRANTOR'S** proper support, care, maintenance, and health, after taking into consideration, to the extent deems advisable, any income or other resources of the **SURVIVING GRANTOR** outside the Trust Estate, known to the Trustee.

(D) After death of the **SURVIVING GRANTOR** and subject to the provisions of Paragraph E of this Article Third, the Trustee may, in the Trustee's discretion, pay out of principal of the Trust to the **SURVIVING GRANTOR'S** executor or administrator, obligations incurred for the **SURVIVING GRANTOR'S** support and any estate or inheritance taxes (including interest and penalties) arising by reason of the **SURVIVING GRANTOR'S** death.

(E) Following the death of the **SURVIVING GRANTOR**, the Trustee shall distribute the balance remaining, if any, of the Trust (including both principal and any accrued or undistributed income)

REVOCABLE TRUST
PAGE 4

to such one or more persons or entities, including the **SURVIVING GRANTOR'S** own estate, and on such terms and conditions, either outright or in Trust, as the **SURVIVING GRANTOR** shall appoint by a Will or Codicil thereto specifically referred to and exercising this power of appointment.

(F) After the **SURVIVING GRANTOR'S** death, the Trustee shall distribute any portion of the Trust not disposedas provided in Paragraph (D) and (E) of this Article Third as follows:

The Trustee shall divide the Trust into as many parts or shares for the Grantor's children: _____

_____

_____ .

Should any child predecease both of the Grantors with surviving children or descendants, then said descendants shall take the share of the deceased child. The shares of the children surviving to be equal and the shares of the descendants of each deceased child to be in the aggregate the amount of the share that would have been set aside for the benefit of such deceased child had he or she survived and to be equal among themselves by right of representation, **per stirpes** and not per capita. Each part or share shall be held and administered as a distinct and separate Trust Fund for the benefit of the child or descendant of the child in respect to whom that part or share of the Trust shall have been

<u>REVOCABLE TRUST</u>

PAGE 5

reserved as aforesaid (said child or descendant being hereinafter sometimes called "**THE BENEFICIARY**".

Should a child predecease the Grantors without surviving descendants then that child's share of the Trust shall go to the remaining child or children that survive the Grantors or which have descendants surviving the Grantors.

The Grantors expressly intend not to distribute anything to _____ except in the event _____ _____ should predecease the Grantors without surviving descendants. In such an event, the entire trust estate shall be distributed to _____ _____.

The Trust with respect to each part or share shall terminate upon either the beneficiary's death or the beneficiary attaining the age of eighteen (18) years. Any beneficiary over the age of eighteen years, at the time of the **SURVIVING GRANTOR'S** death is to receive his or her distribution immediately.

    (a) With respect to each such Trust, the Trustee shall hold, invest, and reinvest the principal or corpus thereof and exercise the powers hereinafter granted with respect thereto and shall collect and receive rents, issues, dividends, interest and

income therefrom and shall pay all of the income derived therefrom to the beneficiary each and every year during the life of the beneficiary.

(b) If any property held shall be distributable or payable to a minor, the Trustee in its sole discretion may:

(i). Transfer and pay over all or any such property to a Guardian of the property of such minor wherever appointed without requiring ancillary guardianship or to a parent or person having care and custody of such minor without requiring such parent or person to qualify as guardian in any jurisdiction or a custodian for such minor under the Uniform Gifts To Minors Act of any State. The Trustee shall have no obligation to see to the use or application thereof or to make inquiry with respect to any other property available for the use of such minor, and the receipt therefor of such guardian, parent, person or custodian shall completely discharge the Trustee as to such transfer or payment; or

(ii). Set aside all or any such property, title to which shall have vested absolutely in such minor, in a separate fund and hold the same until the minor shall become of age or sooner die. During such period, the Trustee may at any time or from time to time in its sole discretion pay over all or any portion of such fund as provided in subparagraph (i) hereof, or invest and reinvest the same and pay or apply to or for the use of such minor, all or so much of the principal thereof and net income therefrom (including accumulated income), and accumulate any income not so paid or applied, as the Trustee may in its sole discretion determine, irrespective of any other property available for the of such minor.

The Trustee holding such fund shall not be required to give bond or security or to render periodic accounts and shall be entitled to compensation as if the fund was a separate Trust.

(c) Upon termination of any Trust, the Trustee shall transfer, convey, and pay over the principal or corpus of said Trust, together with any and all accumulated income that may remain in the Trustee's hands to the beneficiary thereof, if living, or if such beneficiary is not then living, then to the descendants of the beneficiary then living or in being, by right of representation, **per stripes**, and not per capita, or if there be no such descendants then living or in being, then to the Grantors' descendants then living or in being, by right of representation, **per stirpes**, and not per capita.

(d) The Trustee is authorized at any time or times and from time to time to pay to the person entitled to receive income from any Trust so much of the principal or corpus of such Trust as in the sole discretion of the Trustee may seem necessary or desirable (after taking into account the income from all other sources of such person and any other property which may be owned by such person) for the maintenance, support, or education of such person. To the extent of any such payment, the Trust shall terminate.

REVOCABILITY

FOURTH: During the lifetimes of both Grantors, this Trust may

REVOCABLE TRUST

PAGE 8

be revoked in whole or in part by either Grantor by delivering written notice to the other Grantor and to the Trustee. In the event of such revocation, the entire community estate or the revoked portion thereof shall revert to both Grantors as their community property. In the event of revocation, the separate estate or revoked portion thereof shall revert to the Grantor contributing it. This Trust may not be amended during the lifetimes of both Grantors without the consent of both of them. **FROM AND AFTER THE DEATH OF EITHER OF THE GRANTORS, THE SURVIVING GRANTOR MAY ALTER, AMEND OR REVOKE THE TRUST IN ANY MANNER INCLUDING TERMINATION OF THE TRUST AND TAKE RECEIPT OF ALL OF THE ASSETS CONTAINED THEREIN AS THE SURVIVING GRANTOR'S OWN SOLE AND SEPARATE PROPERTY.**

PAYMENTS OF TAXES, BEQUESTS, ETC.

FIFTH: Any estate, inheritance, succession or other similar taxes that may be imposed as a result of a Grantor's death, as well as funeral, last illness, and administration expenses, debts and other proper charges against the estate, may be paid out of the principal of those properties allocated or to be paid to the Trust that are otherwise includible in the Grantor's gross estate for federal estate tax purposes, to whatever extent the Trustee, in his or her sole discretion deems to be expedient and in the best interest of the deceased Grantor's beneficiaries. Written statements by the fiduciary or fiduciaries of the Grantor's probate estate of the sums to be paid hereunder shall be sufficient evidence of the amount and propriety thereof for the protection of the Trustee, and the Trustee shall be under no duty to see to the application of such payments.

If at any time or times prior to the closing of a Grantor's probate estate, the Trustee of the Trust hereunder receives a written statement signed by the fiduciary or fiduciaries of such estate certifying that any monetary bequest that is contained in the Grantor's Will as duly admitted to probate is not payable in full because of insufficiency of the net assets of such estate, such Trustee within a reasonable time thereafter shall pay such bequest (or the portion thereof that the fiduciaries certify cannot be paid by said estate) out of the principal of those properties allocated to the Trust that are otherwise includible in the deceased Grantor's gross estate for federal estate tax purposes.

All other provisions hereof to the contrary notwithstanding, under no circumstances shall a Grantor's probate estate nor any legatee under a Grantor's Will receive or in any way benefit from anything that is received or receivable by the Trustee hereunder, that, if paid to a beneficiary other than the Grantor's estate, would be excludable from Grantor's estate under Section 2039 of the Internal Revenue Code or any amendment thereof, or would be exempt from estate or inheritance taxes under applicable state tax laws.

TRUSTEE POWERS

SIXTH: In the administration of this Trust, the Trustee shall

REVOCABLE TRUST

PAGE 10

have the following powers, all of which shall be exercised in as fiduciary capacity:

1. To retain any such property without regard to the proportion such property or similar property held may bear to the entire amount held and whether or not the same is of the class in which fiduciaries are authorized by law or any rule of court to invest funds.

2. To sell any such property upon such terms and conditions as may be deemed proper at either public or private sale, either for credit for such period of time as may be deemed proper or for cash and with or without security; and the purchaser of such property shall have no obligation to see to the use or application of the proceeds of sale; to exchange, lease, sublease, mortgage, pledge or otherwise encumber any such property upon such terms and conditions as may be deemed advisable; to grant options for any of the foregoing and to make any lease or sublease, including any oil, gas or mineral lease, for such period of time and to include therein any covenants or options for renewal as may be deemed proper without regard to the duration of any Trust and without approval of any court.

3. To invest and reinvest in and to acquire by exchange property of any character, foreign or domestic, or interests or participations therein, including by way of illustrations but not limitation, real property, mortgages, bonds, notes debentures,

certificates of deposit, capital, common and referred stocks, and shares or interests in investment trusts, mutual funds or common trust funds, without regard to the proportion any such property or similar property held may bear to the entire amount held and whether or not the same is of the class in which fiduciaries are authorized by law or any rule of court to invest funds.

    4. To hold any personal property in any state; to register and hold property of any kind, whether real or personal, at any time held hereunder in the name of a nominee or nominees, and to take and keep stocks, bonds, or other securities unregistered or in such condition as to pass by delivery.

    5. To employ in the exercise of absolute discretion, investment counsel, accountants, depositaries, custodians, brokers, attorneys and agents, irrespective of whether any person so employed shall be a fiduciary hereunder or a firm or corporation in which a fiduciary hereunder shall have an interest and to pay then the usual compensation for their services out of the principal or income of the property held hereunder in addition to and without diminution of or charging the same against the commissions or compensation of any fiduciary hereunder; and any fiduciary who shall be a partner in any such firm shall nevertheless be entitled to receive his share as partner of the compensation paid to such firm.

    6. To retain any property or interest in property in the form received.

REVOCABLE TRUST

PAGE 12

7. To invest funds in stocks, bonds, notes, debentures or other securities, or property, real or personal (including any common or commingled fund), notwithstanding such securities or property may not be eligible investments for fiduciaries under statutory or general law, either as to the nature of the security or in relation to the other investments. It is the Grantor's intention that the Trustee shall have the power to make such investments as it may, in its unrestricted judgment, deems best.

8. To register any stock, bond, or other property in the name of a nominee, without the addition of words indicating that such security is held in a fiduciary capacity; but accurate records shall be maintained showing that such security is a trust asset and that the Trustee shall be responsible for the acts of the nominee.

9. To retain and carry on any business which may be accepted as a part of the trust fund, to acquire additional interest in any such business, to agree to the liquidation in kind of any corporation in which this Trust may have any interest and to carry on the business thereof, to join with other owners in adopting any form of management for any business or property, in which this Trust may have an interest, to become and remain a partner, general or limited, in regard to any such business or property, incorporate any such business or property and to hold the stock or other securities as an investment, and to employ agents and confer on them authority to manage and operate such business,

property or corporation, without liability for the acts of any such agent for any loss, liability or indebtedness of such business if the management is selected or retained with reasonable care.

10. To determine any questions which may arise as to what constitutes income and what constitutes principal, and such determination shall be conclusive as to all persons interested in the Trust (but, subject to such power and in except some unusual instance where it may be exercised to the contrary, shares of stock received by way of a stock dividend shall be deemed principal and not income).

11. To employ such agents and counsel and other persons as may be necessary, in the opinion of the Trustee, and to determine and pay them such compensation as may be deemed appropriate by the Trustee.

12. To sell any property to or purchase any property from any other trust or share thereof created by a Grantor during the Grantor's life, or the Grantor's estate or of the estate of a Grantor's spouse or form any trust created by a Grantor's spouse by Will or during the Grantor's life, at the fair market value thereof as determined by the Trustee, even though the same person or corporation may be acting as Trustee of any such other Trusts, as Executor of the estate of the Grantor's spouse, or as the Grantor's Executor or Trustee of any Trust established by the Grantor.

13. To commingle, for the purposes of management and

REVOCABLE TRUST

investment, the funds of this Trust with funds of any other Trust or Trusts created by a Grantor.

14. To make loans, either secured or unsecured, in such amounts, upon such terms, at such rates of interest, to such persons other than a Grantor and to such firms or corporations other than those controlled by a Grantor, as the Trustee may deem advisable, including but not limited to the beneficiary of this Trust. It is the Grantors' intention that this provision be used to assist the beneficiary when the beneficiary is in need of funds without having to make a final distribution of principal to the beneficiary.

15. To exercise any and all powers not included herein which are authorized by the laws of the State of _____ which by reference is specifically incorporated herein as though fully set forth in its entirety.

16. In its fiduciary capacity, to exercise all powers in the management of the Trust Fund which any individual could exercise in his or her own right, upon such terms and conditions as it may deem best, and to execute and deliver any and all instruments and to do all acts which may be deemed necessary or proper to carry on the purposes of this Agreement.

17. To prosecute and defend actions, claims or proceedings for the protection of trust property and of the Trustee in the performance of the Trustee's duties.

REVOCABLE TRUST

18. To pay any sum distributable to a beneficiary, without regard to whether the beneficiary is under a legal disability, by paying the sum to the beneficiary or by paying the sum to another person for the use or benefit of the beneficiary. No distribution under this instrument to or for the benefit of a minor beneficiary shall discharge the legal obligation of the beneficiary's parent's to support him or her in accordance with the laws of the state of the parent's domicile from time to time, unless a court of competent jurisdiction determines that this distinction is necessary for the minor's support, health, or education.

SUCCESSOR TRUSTEE

SEVENTH: On the death, resignation, or incapacity of either Grantor, the Surviving Grantor shall become the sole Trustee of all Trusts created under this instrument. In the event that both Grantors shall cease, for any reason to serve as Trustee of the Trust, then _____ shall serve as Successor Trustee. In the event _____, shall fail, for any reason to serve as Trustee, then _____ shall serve as Successor Trustee. In the event that _____ _____shall fail, for any reason to serve as Trustee, then the Court having appropriate probate jurisdiction over the Surviving Grantor's estate shall appoint the Successor Trustee.

Physical and mental incapacity shall be conclusively established

REVOCABLE TRUST

if a doctor, authorized to practice medicine in the Grantor's state of domicile, issues a written certificate to that effect. In the absence of such a certificate, the Successor Trustee or the beneficiaries may petition the court having jurisdiction over the Trust to remove the Trustee and replace him or her with the Successor Trustee. The Successor Trustee or the beneficiary who so petitions the court shall incur no liability to any beneficiary of the Trust or to the substituted Trustee as a result of this petition, provided the petition is filed in good faith and in a reasonable belief that the Trustee is physically or mentally incapacitated or otherwise cannot act.

The Grantors shall have the right at any time and periodically to appoint or to remove any Trustee and thereafter appoint a Successor trustee even though a Successor Trustee may be named in this Agreement. In such an event, the Successor Trustee named in this Agreement will follow the Successor Trustee appointed by the Grantors. The removal or appointment of a Successor trustee shall be made in writing, shall be attached to this Agreement at the time made, and shall take effect at the time stated in the instrument. All Successor Trustees shall have the same duties and powers as are conferred upon the Trustee.

BOND

EIGHTH: No bond shall be required of any Trustee named in this Trust Agreement.

ACCOUNTINGS

REVOCABLE TRUST

NINTH: Annual accounting may be waived by a waiver executed in writing by both the Grantors, the Surviving Grantor, or all of the beneficiaries of the Trust.

ACCEPTANCE BY TRUSTEE

TENTH: The Trustee by joining in the execution of this Agreement hereby signifies their acceptance oi this Trust.

BROAD SPENDTHRIFT CLAUSE

ELEVENTH: To the extent permitted by law, no interest of any beneficiary in the income or principal of any Trust hereby created shall be subject to pledge, assignment, sale, or transfer in any manner, nor shall any beneficiary have power in any manner to anticipate, charge, or encumber his or her interest, nor shall any interest of any beneficiary ne liable or subject in any manner while in the possession of the Trustee for the debts, contracts, liabilities, engagements, or torts of such beneficiary.

TRUSTEE COMPENSATION

TWELFTH: For services as Trustee, all Trustees shall receive reasonable compensation for such services, provided, however, that any Trustee who contributes to the principal of any share of a

Trust created under this Agreement shall not receive any fee for his or her services. A Corporate Trustee shall receive a fee based upon those set forth in the Trustee's regularly published fee schedule for similar services or such other fee as may be agreed upon the Trustee's appointment.

REVOCABLE TRUST

APPLICABLE LAW

THIRTEENTH: This Trust has been created and accepted by the Grantors and the Trustee in the State of _____, and the validity, construction and all rights under this instrument shall be governed by the laws of the State of _____. If any provision of this instrument shall be invalid or unenforceable, the remaining provisions shall continue to be fully effective.

Titles and heading contained in this instrument shall not be deemed to govern, limit, modify or in any manner affect the scope, meaning or intent of the provisions hereof.

NO-CONTEST CLAUSE

FOURTEENTH: Except as otherwise provided in this instrument, the Grantors have intentionally and with full knowledge omitted to provide for their heirs. If any beneficiary under this Trust, singly or in conjunction with any other person or persons, contests in any court the validity of this Trust or of either Grantor's Last Will or seeks to obtain adjudication in any proceeding in any court that this Trust or any of its provisions or that such Will or any of its provisions is void, or seeks to otherwise to void, nullify, or set aside this Trust or any of its provisions, then that person's right to take any interest given to him or her by this Trust shall be determined as it would have been determined if the person had predeceased the execution of this Trust without surviving issue. The provisions of this paragraph shall not apply

REVOCABLE TRUST
PAGE 19

to any disclaimer by any person of any benefit under this Trust or under any Will. The Trustee is hereby authorized to defend, at the expense of the Trust Estate, and contest, or other attack of any nature on this Trust or its provisions.

PERPETUITIES SAVINGS CLAUSE

FIFTEENTH: Any Trust created under this instrument shall, unless terminated earlier, terminate twenty-one (21) years after the death of the last survivor of the Surviving Grantor and all of the Grantors' issue living on the date of the last Surviving Grantor's death. The Trust Estate shall then be distributed by the right of representation to those persons who are then entitled or authorized at the Trustee's discretion, to receive income distributions from the Trust.

CLAIMS OF CREDITORS

SIXTEENTH: The Trustee shall not be personally liable to any creditor or to any other person for making distributions from any Trust under the terms of this instrument if the Trustee has no notice of the claim of such creditor.

SEVERABILITY CLAUSE

SEVENTEENTH: If any provision of this Trust instrument is unenforceable, the remaining provisions shall nevertheless be carried into effect.

NAME OF THE TRUST

EIGHTEENTH: This Trust and the Trust contained herein may be

REVOCABLE TRUST

referred to collectively as the _____
_____ or by the identifying name of the named
beneficiary of any Trust hereunder from time to time or by such other
designation as the Trustee may from time to time deem appropriate.

    Property shall be deemed transferred to the Trustee and
subject to the terms of this instrument if it has been registered
in or assigned to the Trustee as Trustee of the _____
_____, or to the Trustee as Trustee under a
Declaration of Trust followed by the same date of this instrument, or to
the Trustee U/D/T dtd (UNDER DECLARATION OF TRUST DATED) followed by the
date of this instrument, or in any other manner indicating its transfer
to the Trustee as Trustee hereunder or under this Declaration of Trust.

    IN WITNESS WHEREOF, the parties have executed this instrument
as of the date and year first written above.

GRANTORS

_____

_____

TRUSTEES

_____

_____

REVOCABLE TRUST
PAGE 21

<u>REVOCABLE TRUST</u>

DATED:

SCHEDULE A

All real and personal property wheresoever located including but not limited to the following:

COMMUNITY PROPERTY

1.
2.
3.
4.
5.
6.
7.

SEPARATE PROPERTY

1.
2.
3.
4.
5.
6.
7.
8.

Grantor will change the title to all property to reflect the transfer into the Trust Estate.

REVOCABLE TRUST

PAGE 22

CERTIFICATE OF ACKNOWLEDGMENT OF NOTARY PUBLIC

STATE OF

COUNTY OF

On this day of _____ in the year _____, before me appeared_____

_____ personally known to me (or proved to me on the basis of satisfactory evidence) to be the persons whose name are subscribed to this instrument, and acknowledge that they executed it. I declare under penalty of perjury that the name of the person whose name is subscribed to this instrument appears to be of sound mind and under no duress, fraud, or undue influence.

_____

REVOCABLE TRUST

PAGE 23

INDEX (chapter and question number)

CHILD CUSTODY AND SUPPORT (CC)

ADOPTION	CC 12
CHILD-NAPPING	CC 16,17
CHILD SUPPORT AGREEMENT AMONG PARENTS	CC 27
ATTACHMENT TO PAY	CC 24
COST OF LIVING INCREASES	CC 25
DURING DIVORCE	CC 22
MANNER OF MAKING	CC 28
REMARRIAGE OF CUSTODIAL PARENT	CC 32
TERMINATION	CC 23
COLLECTION OF CHILD SUPPORT	CC 26
COLLEGE FOR CHILD	CC 29
CONSENT TO ADOPTION	CC 14
DETERMINATION	CC 1
FACTORS	CC 2
GRANDPARENT VISITATION	CC 20
HEALTH COVERAGE	CC 30
JOINT CUSTODY	CC 7
NAME CHANGE OF CHILD	CC 10
NOMINATION OF GUARDIAN IN WILL	CC 13
PARENT LIVING WITH OPPOSITE SEX	CC 4
PARENT VISITATION	CC 18
RELIGION OF CHILD	CC 8
REMARRIAGE OF PARENT	CC 9
SELECTION BY CHILD	CC 3
STEP-PARENT ADOPTION	CC 14,15;UP 24
DANGER TO CHILD	CC 11
TAKING CHILDREN OUT OF STATE	CC 5,19
TAKING CHILDREN FROM BOTH PARENTS	CC 6
UNIFORM CHILD CUSTODY AND SUPPORT ACT	CC 31
WITHHOLDING SUPPORT BECAUSE OF DENIAL OF VISITATION	CC 21

UNWED PARENTING AND ADOPTIONS (UP)

ACKNOWLEDGMENT OF PATERNITY	UP 5
ADOPTION BY UNMARRIED COUPLE	UP 13
ADOPTION BY SINGLE PARENT	UP 14
ADOPTION BY HOMOSEXUAL	UP 15
ADOPTION AGENCY	UP 21
ADOPTION BY FAMILY MEMBERS	UP 25, 31
ADOPTION PROCEDURE	UP 22,23,26
ARTIFICIAL INSEMINATION	UP 9
ATTORNEY IN ADOPTION	UP 17
BABY BLACK MARKET	UP 18
BLOOD TESTS TO DETERMINE PATERNITY	UP 7
CHANGE OF MIND ON ADOPTION	UP 28
CHILD SUPPORT: GRANDPARENTS' OBLIGATION	UP 10
HUSBAND NOT THE FATHER	UP 8
ILLEGITIMATE CHILD PATERNITY ACTION	UP 9 UP 12
FOREIGN CHILDREN ADOPTION	UP 19,20
ILLEGITIMATE CHILD	UP 1,2
MARRIAGE OF MOTHER TO FATHER	UP 3
MARRIAGE OF MOTHER TO MAN NOT THE FATHER	UP 4
PATERNITY SUIT	UP 6,11,12
PRIVATE ADOPTION	UP 16
STEP-PARENT ADOPTION	UP 25,29
SURROGATE CONTRACT	UP 33,34,35,36
SURROGATE MOTHER	UP 32,33
SURROGATE CONTRACT-LEGAL PARENT	UP 35, 36
UNMARRIED FATHERS' RIGHTS	UP 27

DRUNK DRIVING (DR)

ACCURACY OF TEST	DR 11,18
ADMINISTRATIVE REVOCATION	DR 26
BLOOD ALCOHOL LEVEL	DR 2
CHEMICAL TEST	DR 6
DEFINITION	DR 1
FIELD SOBRIETY TEST	DR 3
FORCED BLOOD TESTS	DR 5
IMPLIED CONSENT	DR 4
JURY	DR 15,20
JUVENILES	DR 25
MOVEMENT OF VEHICLE	DR 7
NYSTAGMUS TEST	DR 16,17
PRESERVATION OF BREATH SAMPLE	DR 14
PRIOR ENHANCEMENT	DR 23
PROBABLE CAUSE FOR STOP	DR 8
RADIO FREQUENCY INTERFERENCE	DR 19
RECKLESS DRIVING	DR 22,24
SEARCH OF VEHICLE	DR 21
SCIENTIFIC STANDARD FOR TEST	DR 12
SMELL OF ALCOHOL	DR 9
SOBRIETY ROADSTOP	DR 10

380 YOUR PERSONAL LEGAL GUIDE

ESCROW (E)		USE OF ESCROWS	E 4
ASSUMPTION	E 35		
ATTORNEY'S CERTIFICATE		*ESTATE PLANNING (ET)*	
OF TITLE	E 11	A-B TRUST	ET 15
BUILDING INSPECTION	E 26,27	ACCOUNTING OF TRUST	ET 47
BUYER'S ACTS ON CLOSING	E 50	ANNUAL EXCLUSION	ET 12
BUYER NON-RESIDENT		ATTACHMENT OF TRUST	
ALIEN	E 52	CREDITORS OF TRUSTOR	ET 34
CC&Rs	E 16	CREDITORS OF BENEFICIARY	ET 35
CLEARING A TITLE	E 14, 15	AVOIDANCE OF PROBATE	ET 3
CLOSE OF ESCROW	E 48	BANK ACCOUNTS	ET 50
CLOSING FUNDS REQUEST	E 47	CHANGING COMMUNITY	
COMMISSIONS	E 44	PROPERTY	
CO-OPERATIVE	E 39	TO SEPARATE PROPERTY	ET 49
DEDUCTIBILITY OF		CHARITABLE GIFT	ET 28,29
ESCROW FEES	E 53, 54	CHARITABLE REMAINDER	
DEFINITION	E 1	TRUST	ET 30
DOCUMENTARY		CONSERVATOR CREATING	
TRANSFER TAX	E 43	TRUST	ET 25
DUE ON SALE CLAUSE	E 37	COSTS OF PROBATE	ET 2
DUTIES OF ESCROW HOLDER	E 5,9	COSTS FOR ESTATE PLAN	ET 45
EASEMENT	E 17	COURT REVIEW OF TRUST	ET 41
ENCUMBRANCE	E 19	DEFINITION	ET 1
HOME WARRANTY POLICY	E 28	DOWER AND CURTESY	
IMPOUND ACCOUNTS	E 34 I	REPLACEMENT	ET 36
NFORMATION TO PROVIDE		DURABLE POWER	
TO ESCROW HOLDER	E 8	OF ATTORNEY	ET 5
INSTALLMENT		ESTATE TAX RATE	ET 21
SALES CONTRACT	E 38	FEDERAL ESTATE	
INSPECTIONS OF		TAX RETURN	ET 26
THE PROPERTY	E 21,22,25,26	GENERATION SKIPPING	
INSTRUCTIONS	E 3	TRUST	ET 19,20
LIEN	E 18	GIFT TAX ON TRUST	
PAYMENT OF		CREATION	ET 37
ESCROW HOLDER	E 6	GIFT TAX RATE	ET 22
PAYMENT FOR		GIFT TAX RETURN	ET 23
TITLE REPORT	E 13	HOUSE: EXCLUSION OF G	
PRELIMINARY REPORT	E 12	AIN ON SALE	ET 40
PRORATIONS	E 29	INCOME TAX ON TRUST	ET 18,39
INTEREST	E 30	IRREVOCABLE TRUST	ET 24
INSURANCE POLICIES	E 32	JOINT TENANCIES	ET 3,4
MAINTENANCE FEES	E 33	JOINT TRUST	ET 45
RENTAL INCOME	E 31	LIFE INSURANCE TRUST	ET 9
RECORDATION	E 40	LIVING WILL	ET 6
RESPA	E 49	MARITAL DEDUCTION	ET 10
REQUIREMENTS	E 2	PROPERTY PLACED IN	
SELECTION OF		REVOCABLE TRUST	ET 16,33
ESCROW HOLDER	E 7	POUR OVER WILL	ET 8
SELLER'S ACTS ON CLOSING	E 51	QTIP TRUST	ET 14
SETTLEMENT	E 46	REASSESSMENT OF	
SUBJECT TO ACCEPTANCE	E 20, 36	PROPERTY TAXES	ET 33
TAX-FREE EXCHANGE	E 41,42	RECORDATION OF TRUST	ET 51
TERMINATION	E 45	REVOCABLE TRUST	ET 7,13,17
TERMITE INSPECTION	E 21,22	REVOCATION OF TRUST	ET 46
TITLE SEARCH	E 10	SELLING PROPERTY	
TITLE AT CLOSE OF ESCROW	E 23,24	IN A TRUST	ET 38

STEPPED UP BASIS	P 51	*INCOME TAX (IT)*	
TAX-FREE BONDS	ET 31	ACCRUAL METHOD	
TERMINATION OF TRUST	ET 27	OF ACCOUNTING	IT 13
TRUSTEE INCOMPETENCY	ET 48	AUDITS	IT 63,64,65
RESIGNATION	ET 42	BASIS COST	IT 49
BOND	ET 43	ADJUSTED	IT 50
UNIFIED CREDIT	ET 11	GIFT	IT 51,52
ZERO COUPON BOND	ET 32	INHERITED PROPERTY	IT 53
		STEPPED UP, COMMUNITY	
IMMIGRATION (IM)		PROPERTY	P 51
ABSENTIA ORDER		CANCELED DEBT	IT 42
OF DEPORTATION	IM 46,47,48	CANCELED STUDENT LOAN	IT 40
AGGRAVATED FELONY		CASUALTY LOSS	IT 56
BY ALIEN	IM 49,50	CAPITAL ASSETS	IT 46
ALIENS NOT SUBJECT		CAPITAL GAIN OR LOSS	IT 47
TO LIMITS	IM 3	CAPITAL LOSS CARRYOVER	IT 48
ALIENS WITH		CASH METHOD OF	
EXTRAORDINARY ABILITY	IM 8	ACCOUNTING	IT 12
B VISA	IM 15	COURT AWARD	IT 39
CRIMINAL CHARGES		CREDIT OR THE DISABLED	IT 62
FOR EXCLUSION	IM 34	DECEDENT TAX RETURN	IT 8,10,11
D VISA	IM 16	DEPENDENTS	IT 5,6
DEPORTATION	IM 41	DEPRECIATION	IT 30
DIVERSITY PROVISIONS	IM 9,10,11	DEATH BENEFIT	IT 34
E VISA	IM 17	DISABILITY INCOME	IT 37
EMPLOYER DEFENSES	IM 54	EMPLOYEE BUSINESS	
EMPLOYER SANCTIONS	IM 51,52,53	EXPENSES	IT 60,61
EMPLOYMENT BASED	IM 6	ESTIMATED TAX	IT 22,23
EXCLUSION	IM 33,34,35,	EXPIRED TAX ITEMS	IT 14
	36,37,38	FEDERAL COURT	IT 67
F VISA	IM 18,19	FILING STATUS	IT 3
H-1 VISA	IM 20,21	FRINGE BENEFITS	IT 16,20
H-2B	IM 22	INCOME RESPECT	
H-3	IM 23	TO DECEDENT	IT 11
FAMILY PREFERENCE	IM 5	INDIVIDUAL RETIREMENT	
FAMILY SPONSORED	IM 4	ACCOUNT (IRA)	IT 45
FILIPINOS	IM 59	ITEMIZED DEDUCTIONS	IT 55
FIREARM OFFENSE	IM 43	IRS FREE SERVICES	IT 1
HONG KONG IMMIGRANTS	IM 12	LOSS OF DEPOSITS	IT 58
L-1 VISA	IM 24	MOVING EXPENSES	IT 59
MARRIAGE FRAUD	IM 42	MULTIPLE SUPPORT	
NATURALIZATION	IM 57,58	AGREEMENTS	IT 6
NUMERICAL LIMITS	IM 2	NON-PROFIT ACTIVITY	IT 41
O VISA	IM 25, 26, 27,	PASSIVE ACTIVITY	IT 32
	28,29	PENSIONS	IT21,33,35,38
ORDER TO SHOW CAUSE	IM 44,45	PROBLEM RESOLUTION	
P VISA	IM 31	PROGRAM	IT 1
PRIORITY WORKERS	IM 7	RAILROAD RETIREMENT	
PUBLIC CHARGE	IM 35	BENEFITS	IT 38
R VISA	IM 32	RETURN OF CAPITAL	IT 27
REGULATION	IM 1	RENTAL INCOME	IT 28,29
RE-ENTRY DOCTRINE	IM 39,40	RENTAL LOSSES	IT 31,32
RELIGIOUS WORKERS	IM 14, 32	REQUEST FOR PROMPT	
SPECIAL IMMIGRANTS	IM 13	ASSESSMENT	IT 9
TEMPORARY PROTECTED		SALE OF HOUSE	IT 42,43
STATUS	IM 55,56	SOCIAL SECURITY	IT 36

SELF-EMPLOYMENT TAX	IT 15	TENANCY AT SUFFERANCE	LT 5
TAX COURT	IT 66	TENANCY AT WILL	LT 3
TAX FREE-EXCHANGE	IT 54	TENANT LIABILITY TO	
TAX EXEMPTION	IT 4,5,7 TAX	THIRD PARTIES	LT 11
EXEMPT OBLIGATIONS	IT 26	TENANT'S MAINTENANCE	LT 12
TIPS	IT 17,19	UNLAWFUL DETAINER	LT 27,28,44
THEFT LOSS	IT 57	WRIT OF POSSESSION	LT 32
W-4	IT 18		
WITHHOLDING	IT 20,21	*PROBATE (P)*	
		ACCOUNTING AND I	
LANDLORD TENANT (LT)		NVENTORY	P 50
ABANDONMENT OF LEASE		AFTER-DISCOVERED	
BY TENANT	LT 23	PROPERTY	P 52
ASSIGNMENT	LT 14,15	ANCILLIARY PROBATE	P 35
CONDEMNATION OF		ATTORNEY	P 20
LEASED PROPERTY	LT 24	CHANGING WILL	P 27,34
CONSTRUCTIVE EVICTION	LT 22	CODICIL	P 26,27
COVENANT OF QUIET		COMPETENCY FOR	
ENJOYMENT	LT 21	MAKING WILL	P 5
COVENANT TO REPAIR	LT 13	COMMON LAW STATES	P 17,18,19
DEFENSES TO UNLAWFUL		COMMUNITY PROPERTY	
DETAINER	LT 29	PROBATE	P 10,11
DESTRUCTION OF		COMMUNITY PROPERTY	
THE PROPERTY	LT 43	STATES	P.10
DISCLOSURE OF DEFECTS	LT 7	CONSIDERATIONS FOR WILL	P 31
EFFECTS OF ASSIGNMENT		COPY OF WILL	P 22,23
AND SUBLEASE	LT 18,19	CREDITOR CLAIM	P 43,44
EFFECTS OF MORTGAGES		CURTESY RIGHTS	
ON THE LEASE	LT 45, 46	OF HUSBAND	P 16,17,18,19
ESTATE FOR YEARS	LT 4	DEFINITION	P 1
FIXTURES	LT 38,39	DISINHERITING CHILD	P 28
FORCIBLE ENTRY		DIVORCE EFFECT ON WILL	P 32
AND DETAINER	LT 30, 31	DOWER RIGHTS OF WIFE	P 15,17,18,19
HOLDING OVER BY TENANT	LT 25	ESTATE TAX	P 24,48,49:
INJURIES IN			ET 21
COMMON AREAS	LT 8	FAMILY ALLOWANCE	P 45
IMPLIED WARRANTY OF		FINAL JUDGMENT	
HABITABILITY	LT 10	OF DISTRIBUTION	P 51
INSURANCE	LT 50	FUNERAL BILLS	P 42
LANDLORD LIABILITY		HOLOGRAPHIIC WILL	P 6
FOR DEFECTS	LT 6	INTESTANCY	P 7,9
LANDLORD LIEN	LT 36,37,39, 40,41	INVALID WILL	P 7
		JOINT PROPERTY: SEIZURE	
LANDLORD'S MAINTENANCE	LT 9	BY TAXING AGENCIES	P 36
LEASE	LT 1	JOINT WILL	P 25
LIQUIDATED DAMAGES	LT 33	LETTERS OF PROBATE	P 14
LOCKING A TENANT OUT	LT 30	LOST WILL	P 22
PERIODIC TENANCY	LT 2	MISSING HEIR	P 53
POSSESSION	LT 47, 48, 49	PERSONAL REPRESENTATIVE	P 13,38,41
RIGHT OF ENTRY		PERSONAL REPRESENTATIVE'S	
BY LANDLORD	LT 42	DUTIES	P 21,48,49
RETALIATORY EVICTION	LT 28	PRETERMITTED HEIR	P 29,30
SECURITY DEPOSIT	LT 34,35	PRETERMITTED SPOUSE	P 29,30
STATUTE OF FRAUDS	LT 26, R 28	PROBATE COURT	P 2
SUBLEASE	LT 16,17	SETTLEMENT	P 47
SURRENDER	LT 20	SIMULTANEOUS DEATH	P 46

STEP-CHILDREN	P 33	QUITCLAIM DEED	R 33
STATUTORY SHARE	P15,16,17,18,19	RACE NOTICE RECORDING ACT	R 27
STATUTORY WILL	P 4	RACE RECORDING ACT	R 26
WILL	P 3	RECORDATION	R 24
WILL CONTEST	P 37	RECORDING ACTS	R 23
WILL VALIDITY	P 40	REMEDIES FOR SELLER'S FALSE	
WITNESSES	P 39	STATEMENT OR CONCEALMENT	R 49
REAL PROPERTY (R)		SALE OF DEED OF TRUST	R 38
ADVERSE POSSESSION	R 16	STATUTE OF FRAUDS	R 28
AFTER ACQUIRED PROPERTY	R 34	TENANCY IN COMMON	R 8
BREACH OF SALE CONTRACT	R 30	TENANCY IN THE ENTIRETY	R 9
CONDOMINIUM	R 45	TERMINATION OF COVENANTS	
COOPERATIVE	R 44	& EQUITABLE SERVITUDES	R 22
COVENANT	R 19	TORRENS TITLE SYSTEMS	R 55
COVENANTS OF TITLE	R 32	TRUSTEE REPLACEMENT	R 40
COVERTURE	R 5	WATER RIGHTS	R 54
DEED OF RECONVEYANCE	R 39	ZONING	R 51
DEED OF TRUST	R 36,37		
DEFEASIBLE FEE	R 3	*SMALL CLAIMS COURT (SC)*	
DEFICIENCY JUDGMENT	R 41	AMOUNT	SC 8
DESTRUCTION OF PROPERTY		APPEAL	SC 16
IN ESCROW	R 31	ATTORNEY	SC 3,27
DUE ON SALE CLAUSE	R 50, E 37	BURDEN OF PROOF	SC 24
EASEMENT	R 10	COLLECTION OF JUDGMENT	
EASEMENT APPURTENANT	R 11	ATTACHMENT OF WAGES	SC 18
EASEMENT IN GROSS	R 12	SEIZURE OF REAL PROPERTY	SC 19
EASEMENT BY NECESSITY	R 14	LIEN OF REAL PROPERTY	SC 20
EASEMENT BY		COSTS	SC 10
PRESCRIPTION	R 17	BAD CHECKS	SC 30
EASEMENT BY		DEBTOR'S BANKRUPTCY	SC 21
RESERVATION	R 13	DEFENDANT	SC 6
EASEMENT TERMINATION	R 15	DEFENDANT'S CLAIM	
EFFECT OF FORECLOSURE		AGAINST PLAINTIFF	SC 15
OF LIENHOLDERS	R 42	DEFENDANT'S FAILURE	
ENFORCEMENT OF COVENANTS		TO APPEAR	SC 14
& EQUITABLE SERVITUDES	R 21	DEFINITION	SC 1
EQUITABLE SERVITUDE	R 20	BURDEN OF PROOF	SC 24
FEE SIMPLE	R 1	EXAMINATION OF DEBTOR	SC 23
FEE SIMPLE ABSOLUTE	R 2	FORMS	SC 7
HOMESTEAD	R 47	FILING FEE	SC 9
IMPLIED WARRANTY FOR		WHERE	SC 4
FITNESS FOR USE	R 48	WHEN	SC 5
INSTALLMENT LAND		FRIVOLOUS APPEAL	SC 33
CONTRACT	R 43, E 38	JUDGES	SC 26
INVERSE CONDEMNATION	R 52	JUDGMENT	SC 17,31,32
JOINT TENANCY CREATION	R 6	PRESENTATION OF CASE	SC 25
TERMINATION	R 7	SATISFACTION OF	
LIFE ESTATE	R 4	JUDGMENT	SC 22
MARKETABLE TITLE	R 29	SERVICE	SC 12
MECHANIC'S LIEN	R 46	SETTLEMENT	SC 13
MINERAL RIGHTS	R 53	SUING GOVERNMENT	
MORTGAGE	R 35	AGENCIES	SC 28
NOTICE RECORDING ACT	R 25	UNLAWFUL DETAINER	SC 29, LT 35
QUIET TITLE ACTION	R 18	WHO CAN SUE	SC 2

WITNESSES	SC 11

TORTS (T)

ABUSE OF PROCESS	T 30
ADULTERY	T 45
ASSAULT	T 3
ASSUMPTION OF THE RISK DEFENSE	T 38
ATTRACTIVE NUISANCE	T 42
BATTERY	T 4
COMPARATIVE NEGLIGENCE DEFENSE	T 37
CONSENT DEFENSE	T 14
CONTRIBUTORY NEGLIGENCE DEFENSE	T 36
CONVERSION	T 7
DEFAMATION	T 10
DEFAMATION DEFENSES	T 13
DEFENSE OF NECESSITY	T 18
DEFENSE OF OTHERS	T 16
DEFENSE OF PROPERTY	T 17
DEFINITION	T 1
EMOTIONAL DISTRESS	T 19
FALSE IMPRISONMENT	T 5
FRAUD	T 33
INVASION OF PRIVACY	T 32
LIABILITY TO INJURED TRESPASSERS	T 41
LIBEL	T 12
MALICIOUS PROSECUTION	T 29
NEGLIGENCE	T 35
NEGLIGENT MISREPRESENTATION	T 34
NUISANCE	T 20,21,22
PRODUCT LIABILITY	T 40
PUNITIVE DAMAGES	T 2
RES IPSA LOQUITOR	T 44
SELF-DEFENSE	T 15
SHOPKEEPER'S PRIVILEGE TO DETAIN	T 6
SLANDER	T 11
STRICT LIABILITY	T 39
SUING FEDERAL GOVERNMENT	T 43
TRESPASS	T 8
TRESPASS TO CHATTELS	T 9
VICARIOUS LIABILITY	T 23
EMPLOYER FOR EMPLOYEE	T 24
PRINCIPAL FOR INDEPENDENT CONTRACTOR	T 25
PARTNER FOR OTHER PARTNER(S)	T 26
OWNER OF CAR FOR DRIVER'S ACTS	T 27
PARENT FOR CHILD	T 28
WRONGFUL DEATH	T 31